ROCK'N'ROLL
BABYLON

Gary Herman

Plexus, London

Text copyright © 1982 by Gary Herman
This edition copyright © 1982 by Plexus Publishing Limited
Published by Plexus Publishing Limited
30 Craven Street
London WC2N 5NT
First printing 1982

Herman, Gary
    Rock 'n' roll Babylon.
    1. Rock music
    2. Musicians
    1. Title
    784.5'4'0922   ML420

    ISBN 0–85965–040–5
    ISBN 0–85965–041–3 Pbk

Made and printed in Great Britain by
Fakenham Press Limited, Fakenham, Norfolk

CONTENTS

To absent friends

'We are all in the gutter, but some of us are
looking at the stars.' *Oscar Wilde*

'If you're looking for trouble, you've come to the
right place.' *Elvis Presley*

PREFACE

I should make it clear from the outset that I love rock'n'roll. It has, at various times in my life, thrilled me, consoled me, saddened me and gladdened me. It has always, and in both senses, moved me. And, like most of the children of my generation, rock'n'roll stars have seemed to me friends, idols and infiltrators in the camp of an enemy dedicated to the ruthless pursuit of wealth, the promotion of a hypocritical morality and the suppression of youthful energies.

It is difficult to see these stars as traitors – harder still to understand that they may have become the enemy. Yet the rock business is a hard-nosed commercial world, with time for idealism and radical visions only if they sell. The stars – our stars? – can't escape it. They are prey to all the vices that a society obsessed with money and power has cultivated for centuries. Maybe they've been the enemy all along.

That doesn't diminish the music, but it does make rock stars fascinating case studies in the effects of success and failure. This is the subject of this book – the perennially absorbing topic of how the rich and famous occupy their time, translated to a context in which wealth and fame have never been simply seen as unequivocally desirable goals for individuals to pursue.

The book is a product of the post-punk age, for it was the punks who – however naïvely or disingenuously – most precisely focused attention on the lumbering and indifferent dinosaur that rock had become. Babylon, it should be remembered, was the capital of a vast and profligate empire. In the rock world, its citizens may start from humble beginnings, but soon they are ushered into lush hanging gardens where there are no dreams of democracy or change, only dreams of power, wealth and the perfect tan. Rod Stewart's former manager once described the singer as 'a growth industry'. Mick Jagger talked about going into politics but not having 'the right wife'. Gregg Allman hobnobbed with Jimmy Carter and earned with Cher the coveted title of 'the Richard Burton and Elizabeth Taylor of rock'n'roll'. And the Beach Boys played at Ronald Reagan's presidential inauguration.

These are among the survivors. But one way or another the rock world eats its own young. Perhaps life would be better if it didn't or if we could, at least, believe that it didn't. Then again, perhaps the music would be less exciting, the art less moving, if it was rendered safe or its audience simple-minded. I don't know, but for those who care to speculate, I wrote this book.

Gary Herman 1982

THE PROMISED LAND

It was a warm and wet June weekend in 1967. The place was Monterey in northern California. The occasion – the rock culture's first international festival, a musical celebration of the youthful optimism embodied in rock'n'roll. By subsequent standards, the Monterey Pop Festival was a smallish and fairly sedate affair. Although the total attendance was estimated at between 30,000 and 100,000 people, only about 8,000 were allowed into the seated arena at any one time during the five concerts that made up the two and a half day event. Many of the performers were locally based and quite a few were all but unknown.

Despite the same lack of adequate facilities that was to plague future festivals, plentiful and often free supplies of grass, LSD and other hallucinogens, a visible police presence and an entrance fee to the arena of between $3.00 and $6.50, there were no riots, no appeals to stoned insurrection and few hassles. Good vibes were the order of the day – so much so that, by the time the second concert began on Saturday morning, one third of the police present had been sent home. A banner across the stage read 'Music, Love and Flowers' – a slogan which seemed, at the time, both reasonable and radical. Later it would look merely naïve.

The Monterey festival encapsulated all that is good and bad about the phenomenon of rock music. On the one hand, it embraced the dreams and aspirations of the 'class of '67'; on the other hand, it was planned on strict commercial principles. As so often before and since, the performers were floundering in the middle; torn between their sympathy with the hopes of their fans and their desire to fulfil them, and their own sometimes shamefaced eagerness for adulation and the undoubted attractions which only money can buy. Monterey was the microcosm of rock'n'roll Babylon: a signpost to the promised land which was really an open prison.

San Francisco, Monterey's nearest big city, was exploding with new ideas about how to live. The fragrance of liberation hung in the air, like an ether haze waiting to be ignited by the sparks that flew when radical student politics met the uncomplicated hedonism of rock'n'roll. The Beatles' *Sergeant Pepper* album had been released a few weeks before the festival into a world pregnant with possibilities. The Free Speech Movement based on the University of California's Berkeley campus was throwing down challenges to adult authoritarianism. The streets were alive with the look, smell, sound, taste and feel of 'mind-expanding'

drugs, new music, experimental arts and sexual adventures and, through 1966 and early 1967, the astronauts of inner space had danced to the music of pied piper bands like Jefferson Airplane, the Grateful Dead and Country Joe and the Fish at festivals and 'be-ins' all round the Bay.

These happenings had promised much. They had been free and fun. Performers mingled with audiences; politicos and weirdos rubbed comradely shoulders (and – why not? – other parts of their bodies); everybody turned on together. Rock'n'roll had always seemed more important than its detractors could give it credit for, except negatively by condemning it. Youth was beginning to show the sour establishment just how important it was, in social, even world terms, not just as entertainment. White and black, woman and man, gay and straight, worker and student, even (to a lesser extent) young and old were all washing their newly radicalized souls in the revitalizing flood of music. People everywhere seemed to be talking about the 'Summer of Love'. It looked like a tidal wave was truly about to sweep away the old order – and Monterey, it was hoped, would be its frothy, bubbling crest.

Monterey had been planned to feature a wider range and a greater quantity of music than ever before – almost the whole spectrum of pop from supper-club soul to body-shaking boogie, taking in folk, folk-rock, acid-rock, electric blues and even the classical Indian ragas of sitar-playing Ravi Shankar. However it is more significant, though less recognizable at the time, to realize that Monterey had been specifically planned as a media event. The Beatles' former publicist, Derek Taylor, had been hired almost at the outset. Any journalist who asked (and many who did not) got free tickets – some 1,200 in all. The concerts were to be recorded and ABC TV was sold the film and TV rights for some $300,000. People would certainly hear about Monterey, even if only from the pages of a magazine. TV, radio, cinema and record – every angle was covered. Massive publicity would announce to the world at large that Monterey was ushering in the long-awaited Age of Freedom, heralded back in the fifties when Elvis Presley first put on his blue suede shoes.

For a dozen years or more, rock'n'roll had travelled its fitful journey, offering moments of exultation in a joyless world trapped in its cycles of paranoid politics and economic fatalism. Elvis had been a revelation of youthful energy and sexual power. The Beatles were an inspiration, Bob Dylan an education. They and their followers brought pleasure and purpose to a dry and dying world. Parents, the authorities, the establishment did not like it. They tried to put it down, stop the kids from listening, keep them away from parties and dances and 'dangerous' films. But the stars were in the sky for everyone to see. They played the music of resistance. If adult society threatened the world with nuclear weapons of mass destruction, youth had a weapon of mass liberation in rock'n'roll. The young could retaliate – and someday perhaps they could win. If any day looked a likely candidate for the start of the victorious final campaign, it was the first day of the Monterey Festival.

Things were never that simple, of course. The growth of a mass market for a kind of rock'n'roll that was seen as artistically important and socially valid meant that *big* business took over and performers found themselves removed from the crucial close contact with audiences. Finding themselves in a sort of creative vacuum they inevitably fell back on the company of other performers, the rich and the famous. Their friends became the friends of stars, their pastimes the pastimes of stars. Their lives were lived in the glare of spotlights, the confinement of backstage dressing-rooms and the luxury of limousines and expensive hotel rooms. Their fans might have seen them as leaders, but then – as now – it was a hollow sort of leadership. Open to the temptations of fame, wealth, and a life-style of unprecedented hedonism, rock stars have always been liable to turn into monsters – caricatures of their former golden youth, leftovers after rock'n'roll's banquet has passed them by, happy to sink into easy dissipation or simply unable to carry the weight of a generation's dreams.

Years after Monterey, it is easy to see its two opposing aspects. At the time few people recognized the dark face of rock'n'roll lurking around the stage area, roped and cordoned off from the audience. This was the Machiavellian face of hustling and profiteering, the bloated face of grotesque excesses and gross indulgence, the haggard face of failure and recrimination.

Maybe it was because of the sunshine and the amazing light shows that it could not be seen at the time. Or maybe it was the dope, or the raw, energetic sound of rock, inhabiting the narrow margin between chaos and order. The people on stage played the songs of social revolution and personal liberation. They were taking risks with their music as they were with their lives, but they were risks the audience understood and shared. Challenge was in the air. 'This is the love crowd, right?' asked Otis Redding from the stage, and the answer came, 'Yeah!' How could manipulation ever become a dirty word?

As one of the few black performers at the festival, Otis seemed to cement a greater unity than anybody else at Monterey. His performance brought Rolling Stone Brian Jones to the verge of tears, and had one Los Angeles record executive on his feet shouting, 'Heavy!' But it was hard to say if that unity had any

substance. Other black performers invited to Monterey were probably accurate in describing it as 'Whitey's festival', and it's worth noting that the 'Summer of Love' also experienced the worst black riots in contemporary American history.

All the same, rock stars never seemed so close to their audience as at Monterey. To bridge the gap between star and fan is one of rock'n'roll's most cherished dreams. The ligger, the lookalike, the groupie and the hanger-on all pursue that dream. So, frequently, do rock journalists (often accused of being musicians *manqués*). Even the rock'n'roll business establishment is fleshed out with fans who have found a respectable niche for their obsession. Finally, rock stars themselves do not escape the obsession. Few, if any, become rock'n'rollers for the uncomplicated love of money. Most start as fans, attracted by rock'n'roll's other magic ingredients: glamour, adulation, fame or the sheer joy of music-making. Many remain fans, idolizing greater or earlier talents than themselves. Some are even obsessed with their own star-images and forever try to blot out the ordinariness of their off-stage, off-record characters or to reproduce and sustain the sense of a performance's power and magical spontaneity through drugs, drink, frequent and fleeting sexual encounters or the cultivation of manic and egotistical behaviour. The rock'n'roll fan and the rock'n'roll star hold up mirrors to each other's world. Each can recognize themselves or friends or lovers in the mirror but neither can cross through the looking-glass.

Occasionally, the music succeeds in bringing star and fan close. Those are the moments when great rock'n'roll is created. They are moments when star and fan face each other across a narrow divide in their common interest – moments of self-immersion in the great Leviathan of rock'n'roll. Each such moment is a kind of suicide – sometimes bizarrely re-run in actual acts of self-destruction or in that curious conspiracy of need which makes stars the easy targets of angry or disappointed fans and which brought John Lennon face-to-face with his murderer: worshipper and idol finally united in the act of mutual self-destruction.

There is no doubt that Monterey witnessed some great rock'n'roll that summer of '67. Janis Joplin sang her heart out, stomping the stage with her feet as though kicking at a coffin lid. The Who, cuban-heeled English dandies at their most petulant, ended their set with a mind-boggling assault on the senses – a crescendo of feedback, a crazed attack on drums and speaker cabinets, a barrage of smoke-bombs. Pete Townshend rammed the neck of his guitar into a speaker-grille, rasped the fretboard with his microphone stand and hammered the instrument viciously on the stage until the neck snapped and splintered. A pall of smoke hung over the group as Keith Moon smashed into his drums. In a final gesture of gratuitous violence, he kicked the lot over and the group walked off. Jimi Hendrix, half black American and half Red Indian, 'fucked' his guitar, stroked it as though it was his own

member and, finally, set light to it – all the while squeezing pure rock'n'roll from it. And there was Otis Redding, his voice pleading and demanding in the same moment, expressing all the pain and anger of black America in a single song. 'We all love each other, right? Let me hear you say "Yeah"!'

'Yeah.'

But if the Festival was a celebration of the coming-of-age of rock'n'roll's guiltless trip through the wonderland of fun, it was also a prime-time star vehicle, as calculated a piece of exploitation as we are ever likely to see. Monterey was a showcase for new talent, a cattle-market with musicians as the beef. For the record executives in the audience (and there were plenty), considerations of profit far outweighed feelings of love – or, rather, they were the same thing. CBS's Clive Davis later recalled seeing Janis Joplin for the first time. 'I had to go after her,' he said. The festival was quickly followed by a spate of record deals, profitable releases and successful tours, and the chief beneficiary of all the good vibes was the music industry.

Don't get it wrong. Right from the start, rock'n'roll has been a heady mix of commerce and creativity. Rock'n'roll is a twentieth-century phenomenon – a modern folk music serving a community of young people with only their youth and their access to the mass media to tie them together. Without the media rock'n'roll music could not exist – and to be involved in the media so far is to be involved in commerce.

The rock'n'roll star system – designed to keep one name in the public eye and ear, to encourage identification and to promote record and concert-ticket sales – is commerce with a vengeance. The music becomes a commodity, the star little more than a super-salesperson. Even life-styles are sold – blue-jeans, punk chic, long hair, short hair, booze, guitar-strings – promoted through posters, the rock and pop press, TV, the cinema and radio. The star becomes a merchandizing trade-mark, the key to a vast revenue above and beyond that provided by the music alone. Stars are valuable items to be manipulated and yet cossetted. Their whims must be catered to – be they eggs benedict with brown sauce; a champagne supper in every dressing-room; an endless stream of groupies, heroin, cocaine, or all three; chauffeur-driven limousines; parties resembling bacchanalian orgies; or just an ever-present bottle of beer sitting on an amplifier at each gig. Stars must be protected from the press and over-zealous fans, they must be sheltered from the problems of everyday life – for as long, that is, as they keep packing houses, selling records and shifting merchandize. On this side of the rock'n'roll balance sheet, every star has a cash value which can be haggled over in courts of law and revalued in stock markets. Even being close to a star is worth money to the scandal-hungry popular press. The multi-billion dollar music industry happily dispenses with the reality which underpins star images and, in the end, the cash value is sometimes all that is left to mark the passing of a rock'n'roller. Time and again it has been demonstrated that stars like Buddy

Holly, Otis Redding, Jim Morrison, Jimi Hendrix and Elvis Presley can be worth more dead than alive.

Inevitably, a life as carefully priced and as lovingly tended as a rock star's can seem a little distorted at times. For the stars themselves there is a further twist. Rock'n'roll feeds off risk. It is a music that takes chances with everything mundane and predictable. When stardom reaches the mundane and predictable heights of heaven and creative risks are no longer an option under your contract, it is all too easy to play with the self-destructive excitement of drugs or drink or fast cars or guns. The isolation of super-stardom, surrounded by a wall of paid protectors and cash-on-the-nail admirers, can be a powerful invitation to paranoia. And if extreme success seems like a recipe for disaster, think what unexpected decline could make with the same ingredients.

So, as a piece of rock'n'roll exploitation, Monterey was nothing peculiar. Most would-be stars are, in any case, quite willingly exploited in the first place. But from Presley to the Pistols, the lesson has been the same: willing as you may be, exploitation can seriously damage your health. If there is no rock life after forty, the business must take at least as much blame as the rock star's own relentless drive for pleasure. For most people, the pursuit of happiness is a leisurely jog through life with an occasional sprint (if they are allowed to enter the race at all). For rock stars, it has become a sort of Indianapolis 500 on a track fenced and policed by the business. There is no way off except along the track itself. Hardly surprising that the casualty rate sometimes seems staggering. If you do it in the road, you must expect to get run over.

What was unusual about Monterey was just how eager people were to ignore the obvious signs of exploitation and then just how quickly and completely their innocent beliefs were shattered. Monterey was a kind of self-delusion, a con-trick with willing victims, carried out by people who seemed to believe the lies they told.

The Festival was originally conceived by a Los Angeles booking-agent called Ben Shapiro and a promoter from the same city named Alan Pariser. These two originally planned a simple, profit-making venture utilizing the undeniable talents of Derek Taylor to gain maximum media exposure. They went to see John Phillips, leader of the very successful Mamas and the Papas and author of the Summer of Love's big international hit – a timeless ditty which went 'If you're going to San Francisco, be sure to wear some flowers in your hair'. Phillips (and Paul Simon, who was present at the meeting) agreed to perform only if the Festival was organized on a non-profit making basis. Derek Taylor favoured this proposition and Shapiro and Pariser followed suit. Phillips brought in his manager and producer, Lou Adler, and a 'board of governors' was put together including such musical luminaries as Mick Jagger, Paul McCartney, Brian Wilson and Smokey Robinson.

Shapiro and Adler fell out – Shapiro suspecting Adler of 'a lust for contracts and prestige' (in critic Robert Christgau's words). Shapiro was eased out and

a press statement appeared in the American entertainment trade paper, *Variety*, to the effect that Shapiro's ideas were 'not compatible with the original festival concept' but that he had left 'amicably to press on with many movie commitments'.

The calculated hustling began. Derek Taylor announced that the Festival's profits would be donated to San Francisco's hippy relief agency, the Diggers, who gave aid and assistance to the hundreds of young people who daily arrived in the city without food, work or money. It was a piece of office gossip that Taylor presented as fact. The Monterey town council believed it and began to have visions of thousands of starving hippies arriving on their doorsteps with nowhere to stay, incited by drugs and music to 'lewd and violent behaviour'. The Festival organizers hurriedly assured the council that 'the profits will not go to a hippy organization', and that 'we have omitted acts that draw the real young kids, and our publicity has solicited family groups'. 'We haven't invited the sort of groups that inspire acting up on the part of the audience,' said Phillips. 'If that happens, we'll pull them off the stage.' The city fathers were appeased.

The Diggers and a number of groups however were not. Bands had been asked to play for expenses only, but an initial investment of $50,000 had been well covered by ABC TV's $300,000 rights payment. With an expected attendance far in excess of the arena's capacity of 7,500 seats, Adler was planning to charge one dollar admission to the Festival site's unseated surroundings. The Grateful Dead's manager and several other music people from San Francisco planned to counter with a completely free 'anti-festival'. Groups dropped out for various reasons – the Beach Boys could not see themselves in this 'hippy community'; the Young Rascals subsequently talked of Monterey as representing 'a clique among music people'. Everybody wanted to know where the money would go and what, exactly, the Festival was all about. Only the organizers knew for sure – which is why they invited the press and record company executives in such great numbers.

Not surprisingly, the Mamas and Papas topped the bill. Another of Adler's acts, Johnny Rivers, was also featured. Adler himself, who had previously sold his Dunhill record label for nearly $3 million to ABC (who had also bought the Monterey film rights), landed a distribution deal after the Festival for his new label, Ode, with CBS. As Adler later recalled, Clive Davis – soon to be head of CBS Records – 'had gone to the . . . Festival where he saw something happening, and he knew that I had put it on'. Deal followed deal and San Francisco was soon rocketed into the big time under the careful guidance of the LA record industry establishment. Most of the direct profits from Monterey (some $200,000) were donated to a variety of charities, chosen by the festival's directors. These included the Sam Cooke Memorial Scholarship established by Atlantic Records' Jerry Wexler, the Monterey Symphony Orchestra, a fund to buy guitars for Harlem's black kids and the LA Free Medical Clinic. But the fate of the money itself was less important than Monterey's promotional worth.

Months after the Mamas and Papas had closed the show, 'a bad taste remains', wrote critic Michael Lydon some time later. Especially bitter was the fate of many of the stars who had first shone so brightly at Monterey. By the onset of the seventies, Janis Joplin was dead, officially though somewhat mysteriously, from an overdose of heroin probably compounded by an alcohol habit of staggering proportions. Jimi Hendrix was dead, too, having apparently choked on his own vomit after taking an excessive number of sleeping pills. Otis Redding had been killed in a plane crash. Canned Heat's Al Wilson had died from a drug overdose, effectively putting to an end a group career that had blossomed after Monterey. Brian Jones had died from drowning.

There have been further tragedies, great and small. Mama Cass Elliott met an untimely death, as did the Grateful Dead's Ron 'Pigpen' McKernan and the Who's Keith Moon. The list is still growing. There have been drug busts, bouts of alcoholism, bizarre reformations, absurd obsessions. Rock has flirted with the occult, with mysticism, with straight-forward religions, with curious science fiction fantasies, with politics. Veins were awash with heroin, cocaine, methedrine, quaaludes (mandrax); Jack Daniels, Remy Martin, neat vodka; uppers, downers and in-betweeners; anything, it seemed, to unlock the walls of the prison. They had thought the promised land was outside the walls, but they were still – are still – captives in Babylon. For many the only possible gesture of rebellion left after all the groupies had gone home, after all the permutations had been tried twice, after all the damage done in all the wild hotel parties had been paid for, after they had consumed so much alcohol they could consume no more, after the strongest drugs had worn off, after the weirdest visions had all faded . . . was self-destruction, final and complete.

Many stars made legends at Monterey have survived, of course, to live in some sort of elegant ease – but there are no longer any risks involved for them, no sense of urgency, nothing of what once made their music so important. They become preening peacocks, sucking up to the social register, or filled with a dull religiosity that denies the sense of sin that once liberated them, or retired major-generals endlessly refighting the old youth culture campaigns in their heads. Even then, they may meet their nemesis as John Lennon met Mark Chapman – a fan filled with the knowledge of betrayal but desperate to identify, crucifier and crucified. It is of course unfair, but there is no such thing as safe retirement for a rock'n'roll star. The rock star's tragedy is that he or she is forced to live a disorienting series of magic moments, draining every last drop from short-lived success, inhabiting a timeless world in which a list of venues takes the place of a calendar, one darkened studio or concert hall is much like another and Saturday night is a working day.

CRASH LANDING IN TEENAGE HEAVEN

Rock'n'roll is an itinerant phenomenon. It leaps fences and challenges boundaries. In the frightened fifties, when the world seemed to have frozen into the power blocs of a cold war, such casual disregard as rock'n'roll showed for the barriers and conventions of race, geography, sex and age was terrifying to both the masters and slaves of the established order. Fifties rock'n'roll – with its rebel images, its heady mixture of sentimentality and angst and its disobedience to the rules of melody and rhythm and decent performance – helped create a sense of community between the disparate groups of teenagers who discovered in the music the symbols of their darkest dreams. No wonder rock'n'roll was condemned as 'lewd' and 'lascivious' by the self-appointed guardians of morality.

Of course, in many ways rock'n'roll was not an unmixed blessing. It confirmed and deepened shameful divisions between men and women. If it led to progress and liberation, it also created stars whose very success has been an object lesson in reaction and repression. And the very fact of stardom resulted in enormous wastage of resources – not just in material things but also and most often tragically in terms of human life and freedom.

Two deaths, in 1953 and 1954, were auguries for rock'n'roll's notorious profligacy in matters of life and talent. On 1st January, 1953, Hank Williams, the country and western star whose career had burnt brilliantly for a brief four years before being doused by the vast quantities of alcohol he consumed, died in the back of a car while being driven to a show by an off-duty taxi driver. Williams' death from heart failure was brought on by drink and the drugs he obtained illegally from a quack doctor. He had drunk heavily while still a teenager but touring and the isolation of fame combined to deepen his familiar depressions. His sizeable ego, which may well have been necessary to his success as a performer, did not help and he relied increasingly on booze to keep him going. His performances suffered, his marriage fell apart and he started taking pills to wake himself up and more to get himself to sleep. He was 29 when he died, and had done more than anyone else to justify country music's description as 'the white man's blues' – an idea which proved crucial to the development of rock'n'roll.

Johnny Ace was a sweet-voiced rhythm and blues star who had worked with Johnny Otis, Bobby 'Blue' Bland, Junior Parker and B. B. King. He had R&B hits in the early fifties, but died bizarrely during the intermission of a concert in Huston's City Auditorium on Christmas Eve, 1954, whilst playing Russian Roulette. In 1955 his posthumous release, *Pledging My Time*, topped the American R&B charts. Bob Dylan once commented that 'the singers and musicians I grew up with transcend nostalgia – Buddy Holly and Johnny Ace are just as valid to me today as then'. It was not merely clever talk to say that Johnny Ace and Hank Williams parenthesize rock'n'roll. It is all there in their lives and deaths – sweetness and bitterness, darkness and light, black and white, anger and joy, success and failure and, above all, the tragedies and pleasures of youth.

While teenagers saw their fifties idols as symbols of a positive rebellion against the sterile and passionless world of their elders, many adults were plainly shocked by the lives and works of their children's new heroes. Rock'n'roll music blared from the ubiquitous radio and the increasingly commonplace phonograph. It seemed like a precise statement of the rootless and narcissistic hedonism that they thought sexual awareness might unleash in their children. Songs about 'shaking', 'rocking', 'rolling', 'loving' and 'playing' were sung by young men whose actions and attitudes were unmistakably *dirty* and whose style was borrowed wholesale by the young and worshipped as in some latter-day idolatry.

The music often sounded to adult ears like a caterwaul. Lyrics seemed nonsensical if not obscene. The *Encyclopedia Britannica Yearbook* for 1956 described rock'n'roll as 'insistent savagery . . . deliberately competing with the artistic ideals of the jungle'. The following year, Frank Sinatra refrained from mincing even more words when he described it as 'the most brutal, ugly, vicious form of expression', a 'rancid-smelling aphrodisiac' and 'martial music of every delinquent on the face of the earth'. A Chicago radio station instituted a regular and highly publicized practice of breaking rock'n'roll records over the air. Juvenile delinquency, a legal catch-call that had caught the imaginations of fifties sociologists and criminologists, was blamed on rock'n'roll and records were banned by Crime Commissions. Britain, which at first had nothing significant in the way of home-grown rock'n'roll, was astounded by the thousands of kids who turned out to greet Bill Haley on his 1957 tour of the country and initial amused tolerance gave way to strident aversion in the face of the gleeful destruction

The King of Rock'n'Roll enjoying some close attention in the way he liked best: from both sides at once.

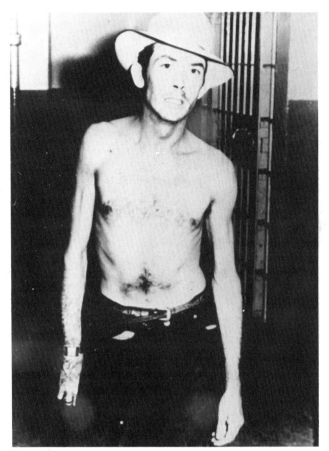

Hank Williams sets the pattern for countless rockers to follow: jailed after yet another drunken binge in Alexander City, Alabama on 18th August, 1952, he's obviously not far from an early death.

itself – in which five people were arrested and at least one stabbed – but the fact that the 25,000 kids included black and white. That was how most newspapers reported it anyway, although their estimates varied from about 60 per cent white to amost totally black. If the public (in the shape of those kids) no longer believed in segregation in music, how much longer could it survive in politics and business at large?

Sam Phillips, who owned a small Memphis recording studio and record label called Sun, found the formula for a more acceptable market crossover in the early fifties. The opportunity to meet market demand while circumventing racist objections presented itself to Phillips in the shape of Elvis Presley, a boy who walked into the Sun studio in 1953 to make a private recording as a birthday present for his mother.

Elvis's talent remains difficult to grasp, his personality an enigma, his biography subject to constant distortion and endless reinterpretation. 'God gave me a voice,' Elvis once said. 'If I turned against God I'd be ruined.' And yet he also recognized the devil's part in his success, saying that 'my voice is ordinary; if I stand still while I'm singing, I'm dead, man'. It was, indeed, Elvis's provocative hip-shaking that caused most consternation among critics of rock'n'roll. *Look* magazine was fairly polite when it opined that Presley's 'gyrations, his nose wiping, his leers were vulgar'. (Nose wiping?) The novelty, of course, was that unlike his equally 'vulgar' predecessors, Elvis was young, white and pretty – not a model rapist but a model seducer.

Elvis was well aware of the sexual delights he con-

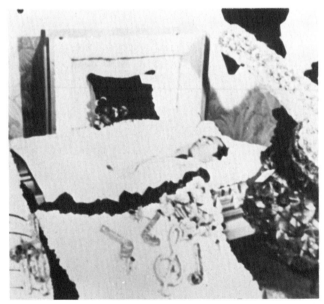

Sure enough, it is only four months later that thousands file past Hank's open coffin at Montgomery's Municipal Auditorium.

jured up. But the sexual power of Elvis the performer gradually infused his off-stage world. His own sexuality was soon reduced to power alone and Elvis, voyeur and masturbator, found it impossible to handle one-to-one relationships. In the early days, his most satis-

'All that glisters . . .' Elvis's gold suit conceals the corruption within.

of cinema and concert-hall seats wherever rock'n'roll inspired the urge to dance.

The traditional combination of racial prejudice and sexual jealousy encouraged hatred of the music and its exponents. The well-spring of rock'n'roll was, after all, black music with its bawdy lyrics, its sensual rhythms and expression and its general air of the bar-room and brothel. Even the phrase 'rock'n'roll' was composed of two sexual metaphors common in black music. It was predictable when, in 1956, the Secretary of the North Alabama White Citizens Council condemned rock'n'roll as 'a means of pulling the white man down to the level of the negro'. But it was harder to understand why the reputable entertainment trade paper, *Variety*, offered that same year 'A Warning To The Music Business', guarding them against a music that turned 'dirty postcards into songs'.

No doubt, the music business (and *Variety*) saw itself as more of a conservative industry with established marketing arrangements than a guardian of the moral order. What *Variety* was really objecting to was market crossover – the tendency for white kids to search out 'authentic' black music. When 30-year-old Alan Freed, the Cleveland disc jockey, organized his first rock'n'roll concert featuring black artists in his home town in 1952, and 25,000 kids turned up to chase 10,000 seats, what frightened the music industry and the rest of the establishment was not the ensuing riot

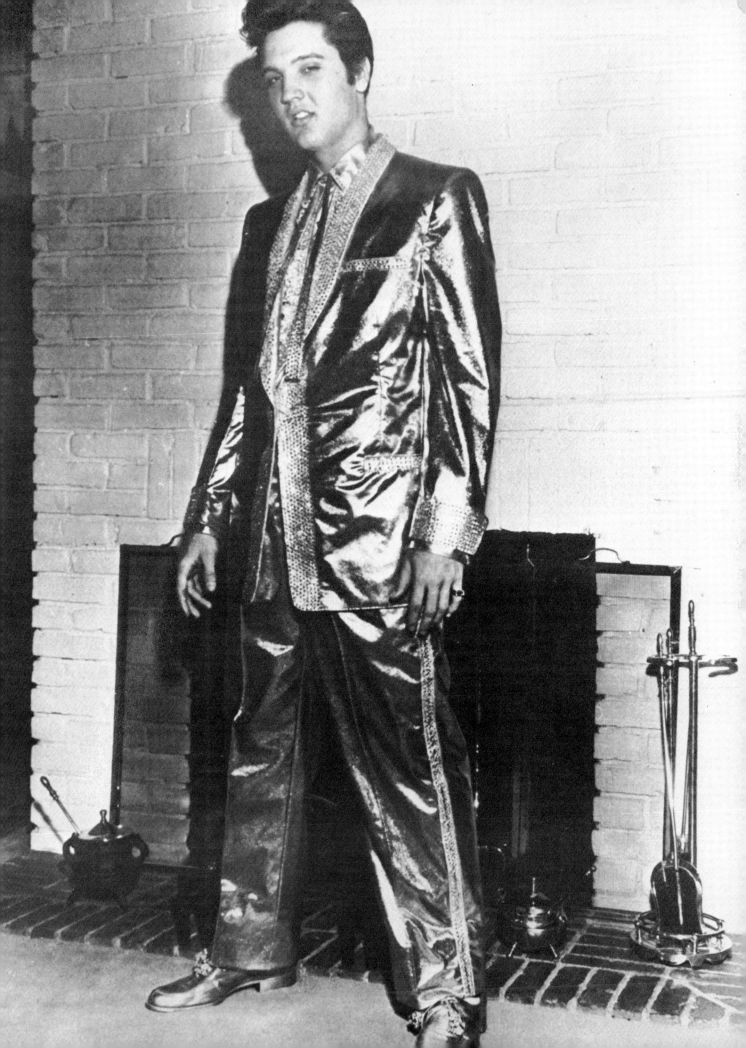

Even Presley couldn't be kept out of court in the early years: on 19th October, 1956, Elvis (third from right) explains how a scuffle with two garage attendants (left) led to a charge of assault.

fying 'sexual' relationship was with three teenage girls who regularly and collectively assisted him in re-creating innocent adolescent horseplay in the privacy of his own bedroom. In the sixties, his home was the venue for regular orgiastic parties, climaxing in the King getting carried away by the sight of two or three girls wrestling naked but for tight white panties stretched over their crotches. He also enjoyed filming his and other people's performances. By the seventies – wrecked by drugs and gross over-indulgence – Elvis's appetite could only be whetted by the sight of other people exciting themselves. Sometimes it was men and women. Mostly it was women only. The furtive voyeurism of a few years earlier became a deadening ritual in which three or four chorus girls would, by special arrangement, perform for Elvis and his video cameras in one or other of his sumptuous bedrooms. Meanwhile, he continued to have curious 'love affairs' with individual women which rapidly became purely platonic and which were almost always directed towards marriage. It is characteristic that the only woman he actually married, Priscilla Beaulieu, was just fourteen when they first met. It was inevitable that, grown up and a mother, Priscilla would leave Elvis (for the Presleys' karate coach, Mike Stone). Elvis, equally inevitably, became so distraught that he seriously planned to murder her lover.

Elvis lived in a fantasy world of power in many forms. He dreamed of demolishing large buildings; he had a mania for collecting all manner of guns – rare, antique, finely-tooled, efficient weapons of death; paranoid about potential assassins, he even reached the point of packing a derringer on stage during performances; he collected police and other law-enforcement agency badges and the honorary titles that went with them as shamanic tokens of his invulnerability. In 1970, after prolonged negotiations, President Richard Nixon agreed to see the drug-soaked Elvis and appointed him as honorary narcotics agent. Most cynically, it was good press for Nixon; most realistically, it suited Nixon's political effort to deflect the efforts of the anti-Vietnam War movement by promoting a 'greater' evil – the 'drug menace' – and one that conveniently also attacked those people most vocal about America's need to get out of Indochina. For Elvis, the schizoid gesture of a drug-happy rock'n'roller becoming a fighter against drug abuse was but another indication of his terminal notion that he could bend reality to his will. The King and the Emperor stood together for a while, and nobody can be sure who had the newest clothes.

His personal relationships were infused with a sense of his own godhead. He expected instant obedience from his minions – not tolerating the slightest demurral to even his most outlandish demands. He strode through his mansions like some despotic, frightened Khan – supervising orgies and violent, childish games with names like War and the Whip, taking vindictive and petty revenge on those who enjoyed themselves too much or displayed the sin of

Priscilla Beaulieu was a fresh-faced schoolgirl of just fourteen years when Elvis first set greedy eyes on her – ten years before their marriage in 1968. The bride wore white, the groom didn't.

lèse-majesté. He would take women home and cajole them into taking drugs he had come to depend on; he used his friends to experiment with LSD in 1964 (evidently eager to learn of the new drug's effects but too scared to risk his own delicate balance by experiencing them himself). Of course, he could be loving and kind (sometimes, if we are to believe some of his associates, to a rare degree) but, if he could not be God, at least he could be His Second-In-Command. His former bodyguards, Red and Sonny West and Dave Hebler, recalled him reading out selections from the Bible, and taking special note that when Jesus said 'It is harder for a rich man to enter heaven than for a camel to go through the eye of a needle', the Messiah was definitely not referring to Elvis.

Elvis's attempt to cope with the illusion of sexual omnipotence fostered by rock'n'roll stardom was to try and become divine – an attempt whose very audacity was only possible because Elvis, as his early friends and colleagues remember, was a colourless youth with little in his life but his burning ambition to succeed. And his success was not based on any extraordinary ability to be everything, but on his need to be nothing but the passive instrument of his own myth.

The truth about Elvis is that this myth was the realest thing about him. His image and even his style were carefully nurtured by men like Phillips, Colonel Tom Parker and Steve Sholes of RCA Records (who bought his contract from Phillips for the then unpre-

cedented figure of $35,000). Colonel Tom, the quintessential showman, was one of those who recognized Elvis's ability to appeal to both sides at once. He even manufactured 'I Love Elvis' T-shirts and 'I Hate Elvis' badges at the same time. It was Parker too who engineered the subtle change from rebel to nice guy.

When Elvis's 'bumps and grinds' started getting flak from the press and the pulpit early in 1956, after appearances on the Dorsey Brothers' and Milton Berle's networked TV shows, Elvis appeared on the Steve Allen show, in July that same year, standing still, dressed in white tie and tails and playing a little light comedy as well as singing *Hound Dog.* Ed Sullivan, whose show on another network was in direct competition with Allen's, had at first refused to consider featuring the singer. But Elvis's success on Allen's show persuaded him to change his mind, if Elvis would agree to be shown from the waist up only. Elvis, and Col. Parker, were happy to agree. For some even this was not enough. The *New York Times* TV critic, Jack Gould, complained about Elvis's 'singularly distasteful . . . movements of the tongue' during the Sullivan show in September 1956. But the Elvis camp had an answer for all objections.

They announced that the first thing Elvis did with all the money he was making was buy a new home for his parents. See, they said, he really was a home-loving, parent-respecting boy. On the Ed Sullivan show, Elvis announced his first movie and sang the title song, *Love Me Tender.* See, he really was gentle and believed in Romantic Love and marriage and that stuff. Elvis's output of rock'n'roll numbers declined

19

and his output of ballads and religious songs increased. See, he was as good as any singer *and* he was a Christian. In 1958, Elvis was drafted and meekly joined the army accompanied only by a mammoth press campaign. He had his hair cut to regulation length. See, Elvis was a patriot. After his discharge in 1960, Elvis appeared on TV arm-in-arm with his arch-rival Frank Sinatra (yes, the one who thought rock'n'roll was a rancid aphrodisiac). See, Elvis was just another pillar of the show-biz establishment.

Thus, Elvis came to obey all the commandments that Americans hold dear. He was once poor but now he was rich. He loved God and his mom, but boy did he know how to party. He resolved America's contradiction between the desire for pleasure and success and the need for guilt and failure just by being Elvis. And in his private imagination only the myth could compensate for or explain the confusing reality. So, helped by the drug habit he had picked up in the army – where his platoon was regularly issued with benzedrine to help it through manoeuvres – Elvis grew to believe the myth and it grew to kill him.

Fifties rock'n'roll couldn't have produced two stars like Elvis, although that didn't stop performers and record companies striving for comparable success. The $35,000 RCA paid Sam Phillips for Elvis's contract helped Sun promote the careers of a number of contenders – all of them, like the title-holder, country-

Self abuse with drugs and junk food turned the King into a sweaty hulk of blubber which, by 1977, the year of his death, he'd given up trying to hide.

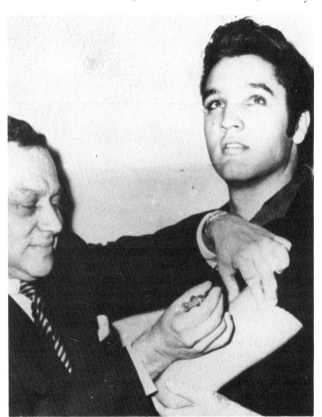

Elvis taking his shots in Germany before joining the Army there in 1958. He picked up his prodigious drug habit in the Army, where troops were regularly dosed with benzedrine to keep them going on manoeuvres.

bred, poor Southern whites. Carl Perkins might have made it, except that he was a little too old, a family man without the required youthful good looks. Besides, a car crash in 1956 on the way to a gig put Perkins out of action for several months at a crucial stage in his career. He had just released a record of his self-composed *Blue Suede Shoes* and was scheduled for all-important appearances on the Perry Como and Ed Sullivan TV shows. The crash killed Perkins' manager outright and led to the death from injuries of his brother Jay, a member of Perkins' band. The singer took a long time to recover from the crash emotionally and professionally. His career began to flounder as he relied increasingly on the bottle. The Beatles subsequently recorded some of his songs, but Carl had missed his early chance for stardom.

The nearest Carl Perkins got to greatness in the fifties was when *Blue Suede Shoes* was also recorded by Elvis. His success with the song helped to payroll Sun for some time. Sam Phillips was so grateful to Perkins that, star or not, he held a party in the songwriter's honour, during which a very drunk Carl was presented with a pink Cadillac, the very accolade of achievement in fifties rock'n'roll. Of course, since Elvis's death, Carl Perkins' career has enjoyed a resurgence of success, and he has been given the recognition he deserved all along as one of rock'n'roll's originators.

Roy Orbison, hugely successful in the sixties, found it difficult to accept Sam Phillips' dictat in the fifties. His records on Sun did not sell well – and in any case, his squirrelish face and horn-rimmed glasses were not the stuff of which Presleys were made. He seemed, if anything, a misfit – and it was only when he developed a style to match his loser image that he met with, success. The songs, with titles like *Only The Lonely* and *It's Over*, exercises in melodramatic emotionalism and delivered with heaps of saccharin and soya sauce feeling, were perfect accompaniments to adolescent crises in the early sixties. Orbison's looks

Roy Orbison, determined not to be lonely after the motorcycle crash in 1966 that killed his wife Claudette at Galattan, near the Orbison home in Nashville, Tennessee. Big O interviews nice English nannies to look after his three children while he goes on tour.

and his dark glasses (adopted after leaving his ordinary glasses at home, so he says, when touring Britain in 1963 with the Beatles), seemed to confirm a truth behind his whinnying, strained vocal agonies. On stage he scarcely moved, which was okay as long as his audience could assume it was fear that rooted him to the spot. But when real tragedy struck it revealed Roy in Orbison a mixture of independence and callousness.

His wife Claudette was killed in a motorcycle accident in 1966, and two of his three children died in a fire at his house two years later. Orbison continued working, his attitude – expressed some years later – was that tragedy should not be allowed to 'turn you all the way round'. 'My object is to be stable,' he said, 'to not let anything throw me too far.' Admirable though this object is, one cannot help but feel that had Orbison been less his own man he might have been more to rock'n'roll. On the other hand, he might have died or gone mad instead.

Johnny Cash was more obviously the stuff of stardom in the first phase of rock'n'roll. But he became hooked on pills, taking them first, he said, 'So I wouldn't be shy when I went on stage.' A promising career went sour as Cash began to rely more and more on 'artificial energy'. He became increasingly ill as a

Just two years after the death of Roy Orbison's wife, on 15th September, 1958 rescue workers remove the body of eleven-year-old Roy Orbison Jr. from the burnt-out Orbison home in Hendersonville, Tennessee. Orbison's six-year-old son Tony also died in the blaze.

21

Hell-raising Johnny Cash winds up in handcuffs at a court in El Paso, October 5th, 1965, charged with illegally importing over 1,000 pep pills and tranquillizers into the United States from Mexico.

greater sense of sin. He shared Presley's Christian background. Unlike Presley, however, Jerry Lee tried to practise what he had been brought up to believe. His faith – profound but inarticulate – led on at least one occasion (the recording session for the undeniably blasphemous *Great Balls of Fire*) to a hold-up in the proceedings while he and Sam Phillips argued at length about the propriety of turning divine imagery into a blatant sexual metaphor. 'I have the devil in me!' Jerry Lee confessed on the tape of the session, while Phillips tried to argue that Lewis's music 'can save souls'. It sounds like a combination of theology seminar and revival meeting and, although Jerry Lee eventually agreed to make the record, you can tell he still thought it evil. Even so, the result was definitive rock'n'roll.

The curiously similar Little Richard – he too assaulted his piano, seemed to talk in tongues ('A Wop Bop A Lu Bop, A Wop Bam Boom'), was possessed by sexual devils and hid behind a façade of aggressive and flamboyant arrogance – 'gave up rock'n'roll for the Rock of Ages' after, so he says, a divine revelation of uncertain nature. Some say the retirement in 1957 at the peak of Richard's success was in order to avoid the ravages of taxation on massive earnings. Richard's own version of the story, which varies from telling to telling, locates his impulse in a dramatic vision received while flying over Australia during a tour. Apparently, the plane was in difficulty and Richard's resolve to abandon rock'n'roll in the wake of a glimpse at his own damnation acted as a sort of spiritual turbo-prop. Safely back on firm ground, the former gospel singer threw his whole supply of garish jewellery into the sea and made more-or-less straight for an Alabama bible school where he trained for the evangelical life. His record company, meanwhile, continued to release Little Richard records from earlier sessions or radio shows as if nothing had happened. Richard himself returned to rock'n'roll seven years later – never having been able to give up completely the fleshly delights of secular music. His career floundered as it swung between periods of ever more grotesque and sacrilegious display and frequent interludes of public self-chastisement.

In those days such behaviour was often considered no better than could be expected from an 'uncivilized' black man. Jerry Lee Lewis, being white, was never allowed the liberty of his own self-doubts. When it was revealed in May 1958, during a tour of Britain, that he had married his thirteen-year-old cousin Myra, the media-led scandal that erupted drove him out of England, out of the charts and almost out of work. Elvis's subsequent relationship with Priscilla Beaulieu, whom he met in Germany when she was still a schoolgirl, and Buddy Holly's marriage to a Mexican woman (also in 1958) were both closely-guarded secrets. Lewis had tried to keep his marriage a secret too, even

result. He crashed his car, sustaining minor injuries. In the mid-sixties he had several brushes with the law. In October 1965, he was busted for illegally importing pills; in 1966, for possession of marijuana; and early in 1967 he was kept in prison overnight on a vagrancy charge. By this time, his career and his first marriage were in shambles. A reputation for unreliability and hell-raising, (he once painted an entire motel room black, and on another bender installed a donkey and a supply of hay in a rented room), preceded him. His friend Waylon Jennings considers that Cash came near to death on a number of occasions. There was also a suit for damages resulting from a forest fire in 1966. Cash was blamed for starting the fire but it was in fact two years before the case was settled and he was eventually fined. When his family decided they wanted to hospitalize him, and after he had been arrested for the third time in 1967, Johnny Cash finally got a grip on himself and began to climb back, achieving great success as a country musician.

On the other hand, one of rock'n'roll's most desperate victims could easily have been Sun's greatest star. Jerry Lee Lewis was a true rock'n'roll primitive; flamboyant, menacing and mischievous on stage and on classic recordings like *Whole Lotta' Shakin' Goin' On* and *Great Balls of Fire*. Lewis would smash up or even burn his piano, throw chairs on stage and abuse his audience. He had none of Presley's manners but he probably had more passion – and he certainly had a

---

The devil looks after his own – has Jerry Lee Lewis survived the ravages of the rock'n'roll life style by playing the devil's music?

POLICE CHECK UP ON CHILD BRIDE

Get out, Lewis!

Little Myra Lewis spoonfeeds the Killer. When Jerry Lee Lewis arrived in Britain in 1958, he barely managed to play a note before word got out about his marriage to Myra Gale Brown, his thirteen-year-old second cousin. Literally booed off stage, Lewis returned to America, unrepentant but in disgrace, and his career took a nosedive. At the time of the scandal, fellow musician Ronnie Hawkins commented: 'We didn't know what the fuss about Jerry marrying a thirteen-year-old was all about. All us Southern boys knew she was only twelve.'

CHILD BRIDE MIX-UP MAY CUT JERRY'S TOUR

POLICE TO ACT IN CASE OF Mrs 'ROCK' AGED

though Myra wasn't underage in the State where the ceremony took place, but once the fuss ensued he went out of the way to show her off. She was his third wife.

Lewis had started to drink heavily in his early teens. Like so many early rockers he got into speed, too. Tragedy followed him throughout his life. His and Myra's son was drowned in the family swimming pool in 1962, aged only three. In 1970 Myra left him; he says she caught him 'cheating'; Jerry Lee was highly sexed or promiscuous, depending on your point of view. The wrath of the Lord continued to dog him – his other son, Jerry Lee Jnr, died in a car crash in 1972, aged only seventeen. Jerry himself crashed his Rolls Royce in 1976, and, in that same year, accidentally shot bassist Butch Owens with a .357 Magnum. Jerry was hospitalized in 1977 for gall-bladder removal, collapsed lung, pleurisy and back trouble, and broke up with his fourth wife some time later. In 1981, he almost died from an ulcerated stomach. Hospitalized again and on the critical list for some weeks, Lewis nevertheless pulled through – at least, for the time being – and declared himself irrevocably committed to gospel music. From the mid-fifties to the time that rock'n'roll sends him to hell – as he is certain that it will – Lewis has been and will remain a survivor. Or, in his own words, 'a drunken oaf who thinks he's the best' and probably is. The final irony has been a running battle with the IRS (Internal Revenue Service) who twice

Difference of opinion among the Lewis family and their advisers. On 30th January, 1959, Jerry Lee asked a court to reduce alimony payments to his second wife Jane, and get custody of their two children awarded to his parents. L. to r.: manager Jud Phillips, Jerry's father, Elmo, Lewis himself and his lawyers, Harry and Allex Barnett.

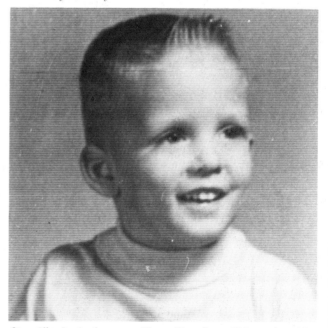

Steve Allen Lewis, three-year-old son of Jerry Lee and Myra, who toddled into the family swimming pool and drowned on 22nd April, 1962.

Bible-thumping Little Richard thinks there's nothing better than curling up in bed with The Good Book. He may have thrown his jewelry into Sydney Harbour in 1957, but by 1964 he was back rocking in the service of the Lord.

confiscated all his cars for non-payment of taxes and have since led him to auction some of his historic memorabilia in order to meet a bill he should never have been unable to pay in the first place.

Unlike many other early rockers, Chuck Berry, arch-stylist of the teen scene, clearly had a substantial hand in determining his own orientation. Berry – perhaps the greatest of the rock'n'roll lyricists – made the point when he said, 'I didn't write *School Days* in a class room. I wrote it in the Street Hotel, one of the big, black low-priced hotels in St Louis.' He deliberately moved away from his black R&B roots in his lyrics and approach, if not his musical style, towards images of Middle American teenage life with an attitude to sexuality distanced by comedy or sentimentality. It was always Berry's technique to cover his tracks with laughter, using teenage slang to talk about things no teenager's parents would have wanted to hear. His car imagery was particularly revealing. His first hit, the countrified R&B number *Maybelline*, used the metaphor of competitive car driving ('As I was motivating up the hill/I saw Maybelline in a Coupe de Ville'.) The words touch the perennial concern of teenagers with driving but are clearly designed also to stand for fucking.

Chuck Berry has revealed over the years an astute commercial mind, able to gauge precisely the concerns and attitudes of his audience. 'The dollar dictates what music is written,' the former Baptist choirboy and apprentice hairdresser once said simply. 'In my case musical and mathematical aptitude go together,' he said in typically immodest fashion in 1964. 'I manage my own affairs, including my investments.' By 1981, Berry's investments – including apartment blocks, houses, a recording studio and a 98-acre country club and leisure zone called Berry Park, situated near Chuck's home-town of St Louis, Missouri – were estimated to be worth around $20 million. Despite all of which, in 1979 Berry was actually jailed for tax evasion (the alternative was a large fine) after under-reporting his annual income for 1973 (in excess of half-a-million dollars) by more than $200,000.

This may demonstrate no more than Berry's legendary meanness. 'My contract is my Bible,' he says – and he has a pretty fundamentalist interpretation of it. In 1975 there were angry scenes after Berry left the stage at London's Hammersmith Odeon, according to fans who were present, 'about eight numbers into the set'. Without doubt, he had fulfilled his contract (in fact, he claimed to have played 58 minutes against a required 45) but the performance was desultory. 'You learn to live with it all,' Berry replies to those who condemn his performances. 'Remember they criticized Jesus as well.'

This latter-day Christ seems to have taken the American Dream to heart in a big way. On one tour outside the US, Berry is said to have checked the exchange rate of the dollar against the local currency every morning, insisting on a cash supplement to cover any devaluation of his fee before setting foot on stage. One night this supplement came to around 25 cents – but he still insisted on full payment.

But there are good reasons for Berry's cussedness. There's no doubt he had a tough past. A poor black who, but for rock'n'roll, would have become a ghetto hairdresser or followed his father's trade as a carpenter, he has been a victim of America's general racism and the music business's exploitative practices. At fifteen, he was sent to reform school for attempted robbery: in 1959, he was arrested in Mississippi for trying to pick up a white girl; and that same year saw him arrested on a statutory rape charge under the Mann Act. Berry had brought a fourteen-year-old Indian prostitute to St Louis to work in his night-club as a hat check girl. He says she told him she was twenty and that he had no knowledge of her profession. He subsequently sacked her for being involved in a fight but she went to the police with her story.

Berry's first trial was abandoned because it was openly racist. The judge persistently referred to him as 'this negro'; meanwhile the press ran riot: 'ROCK'N'ROLL SINGER LURED ME TO ST LOUIS SAYS 14-YEAR-OLD' screamed the headlines. A second trial in 1962 convicted him and he was fined $5,000 and sent to jail for three years, ultimately serving sixteen months. In 1964, Chuck Berry claimed he owed his then current popularity to the jail sentence. 'My only consolation was to think about music,' he said. 'I made notes of new songs and now think the public will forget and accept me as a performer, not as an ex-jailbird.' By 1972, Berry was denying that he was ever jailed. 'I was acquitted,' he said, claiming that the affair was connected with a rivalry between his club and a whites-only club 'across the street'. The vehement denials that he had ever served time had disappeared by 1975, but not the suggestion that his trial was 'a frame-up to ruin me and drive me out'.

What are we to make of Berry's contradictions? He's been married to the same woman since he was 22 but is persistently seen in the company of pretty young blondes. Within the space of a few months, he can deny knowledge of Mick Jagger and Keith Richard, who helped to resurrect Berry from an early decline, and then profess admiration and love for those same

Chuck wouldn't name the pretty blond accompanying him back home to the USA from London in July 1979 to face a jail sentence for tax evasion, but it certainly wasn't his wife of 22 years' standing.

two rock'n'rollers. He can be short-tempered to the point of violence: he once destroyed the camera of a fan who annoyed him by trying to take his picture before a performance; in 1981, he punched Keith Richard, when Keith approached him while he was leaving a club. Like Elvis, but in a different way, Berry embodies both the disturbing dreams of rock'n'roll and the comforting dreams of the 'average American'. An ardent believer in free enterprise, democracy and the motor industry, perhaps Berry just cannot accept his rebellious soul. 'At times I become very hot and cold, moody, very schizophrenic,' he once said. 'It's really controlled schizophrenia, and I'm controlling it.'

Without Berry there would have been no clean rock'n'roll. The record industry majors had a lot to thank him for. Shorn of its unmistakeable lyrical *doubles entendres* and its most lascivious bodily movements and vocal inflections, rock'n'roll turned into pop music. Television was especially influential as a launch pad for clean rock'n'rollers. *American Bandstand*, a networked show produced in Philadelphia and hosted by Dick Clark, pushed numerous would-be stars up the ladder of success. Most of them were called Bobbie or Frankie. Few had much talent and even those who had, suffered from the trivializing impact of relentless TV exposure. This was the much-lampooned era when good-looking boys were virtually pulled off the street and asked if they wanted to be stars. The record industry buzzed with the sound of white boys with Latin looks and duck's arse hairstyles scratching their names on contracts. With Elvis in the army, there was now to be an army of Elvises.

Fabian (real name Fabiano Forte Buonaparte) was thirteen when he was signed up by two local Philadelphian entrepreneurs. He was happy to admit that he couldn't sing (one legendary recording session lasted for 88 takes before Fabian got it right) but that did not matter. Fabian looked great.

Bobby Vee (real name Robert Velline) had the good fortune to be in the band that stepped into the empty spot left in the show at Moorhead, Minnesota, after Buddy Holly's plane crashed. Subsequently, producer Snuff Garrett heard a record by Vee's group (the Shadows) and took them under his wing. Vee – with the right, boyish puppy lover looks – was groomed for a solo career and even teamed up with Holly's old backing-group, the Crickets, to capitalize on the Holly mystique.

Rock'n'roll in Britain was, at first, hardly more than a marketing operation, a calculated response by the entertainment industry to bridge a gap in the market. The first big star was Tommy Hicks, whose assumed name, Steele, set a pattern to be followed by almost all the other singers managed by the man who virtually ran the British rock'n'roll scene for two or three years – Larry Parnes. Parnes had a penchant for calling his 'stable' by names crudely suggestive of sexual characteristics. There was Marty Wilde, Billy Fury, Vince Eager, Dickie Pride and Johnny Gentle – to name but a few. At one point, Parnes was managing sixteen performers, but by 1961 he had released all of them, bar Steele, Wilde, Fury and Joe Brown – preferring to concentrate on his first love, the 'straight' showbiz of managing theatres and promoting stage shows.

With an evident relish for the theatrical world, Parnes was also attracted to the histrionic posturing of rock'n'roll. As his talent for creating stage-names suggests, rock'n'roll only meant anything to Parnes as a form of theatre. In the mid-fifties, he was running his father's tailoring shops in London and had invested in the partnership of a small club frequented by show people. He bought an interest in a touring play – the publicist was a man named John Kennedy. Kennedy became interested in managing a singer he had seen in London's 2I's coffee-bar, where a number of Britain's skiffle acts and rock'n'rollers made their debuts. The singer was Tommy Hicks, a young merchant seaman, and Kennedy persuaded Parnes to join him in promoting the lad. The two remained partners until 1961, when a dispute over a five hour, £3,500 poker game caused them to fall out – although Parnes' sardonic comment at the time was simply 'I do the business. Kennedy does the publicity. It isn't essential to confer.'

Parnes and Kennedy saw rock'n'roll as a launch pad for more rounded careers. Accordingly, Tommy Steele only made two records with any pretensions to rock'n'roll (*Rock With The Caveman* and *Doomsday Rock*) before beginning the transformation to film-star, actor, cabaret-performer and TV personality which has been followed equally by Cliff Richard and Adam Faith. Commenting on his own success, Tommy Steele said, 'Someone was looking for an exponent of rock'n'roll, and I was there.' TV producer Jack Good's comment on Cliff Richard was even more succinct: 'He was malleable!' But for others, things were less simply encapsulated. Many were unable to cope with the manipulation of their personalities and were therefore unable to cope when their rock'n'roll moment passed. Marty Wilde, who continued to have hits into the early sixties, nonetheless found his earnings dropping from '£10,000 a year to £1,000' in the wake of a much publicized marriage. In 1961, at the age of twenty, Marty was obliged to announce his first come-back.

Billy Fury, despite being the best of Britain's early rockers with a stage act that even the *New Musical Express* described as 'downright disgusting' (those were the days), suffered from acute depression. Having inveigled his way into Marty Wilde's dressing room at a 1958 gig in Birkenhead, in order to play the

star some of his compositions, Fury was catapulted to stardom himself by the ever-rapacious Parnes, insatiably in pursuit of new blood. The would-be songwriter was transformed, Cinderella-style, into a sexual demon. Even Jack Good was moved to comment that, 'Frankly, there are one or two things that Billy does that I would rather he didn't.' He did not elaborate.

Fury's career – parodied in the seventies' film *That'll Be The Day* – was suitably summed up by the name of the character he played in it, Stormy Tempest. He continued in the public gaze until almost the end of the sixties and has subsequently made a couple of abortive comebacks (one ruined by his illness on the eve of a rock'n'roll revival package tour and one as recently as 1981). His image was that of an English James Dean. He was shy but passionate, a lover of animals ('Billy cries whenever he sees an animal hurt,' said the press), infatuated with speed and fast cars (he was pulled up for speeding in 1961, 1962, 1963 and 1968), yet lacking the confidence to talk to girls. (Parnes claimed to have written a script for Fury to use once when breaking up with a girlfriend.) Without doubt, Fury was an erotic performer (even without his gold lamé suit) and a victim of his own melancholy. The idea of simultaneous weakness (he suffered from rheumatism, kidney trouble and bronchitis) and strength (sexually and otherwise – he had been a tug-boat man), of sensitivity and aggression (he read poetry as well as raced cars), was immensely attractive. But Fury actually seemed to prefer his quiet life studying ornithology and owning race-horses to the rigours of the public life as a rock'n'roll performer.

Larry Parnes (centre) gloats as shy, pet-loving Billy Fury, the latest addition to Parnes' rock'n'roll stable, copes with the clamour of his fans. Fury's act was described at the time as 'downright disgusting'.

Britain's answer to Elvis? But Cliff Richard doesn't know where to put his hands when faced with a kiss from delectable Janette Scott. Nowadays Cliff claims to have been celibate for sixteen years.

Parnes was not slow to drop those that did not pull their weight. Vince Eager went on the grounds that he never made hit records. Dickie Pride, who wore pork pie hats and battered leather jackets, was one of the few early rockers who became a heroin addict. He drove a much used sports car and once test-drove a motorcycle through the show-room's plate glass window. Parnes needless to say dropped him because he was a liability and he died in obscurity of an overdose. 'I'm only going to retain the ones who give me whole-hearted co operation and put themselves completely in my hands both on and off stage,' was Parnes's explanation.

30

Terry Dene was the next most likely to succeed on the British rock'n'roll scene, after Tommy Steele. He was spotted, by Jack Good, singing between bouts of a wrestling match in 1957 and Good decided to put him on his TV show. At eighteen, Dene was a classic teen idol – fans chased him down streets, tearing his clothes and hair; he was obliged to make elaborate getaways from stage shows through dressing-room windows; even his mother was knocked down by the screaming hordes. From a £3.50-a-week record packer he was transformed into a public sensation. He lost his head. He took to smashing plate glass windows on impulse, throwing motor-bikes around if he did not like the way they were parked and, on one occasion, smashing a telephone kiosk because he had no money to call his girlfriend, the singer Edna Savage. When he married Edna in 1958, it caused a sensation in the press – two of the country's biggest stars falling in love with each other. In fact, the young Dene had only fallen for a face he had seen in a spotlight and, on their wedding night, the bride waited in vain in her room for her young husband, while he went off on a motorcycle ride that lasted three weeks. 'In our months together,' a sadder and much poorer Edna recalled years later, 'I count only five happy days.'

The couple's very public rows invariably made the news. There was even a joke about them ('Does Terry Dene make Edna savage?'). They lived in the whirlwind of their own fame, spending their easy money and cheap emotions like there was no tomorrow. Needless to say, the marriage did not last very long.

A few weeks before marrying Edna, on the very day that Elvis Presley reported for duty in the US Army, Dene had received his draft papers for the British Army. It was a golden opportunity for his publicists – and for the Army. 'I wanted to go like any other man,' says Dene, 'but the publicity boys thought otherwise.' He hoped that the army would offer a refuge from the pressures of showbiz. But his 'advisers' fought the call-up and in a month Dene was in court on a drunk and disorderly charge. Eventually, Dene was required to report to the barracks, and a posse of reporters and photographers went with him. After they left, he recalls, 'I broke down and wept.' Not even the Army could rescue him. He was sent to hospital for psychiatric tests and two weeks later was sent to a civilian hospital, suffering from a nervous breakdown. Nine weeks after entering the army, Dene was invalided out. Questions were asked in Parliament. 'It seems there is one law for ordinary lads,' said Gerald Nabarro MP, 'and another for Mr Terry Dene.'

At home, Dene started to read the Bible and began to calm down. But at a comeback performance in Blackpool, he was booed off the stage – the British can never tolerate an out-and-out weakling. He started drinking again, a has-been at 21. Then one night in 1964, he 'was walking the streets, alone, fed-up and lost'. In London's Trafalgar Square he was approached by an evangelist. 'He took the time to talk to me about Jesus,' said Dene, announcing his conversion.

Dene became an evangelist. He began ministering to the needs of junkies and alcoholics, sometimes singing hymns and accompanying himself on guitar, but never, never listening to his old records. 'I was a false idol,' he announced, 'a false person.'

Gene Vincent, though American, can fairly be linked with these British names since his most sustained success was in Britain where, again under the guidance of Jack Good, Vincent was given his definitive black leather image. With one massive hit to his name, *Be Bop A Lula*, Gene and his band, the Blue Caps, caused riots in Australia and the US. They drank a great deal, destroyed hotel rooms and generally caused havoc. A hotel manager once asked for a $50,000 deposit against breakages and Vincent's unpleasant temper when drunk (which he was most of the time), led to feuds with his managers and numer-

A Martini-soaked Gene Vincent (left) gives some timely advice to ex-Shadow Jet Harris. It doesn't seem likely that either of them took it – Vincent died in obscurity in 1971, and Harris's career has consisted of one abortive come-back after another.

ous other problems for his career. He was a naïve working-class kid, unable to cope with success. 'I didn't know how to handle a hit, I was only a child, a boy,' he once reflected. The major injury he suffered to his left leg (it was nearly severed at the shin in a motorcycle crash in 1955) was never properly treated. He never took care of his tax situation after his first success. His membership in the American Musicians Union was revoked for unprofessional behaviour. On top of all that, his record company were bent on exploiting him as a new Elvis, while Gene himself found it immensely difficult to talk to DJs or to do interviews – which did not endear him to the publicity machine. Finally, a court case between his management and his agency forced him off the road, at one point, for three months.

Yet Gene Vincent was a born performer and when things got too difficult in America he simply moved to Britain. Jack Good took him under his wing and played up the sense of ugly menace in Vincent's personality. The black leather was one aspect. Good also remembers standing in the wings during one TV show exhorting Vincent to 'Limp, you bugger, limp!' Vincent became one of the biggest ballroom draws in the country (in fact, his compere, ex-singer Don

Don and Phil Everly pass on the experience of several years already spent on the road to a green Cliff Richard, whom they met during a 1958 tour of Britain. The filial harmony was only skin deep.

Arden, became his manager and built an empire from there, eventually centred on the Electric Light Orchestra). But the 1960 crash which had killed Eddie Cochran worsened Vincent's leg injury, and by 1964 the pain and the drinking were beginning to show in Britain. His private life was a public shambles – involving press stories of drunken brawls with and without his wife. His leg desperately needed treatment. For four years he was altogether out of the limelight and his life grew more and more chaotic. He sank into a permanent, Martini-induced haze, came back to Britain in 1969 and was greeted by alimony proceedings instituted by his wife. He was fat and debilitated. In 1970, grateful to a faithful French fan, he was reduced to playing village *fêtes* around the countryside of France and, the next year, he fled Europe for the home of his birth, only to die a few days later of a seizure resulting from a perforated ulcer. Performing and dying were two things that came easiest to him. When he could no longer do one, the other was inevitable.

In America, the manipulation of young, *ersatz* Elvises was seen as something that had happened to a spontaneous form of musical expression under the influence of a controlling industry. The 1959 Payola scandal and the various fates of rock'n'roll's most creative artists – Elvis, Chuck Berry, Buddy Holly, Eddie Cochran, Jerry Lee Lewis and Little Richard were all either killed or effectively silenced – helped that interpretation of events. While British kids believed that real rock'n'roll had been denied them, their contemporary Americans assumed that it had been co-opted.

It was not always as simple as that. The worst victims among America's younger rock'n'rollers were often street-wise kids whose ordinary lives were surrounded by a routine terror. Dion Di Mucci was Bronx-born and started singing at the age of five. By the age of fifteen, he was appearing on TV and, at nineteen, in 1958, he formed Dion and the Belmonts who had a massive hit with *Teenager In Love*. Dion was already using heroin. His neighbourhood was tough and drugs, guns and car crashes were common hazards. Dion took to the drug to 'fill the gap' between what he later described as 'your public and your private face'. It enabled him to cope with everyday life, not just with fame. Certainly, being persuaded by his management to go solo in 1960 – a move which saw him have massive hits with songs like *The Wanderer* – created extra pressures, and by 1964 Dion had dropped out of sight to go through the painful process of overcoming his addiction. On the one hand, heroin had helped him deal with the problems of stardom; on the other hand, however, stardom may well have given him the money and the motivation to throw off

Don Everly arrives in New York with his second wife, Venetia Stevenson, after collapsing from a drug overdose in Britain, in 1962. A doctor had prescribed 'vitamins' to help the Everlys on tour, but they turned out to be amphetamines.

an addiction that might otherwise have proved fatal. Fortunately, his withdrawal was successful and he eventually returned to performing.

One example from the early days of rock'n'roll does seem to indicate clearly how commerce can ruin careers and lives. In 1960, the two brothers, Phil and Don Everly, left the small Cadence label, with whom they had had a string of hits, after a dispute over royalties. They went to the potentially greener pastures of Warner Brothers and, a year later, they also broke acrimoniously with the production-management-writing team that had previously provided them with so many hits. In 1962, they were still being described as 'the world's most successful and richest singing team', but the cracks were beginning to show.

'Everyone has the feeling that all you have to do is to achieve stardom and once you're there you can relax,' said Phil in 1981. 'It's just the opposite. Once you get there, then the war really starts. The pressures get larger because getting hit records is a miracle.' The brothers began to argue, travelling separately, staying in different hotels, eventually hiring separate managers, agents and lawyers. For successful close harmony singers they were the least harmonious of couples. Don, the elder by two years, was married in 1957 and divorced in 1961. He married again in 1962 and within a year his wife was threatening to sue him for divorce on the grounds of mental cruelty. That same

year, a doctor prescribed drugs to the brothers to help them through an arduous tour. The drugs, thought to be some sort of vitamin, turned out to be amphetamines and Don became hooked. While playing in Britain in late 1962, Don was taken to hospital twice in twelve hours. His condition was reported variously as 'food poisoning', 'nervous exhaustion' and – more accurately – 'an overdose of drugs'. He flew home, leaving Phil to complete the visit alone.

A suicide attempt followed before Don successfully came off speed, but the pressures continued. In the early seventies Don fell in love with a woman suffering from spinal meningitis. 'She recovered,' he recalled, 'and I decided she was the most important thing in my life.' After his two previous disastrous marriages, he opted to retire from the Everly Brothers and marry again. Phil had also discovered how difficult living with someone could be. 'I reached the point where I wasn't sure love really existed,' he said after two unhappy marriages. Regrettably, common experiences had not led to common understanding and, at their last show together in 1973, Phil smashed his guitar on stage and walked out of a sixteen-year-old act that had, in Don's words, 'died ten years ago'. Both eventually returned to performing separately, while maintaining their long-lived mutual hostility.

Faced with a host of lookalike/soundalike pretty boys controlled by sharp entrepreneurs it is not surprising to find American kids in the early sixties deserting rock'n'roll for less commercial musics like jazz and folk.

In Britain, kids had all along been fed on largely second rate pap. They rejected the British pop establishment and looked for authenticity overseas in the land of Elvis, Chuck and Eddie. British musicians have always acknowledged this spontaneous searching out of American music for more meaningful forms. Some got caught up in a quest for rock'n'roll, R & B and blues roots – others found inspiration in the emerging soul music which, they believed, ran in a direct line of development from rock'n'roll. In every case they saw that 'black' music (which ironically was often written by whites) stood for a liberation they urgently wanted *and* they saw that rock'n'roll had shown a way in which whites could interpret black soul. Here is the real link with the sixties – for among their number we can count John Lennon, who acknowledged Elvis's influence; Keith Richard and Mick Jagger who, legend has it, first got together over a mutual admiration for Chuck Berry; George Harrison who followed Eddie Cochran around England watching his guitar technique; and Eric Burdon and the Animals, whose Bo Diddley impersonation was admired by Bo himself. After the nightmare race run by the first rockers against the short memory of their public, it was these mainly British artists who revitalized rock music, but who in turn had to face many of the same kinds of battle. Only now it was the sixties, and this was a whole new war.

SEX AND DRUGS
AND ROCK'N'ROLL

Serious drug-taking has always had some part in the rock'n'roll landscape. In fact the excessive use of stimulants and depressants of one sort or another has been associated with the rebel image and with music-making since well before the first bohemians walked the boulevards of Paris. For rock musicians, trapped by tough schedules, unnatural hours and the expectations of entertainment-hungry audiences, drugs can also be a necessary tool of trade. Even back in the Beatles' early years entertaining the thirsty patrons of the Hamburg Reeperbahn bars, John Lennon recalled the need for drugs: 'The only way to survive in Hamburg to play eight hours a night was to take pills. The waiters gave you them . . . the pills and the drink.'

The story was the same wherever the rock music of the sixties was being born. In New York's Greenwich Village, the coffeehouses echoed to the folksy sounds of Bob Dylan, Jim McGuinn, Steve Stills and John Sebastian. In London there was less folk, but more blues, R & B and soul, fuelled just the same by plentiful supplies of booze, speed, marijuana – and sometimes by something a little more exotic, like amyl nitrate or cocaine. One rock star used to surprise fellow performers on British TV's early sixties' show, *Ready, Steady, Go!*, by popping amyl nitrate ampoules in front of their faces just before they went on. (Amyl nitrate is a heart stimulant administered in vapour form. The startling effect of the drug is due to a sudden surge of blood to the brain.) For some die-hards there was always heroin, and for others as the sixties progressed there was LSD.

Rock people who take drugs for fun rarely stop at one kind. There is often a tendency to take combinations of drugs to see what the effect will be and almost every user of an illegal drug will experiment with something new. After all, once the barriers of illegality and fear have been broken down, there's not much besides lack of opportunity to prevent you. Rock stars, with their wealth and their unique access to the underworld of late-night clubs and the pushers who frequent them, have had endless opportunity. They have taken it – partly because they needed it to keep going, partly because it was expected of them as vanguards of the new liberation of youth. The result for too many has

been the trap of addiction and self-abuse, ending in death.

Two days after Janis Joplin's death from a heroin overdose her friend and musical colleague Nick Gravenites talked about the inevitability of death among the rock fraternity. 'There's a lot of people using junk on the rock scene and they're on death row . . . You know they're going to die, you know it. So people were just figuring out ways to cushion the blow when it happens.' This was in 1970 – by this time the list of drug- and booze-related deaths among rock stars had grown so long that it wasn't really a surprise; feelings were numbed and each one was, as John Lennon said of Brian Jones, 'just another victim of the drug scene'. Janis Joplin had been part of the West Coast rock scene, where LSD ruled.

LSD, whose effects were first noted in 1943, gained immense popularity in the sixties thanks largely to the proselytizing efforts of two Harvard university researchers, Drs Timothy Leary and Richard Alpert. Both men were sacked by the university in the early sixties for their very public espousal of the drug. For Leary in particular, LSD became a messiah whose gospel he preached across America, wherever there were people adventurous enough to look for new experiences.

The inheritors of rock'n'roll's rebellious spirit – musicians and other outsiders from Los Angeles, San Francisco, New York and London – were just such people: politicians of pleasure, enemies of the establishment and mostly practised drug users already. They took to LSD like ducks to water. It was an excuse to throw aside the old conventions, a drug that changed you, as Hunter S. Thompson said, 'at the place of definitions'. It certainly changed the style and image of rock music.

1965 was the year. The Beatles (who famously smoked pot in the toilets of Buckingham Palace before collecting their MBEs) and the Rolling Stones (three of whom had more famously been fined for pissing against a filling station wall) had made it in the USA. From out of Greenwich Village, a politically committed nasal folk-singer named Bob Dylan had become – quite unpredictably – a star. As it happened it was Dylan who turned the pill-popping Beatles on to marijuana's more meditative buzz in 1964. It showed in the music – rock'n'roll started to look into itself and created a sound that was built for LSD. By the time the Beatles played San Francisco in 1965, Leary was proclaiming them the advanced guard of his psychedelic revolution, 'mutants' preparing for an imagined golden age.

Sid Vicious doing it his way. Vicious, the archetypal punk – angry, inarticulate, and given to self-mutilation – was thrust into the limelight with the Sex Pistols. Sid, a homosexual and habitual drug-user, couldn't cope. In 1978 he killed his groupie girlfriend, Nancy Spungen, and subsequently died of a self-administered overdose on 2nd February, 1979, before coming to trial for murder.

WILD GIRL OF POP DIES

Singer Janis Joplin is found in a Hollywood hotel .. killed by drugs overdose

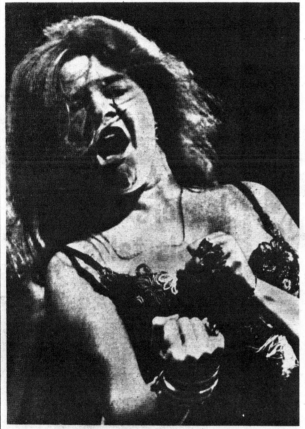

Janis, flashing rings and singing as the fans liked her best . . . loud, agonised and electrifying.

The drug culture was nurtured especially in the fertile ground of California – where LSD remained legal until as late as October 1966. David Crosby, a founder member of the Byrds, remembered the time he spent in San Francisco's North Beach, in Sausalito and further south in Venice, while the Byrds were being born in 1964–65. 'Dino Valenti and David Freiberg and I were dropping acid together years ago,' Crosby said in 1970, recalling times spent hanging-out and playing music with key members of the Californian rock scene. In Venice, Crosby and Freiberg hung out with Paul Kantner – founder member of the Jefferson Airplane. Drifting around the coast there were plenty of other musicians – Jerry Garcia (friend of

Janis Joplin, the wild girl of rock, cuddles her most constant companion, a bottle of Southern Comfort, backstage at San Francisco's Winterland in 1968. The ugly duckling from Port Arthur, Texas, became a swan on stage, but to help her fly she needed vast quantities of booze, speed and, ultimately, the heroin which killed her. The tawdry surroundings of her dressing-room are a long way from the quiet, middle American backwater of Port Arthur – and Janis, who made the journey, never quite knew why or how she'd made it.

novelist and LSD-experimenter Ken Kesey), Ron 'Pigpen' McKernan, Grace Slick, Janis Joplin, Spencer Dryden – all folk, jazz or blues people who now heard the call of rock'n'roll and would soon become familiar names in the first family of San Francisco bands: the Grateful Dead, Jefferson Airplane, Moby Grape, Big Brother and the Holding Company, Quicksilver Messenger Service.

In the Bay Area, LSD quickly became part of a dramatically radical scene which moved from North Beach to the notorious Haight-Ashbury district of San Francisco. There were revolutionary students from Berkeley campus, the Sexual Freedom League, dance troupes, mime troupes and a burgeoning commune movement. The mid-sixties saw a variety of dances, festivals and benefits (among them, Ken Kesey's famous 'Acid Tests') at which musicians, poets, face-painters, Hell's Angels and even ordinary people were piled into one large room dosed with LSD, dazzled with light-shows, seasoned with music, films, make-up and exotic costumes and left to simmer all night. 'Fluid' was the word that fitted.

Jerry Garcia, sometimes known as Captain Trips, and some of his LSD-soaked friends, played music at the early Acid Tests. They were known as the Warlocks, later they became the Grateful Dead. In those days, the band took plenty of drugs – dropping acid, so it was said, before *every* show. For a while, the band was being supported by one Augustus Owsley Stanley III, a drop-out engineering student who had set up his own laboratory and supplied much of San Francisco's LSD. Owsley poured his profits into a sound system for the Warlocks of such unparalleled power and complexity that it took three or four years for the rest of rock to catch up.

'Acid has changed consciousness entirely,' Garcia said at around this time. 'The US has changed in the last few years and it's because that whole first psychedelic thing meant: here's this new consciousness, this new freedom, and it's here in yourself.'

Although the electric heroes of rock were among its first and most avid disciples, by no means all rock stars favoured LSD. Janis Joplin and the Grateful Dead's Ron 'Pigpen' McKernan, for example, rejected LSD in favour of booze, speed or heroin. They seemed scared of LSD's disorientating effects, and sought other drugs and drink in order not to 'expand their consciousness' but to shut it down. But, LSD or not, everyone shared the common attitude of experimentation, hedonism and excess.

With typical exaggeration, somewhere between exuberance and calculated image-building, Janis recalled her mood on arriving in San Francisco in 1963. 'I'd've fucked anything, . . . I did,' she told David Dalton. 'I'd lick it, smoke it, shoot it, drop it, fall in love with it.' She tried acid only once in those days. Sometime later when she inadvertently drank LSD-laced wine, she forced herself to vomit rather than endure the trip.

Yet her consumption of drink and other drugs was prodigious. Within a few months of leaving her Texas home-town in the early sixties she had become heavily dependent on speed; her death in 1970 was due, according to the inquest, to a self-administered heroin overdose; an open bottle of tequila or Southern Comfort had been a permanent companion on and off-stage. As with many other rock stars, the drugs and drink all but eclipsed the music. Janis's later performances became caricatures of the woman she had then become – drunk, drugged, pained and passionate, trapped between torture and orgasm and screaming hoarsely for release. 'It's not what isn't, it's what you wish *was* that makes unhappiness,' she said. 'The hole, the vacuum . . . I think I think too much. That's why I drink. . . .'

If she could hold back, she preferred not to drink till a few minutes before going on stage because she felt that her best times were when performing and she could never remember them if she was too drunk to start with. Running on stage at 'full-tilt boogie' was, for her, as good as an orgasm – 'better than it has been with any man'. Performance was the key term in her personal equation between sex and drugs and rock'n'roll. Lonely and desperate for love, she found solace in men, women and – best of all – anonymous audiences who alone seemed to promise an uncomplicated release.

But release never came – the common ambivalences of her soul were magnified by the heights of adulation she attained. She once commented in evident amazement that her fans paid her $50,000 a year to be like her. And like her they were – especially if they were women. More than anyone else, she was the cultural symbol of a need for liberation that women were only beginning to rediscover and from which men would ultimately gain. She stood for the future, yet she never overcame the memory of her own past – an unpopular pupil at school, an unhappy and alienated child at home. She couldn't admit her stardom; she liked to be 'one of the boys' but needed to be treated as a helpless little woman; she had dreams of marriage and, according to a former boyfriend, Country Joe MacDonald, wanted children, but she lived and died a child herself and a faithless woman among faithless men. Booze and speed charged her up; heroin blanked out the despair. And though she tried to sort herself out, even managing to overcome her addiction to speed, the last shot of smack took its toll on a sad and abused body. On 4th October, 1970, alone in her room in Hollywood's Landmark Hotel, she collapsed and died from an overdose, splitting open her troubled head as she fell to the ground. She had been in the middle of recording what turned out to be her last album, *Pearl*: by all accounts the sessions had been going well. It may not have been suicide, but then a self-administered heroin overdose is hardly an accident.

Pigpen – who inspired the Grateful Dead with his passion for the blues – slowly poisoned himself with

Ron 'Pigpen' McKernan – bulky prototype for a heavy metal kid in 1967 – weighed only 100 lb when he died from drink in 1973, aged 27.

alcohol. Not even the relative anonymity in which he enjoyed success, nor the egalitarian character of the Dead and their relationship with audiences, could protect Pigpen. Like Janis, he was a loner – part of, yet apart from, the San Francisco scene. He too avoided acid, only taking it once – and then because it was daubed on the lip of an unopened drink can. (It was common for the evangelical sixties' acidheads to dose drinks with LSD and give them to unsuspecting victims. Aware of such japes, Pigpen never drank from already opened cans, but that precaution wasn't enough.) In 1971, by the age of 26, Pigpen had ruined his liver beyond repair and illness forced him out of the Dead. He lingered for another eighteen months. On 8th March, 1973, his once bulky body was found in his apartment in Corte Madera, California – his stomach haemorrhaged and most of his internal organs wasted. He weighed just over 100 lbs and looked twice his 27 years.

Acid had also found ready converts in the place already known as Swinging London. Naturally, the rock musicians whose names were almost synonymous with that over-worked phrase were part of the elite band of young aristocrats, artists and photographers, musicians and models, hairdressers and Harley Street doctors' daughters whose names rang out of the gossip columns and who frequented the night-clubs and restaurants of Soho and Chelsea. Money was the great leveller – upwards – and despite the Carnaby Street image of psychedelia on the cheap, the Beatles, Stones and their friends were early on cocooned in a world of privilege where sex was freer, the drugs more available, the clothes and cars more expensive than anything most of their fans could have imagined. 'We were kings,' Lennon remembered. 'We were all just at the prime . . . it was like a men's smoking club, just a very good scene.'

The Beatles tours became, in Lennon's words, 'like Satyricon'. So much money was being made that no one could mock them – and why should they when the boys in the band picked up the tabs for drinks, drugs, meals and whores. Even those who could afford to pay for their own pleasures, felt a need to buy entrance to the most exclusive 'men's smoking club' in the world by offering gifts unavailable to the common herd. In fact it was a dentist who first introduced John Lennon and George Harrison to LSD. Without telling them, he dosed both of them and their wives, Cynthia and Patti, at a dinner party. 'He was saying, "I advise you not to leave",' Lennon said later, 'and we thought he was trying to keep us for an orgy in his house.' (Obviously a common occurrence.) 'We didn't want to know,' added Lennon, and so it was that the trip hit them at a night-club later, with its usual disconcerting delusions. The club was on fire, their table seemed to elongate, and at George's house, John imagined he was in a submarine floating eighteen feet above the ground. George Harrison told journalist Hunter Davies, 'It was as if I'd never tasted, talked, seen, thought or heard properly before.'

Lennon took his second trip in California, during the Beatles' 1965 tour. Jim McGuinn, Dave Crosby and Peter Fonda were there, as well as George, Ringo and the Beatles' road manager, Neil Aspinall. This was the occasion on which Fonda kept whispering 'I know what it's like to be dead', which at least gave Lennon the hook for a song. After that, trips came thick and fast: Lennon claimed he dropped acid a thousand times – all the while taking speed to help get by in recording sessions.

Through 1966 and 1967, LSD spread through the British rock scene like wildfire. Eric Clapton claimed that 'Acid was conducive to exploring music'. After taking it he never played straight blues. The Rolling Stones, leaders of the sixties' rebels of rock, also joined the beautiful people. Brian Jones, who had initially been the drive and musical inspiration behind the Rolling Stones, was particularly prominent. In 1966, the Stones found themselves musically dried up. LSD provided something of an answer, encouraging them eventually to make *Their Satanic Majesties Request*. The only problem was Brian Jones, who spent his time in the studio tripping out in a corner, contributing little or nothing to the recording sessions.

Jones and his Italian-German girlfriend, Anita Pallenberg, inhabited a world of self-obsessive callousness, but on the streets of London they dazzled the world with their androgyne splendour. As part of the underground they were members of a tight little family, whose house magazines were IT (*International Times*) and *Oz*. The 'all-night rave' thrown to launch IT was visited by Paul McCartney dressed as an Arab and accompanied by Jane Asher (the proverbial Harley

Street doctor's daughter). Unhampered by intrusive fans, the Beatles, Pete Townshend, Jimi Hendrix and the Stones could visit John Hopkins' club UFO (standing for Unlimited Freak Out), and at the same IT launch party, Marianne Faithfull, with four top ten hits under her belt, could win a prize for 'the shortest/barest costume' dressed as a nun in a bottomless habit, without anyone being uncool enough to make a fuss about it.

But of course they wouldn't be allowed to get away with it. After all, the drugs they openly used were illegal, and though rock stars were cushioned by privilege and wealth, their fans were following suit and were in the eyes of the media being seduced by the easy pleasure of drug-fuelled liberation. Horror stories began to be unleashed on the public – many of them complete fabrications, issuing from government agencies. LSD was made illegal in California in October 1966, and began to be condemned in unequivocal terms: 'The greatest threat facing the country today . . . more dangerous than the Vietnam war' was how the chairman of the New Jersey Narcotic Drug Study Commission described it. Sexual licence and a breakdown in social order were identified, not altogether inaccurately, with the spread of drug use, and a police crackdown began. Rock stars were prime targets – especially once phenomenally popular heroes of the young publicly confessed to having used (and sometimes enjoyed) illegal drugs.

In July 1966, the folksy Donovan, (full name Donovan Leitch, once heralded as Britain's Bob Dylan), was fined £250 for possession of marijuana. 'I would like you to bear in mind,' said the magistrate, 'that you have great influence on young people, and it behoves you to behave yourself.' A London Sunday paper reported that 'evidence disclosed a shocking scene of debauchery at a reefer smoking party in his flat', and, despite claiming to have given up drugs altogether after the case, Donovan's immediate response was to comment that 'I hope it won't hurt my career'. Of course the press was indignant and took great relish in pointing out that Donovan was, at that time, earning £25,000 a year.

An investigation by the *News of the World* followed Donovan's conviction. The investigation had some far-reaching, if unexpected, consequences. In the course of the paper's four-week series, banner headlined 'DRUGS AND POP STARS – Facts that will SHOCK you', it was 'revealed' that members of the Moody Blues had taken LSD, Pete Townshend (who had previously admitted to taking marijuana and pep pills) had taken LSD, Ginger Baker had gone 'from hash and LSD to heroin and cocaine' and that, generally, drug use among pop stars was rife and clearly demonstrated by the titles and lyrics of numerous songs, like Donovan's *Sunshine Superman*, the Move's *Night Of Fear*, the Beach Boys' *Good Vibrations* and even the Mothers of Invention's *Can't Happen Here*, which, the *News of the World* wrote, was said to have been made on a LSD trip, (by whom, one wonders, since the Mothers' leader, Frank Zappa, is one of the few who definitely *didn't* trip out). The paper also

Back in 1967, rock stars wore suits to go before the law. On 10th May, 1967, Mick Jagger and Keith Richard run the gauntlet of the Chichester citizenry after electing to go to trial by jury following their arrest on drugs charges at Redlands, Richard's house in the Sussex countryside.

Marianne Faithfull, Mick Jagger's girlfriend, was described as Miss X during the Redlands trial. She was supposed to have been naked but for a fur rug.

revealed the 'inside story' of psychedelic events, paying particular attention to 'bare-breasted girls' at 'a freak-out' – complete with pictures, of course.

Many of the paper's revelations were unreliable – a fact which was dramatically demonstrated when Mick Jagger instituted libel proceedings against it. The paper had attributed to Jagger the substance of an interview about drug-taking that two unnamed 'investigators' had in fact had with Brian Jones. However, the real impact of the articles soon became evident. Jagger's libel suit was lodged two days after the *News of the World* article naming him appeared. Five days later, on 12th February, 1967, Keith Richard's house in the Sussex countryside, known as Redlands, was raided, with the resulting arrest of Richard, Jagger and art dealer Robert Fraser. Eight men were present, 'two of whom were hangers-on', according to one of the prosecutors at one of the subsequent trials, 'and the third a Moroccan servant'. (Persistent rumour maintains that that there was a ninth – George Harrison – but although he had been at Redlands that weekend, Harrison had left before the raid.) There was also one woman present – called 'Miss X' in court, but actually Marianne Faithfull (whose name the Stones wanted kept out of the whole affair). But further harassment was to follow. On the day of Jagger and Richard's committal appearance in court, 10th May, Brian Jones

PRINTING HOUSE SQUARE, LONDON, E.C.4.   TELEPHONE: 01-236 2000

WHO BREAKS A BUTTERFLY ON A WHEEL?

MR. JAGGER has been sentenced to imprisonment for three months. He is appealing against conviction and sentence, and has been granted bail until the hearing of the appeal later in the year. In the meantime, the sentence of imprisonment is bound to be widely discussed by the public. And the circumstances are sufficiently unusual to warrant such discussion in the public interest.

MR. JAGGER was charged with being in possession of four tablets containing amphetamine sulphate and methyl amphetamine hydrochloride; these tablets had been bought, perfectly legally, in Italy, and brought back to this cou~~~. They are not a highly danger~~~ ~~ proper dosage a danger~~~ ~~~ ~~ of the benze~~~ factu~~ stim~~ sick~~

They were separate cases, and no evidence was produced to suggest that he knew that MR. FRASER had heroin tablets or that the vanishing MR. SNEIDERMANN had cannabis resin. It is indeed no offence to be in the same building or the same company as people possessing or even using drugs, nor could it reasonably be made an offence. The drugs which MR. JAGGER had in his posses~~~ must therefore be treated ~~ as a separate i~~~

that JUDGE BLOCK should have decided to sentence MR. JAGGER to imprisonment, and particularly surprising as MR. JAGGER'S is about as mild a drug case as can ever have been brought before the Courts.

It would be wrong to sp~~~ ~~ JUDGE'S reasons~~ It is ~~~

~~~ ~oming to ~~~ resent the anarchic ~~y of the Rolling Stones' perform-nces, dislike their songs, dislike their fluence on teenagers and broadly spect them of decadence, a word used ~ MISS MONICA FURLONG in the *Daily Mail*.

As a sociological concern this may be reasonable enough, and at an emotional level it is very understandable, but it has nothing at all to do with the case. One ~~ a different question: has MR. ~~~ the same treatment as ~~ he had not ~~~iti-

'NUDE GIRL AT STONES PARTY'

Jagger leaves jail handcuffs

'Stones' get summonses after raid

Daily Mirror

4d.   Saturday, March 18, 1967

No. 19,667

JAGGER IS ACCUSED OVER DRUGS

Jagger—accused.

BY BARRY STANLEY and JOHN SANDIFORD

TWO of the Rolling Stones pop group—Mick Jagger and Keith Richard—have been accused of offences against the drug laws.

Summonses against the two men—both aged 22—were issued after a police raid on Richard's £20,000 farmhouse home at West Wittering, Sussex.

The summonses, due to be dealt with at Chichester magistr~~ are expected to be served early next week. Two other ~ summoned.

Brian Jones on his way from court on £2,000 bail. He had been charged with possession of cannabis at his Chelsea flat on 21st May, 1968.

With friends like these who needs enemies? Brian, visibly deteriorating, accepts a kiss from girlfriend Suki Potier, and the upright support of fellow Rolling Stones, Keith Richard and Mick Jagger. Brian had just been on the witness stand to deny possession of 144 grains of cannabis. Within a year he was dead.

was arrested on drugs charges at his London flat. The campaign against drug use was hotting up.

Jagger and Richard's trials, held in June 1967, were fated to become spectacular engagements in the phoney war between youth and the establishment. Jagger, charged with possessing four legally purchased Italian amphetamine tablets, was sentenced to six months' imprisonment; Richard, charged with allowing his premises to be used for smoking cannabis, was jailed for a year. On appeal, Jagger's sentence was reduced to a conditional discharge and Richard's was quashed on the grounds that the prosecution put too much emphasis on the role of Miss X. It was felt that the reliance of the prosecution on the evidently carefree behaviour of a young woman who was naked but for a fur rug when the raid took place, suggested moral opprobrium – even prurience – rather than legal consideration. During the trial Jagger was held for two days in Lewes prison, an experience which shocked him deeply.

One exchange between Keith and the prosecution indicates the tone of the original trial. Replying to the prosecution's suggestion that Miss X should have been embarrassed by the state of undress in which she was found, Richard said: 'We are not old men. We are not worried about your petty morals.' The *News of the World* – in a sudden fit of moral rectitude – sub-

sequently admitted passing on information to the police which led to the arrests.

After the Redlands raid and the subsequent trial, Paul McCartney and Brian Epstein both publically admitted to taking LSD – as did Eric Burdon. Burdon claimed to have given it up by then, but later revealed that until 1970 he had spent most of his time on acid. The press and public picked up the smell of vendetta. The role of the *News of the World* in the whole affair raised considerable doubts as to the propriety of the Redlands arrests in the first place. There was a widespread feeling that what highly paid adults did in the privacy of their own homes warranted no intrusion by sensationalist newspapers and killjoy policemen. The picture of Jagger in handcuffs on his way to Lewes prison was a clear image of the victimization of a scapegoat. 'Who breaks a butterfly on a wheel?' asked the *Times*. 'Let him who is without sin jail the first Stone,' said a popular poster.

Restricting people's freedom of movement is one thing, but – as Keith Richard commented about Brian Jones – 'they hounded Brian to death'. At the trial following his bust in May 1967, a psychiatrist described Brian as 'an extremely frightened young man'. A sentence of nine months' imprisonment for possessing cannabis was over-harsh, especially since the sentences passed on Jagger and Richard following the Redlands raid had already been effectively overturned on appeal, following an unprecedented public fuss. But Brian's sentence was particularly stressful since he had already spent some time in hospital, suffering from what was politely called 'strain' and one of the psychiatrists at the trial had commented that Jones had suicidal tendencies. In December 1967, the sentence was at last commuted – to £1,000 fine and three years' probation – but three days later, Jones had collapsed again and was once more in hospital. Six

A floral tribute for Brian Jones from Mick Jagger and Marianne Faithfull who had already left for Australia. While Brian was being buried in England, Marianne was in a coma in a Sydney hospital, after an overdose of sodium amytal tablets.

months later, in May 1968, Brian was arrested again on a drugs charge. This time the fine was only £50 but the real punishment was the psychological damage caused by so much police interest.

The harassment accelerated Brian's general decline. The Stones as a whole found it increasingly difficult to work under the permanent threat of imprisonment and Jones himself was rapidly sinking into complete mental and physical stupor. He believed Jagger and Richard were conspiring against him. Even his girlfriend, Anita Pallenberg, had deserted him for Keith. Brian's total insecurity was reflected in the reputation he had acquired for near satyriasis (60 women a month was the figure bandied about) and, believing himself deliberately shut out of the decision-making, creativity and companionship of the Rolling Stones, he withdrew into drug dependence and manic hedonism. His own suspicions turned into a self-fulfilling prophecy. By the summer of 1968, Jack Nitzsche – scoring the music for Nicolas Roeg's film, *Performance*, which starred Jagger and Pallenberg – observed that the Stones had, in reality, turned against their former golden boy. Brian, in his turn, became literally incapable of making music: when he tried to play harmonica, his mouth started bleeding.

In mid-summer, 1969, Brian quit the band, ostensibly to pursue a solo career, in fact because he was a liability. The Stones were planning a tour and Brian was incapable of undertaking it. A month later, on 3rd July, he drowned in the swimming pool of his secluded mansion in Sussex (once the home of A. A.

Milne and Christopher Robin) – many of his vital organs suffering fatty degeneration that could, in itself, have killed him. Two days later, his replacement, Mick Taylor, made his first public appearance with the Stones at an open-air concert in Hyde Park. Jagger, looking Byronesque in a white Greek-style tunic dress, released hundreds of butterflies and everybody felt sad. Pete Townshend's response to Brian's death was to comment, 'It was a normal day for Brian, he died every day.' And ten years later, Jagger recalled that 'I felt a bit shocked, but it was really inevitable. The guy was unbearable, but maybe it was us that made him unbearable.' Precisely who 'hounded Brian to death' remains an unanswerable question.

In America, drug-related arrests in the sixties were mainly concentrated on the West Coast – mecca of the drug culture. The Grateful Dead's communal house at 710 Ashbury, in San Francisco's notorious Haight-Ashbury district, was raided in 1967 with the consequent arrest of eleven people for possession of marijuana (not including Jerry Garcia, who was warned of the bust on the street outside the house). Interestingly, the police failed to discover a large stash of grass in a glass jar on a kitchen shelf: in fact, infor-

---

The Grateful Dead hold a press conference on 5th October, 1967, after the police raided their communal house in San Francisco, acting on a tip-off. This really was the end of the summer of love. L. to r.: Pigpen, Bill Kreutzmann, Phil Lesh, managers Rock Scully (who has since done time for drug trafficking) and Dan Rifkin, Bob Weir, Jerry Garcia (known as Captain Trips), and the group's lawyer.

It took forty of London's finest to arrest John Lennon and Yoko Ono on charges of possession of marijuana – and about as many to escort them from the court the next day, 19th October, 1968. Yoko suffered a miscarriage a week before John was convicted on 28th November, and the conviction led to immigration problems when Lennon wanted to settle in America.

mers had been used so no search was undertaken. Dino Valenti – who had written *Get Together*, the true anthem of the 'love generation' – was busted at this time, as were Neil Young, Richie Furay, Jim Messina and Bruce Palmer, (all of Buffalo Springfield). Palmer was taken three times and, in fact, Messina was brought in to replace him in the group. Eric Clapton, arrested with the Springfield members in March 1968, was acquitted.

At times, the consequences of this campaign on both sides of the Atlantic were no less damaging to careers than the drug-taking itself. John Lennon, busted in 1968 with Yoko Ono, was denied a resident's permit for the United States as a consequence (although the objections to the permit only emerged after he had released *Sometime In New York City*, an openly revolutionary album, in 1972). Lennon finally got his 'Green Card' in 1975, only to be gunned down outside his New York home in 1980, a few weeks after his fortieth birthday.

If addiction turned some rock musicians into liabilities for their fellows, it was a godsend to the police, always happy to increase their arrest figures and hence their public presence by making a few uncomplicated busts. But the circumstances of John Lennon's 1968 arrest, the culmination of two years of 'exemplary' raids by the narcotics division, actually led to questions in

Parliament. How was it, MPs wondered, that it took 40 policemen to arrest two people (John and Yoko) who weren't thinking of running away, and how was it that two national daily newspapers were already present to witness the arrest before the police even arrived? There was more than a suspicion that the drug squad was scalp-hunting and the press had been tipped off. ('Tipping off' in fact worked both ways, however; a showbiz correspondent had warned Lennon some three weeks earlier and John and Yoko had 'cleaned the house out', because, said Lennon, who was on heroin at the time, 'I'm not stupid.')

The theory is still current that John and Yoko's big-time bust was precipitated by reaction against the release of their album, *Two Virgins*, which featured the couple naked on the sleeve. But this is stretching the power of prudery too far. On the other hand, since there was a general feeling at the time that the Beatles (MBE) were actually immune from arrest, the swoop demands some explanation. Even the *News of the World*, eager to explore the illegal drug use of other rock stars, had shied away from tarring the Beatles with that brush. Leading rock groups, like the Beatles, 'derived their success from sheer native genius,' the paper had written in January 1967. 'But others in the pop world needed or sought artificial means to gain recognition.' The clear implication was that the Beatles were above the use of drugs.

However, eighteen months later in 1968, student riots and protests from Paris to Berkeley and back, had made the threat of youthful rebellion seem sufficiently ominous to outweigh these previous considerations. Busts that might have been unthinkable before the Redlands raid and unwise after it were now zealously pursued (although sentences were usually of saner proportions than had once been the case). As far as the Beatles were concerned, it was significant that Brian Epstein was dead (ironically, from a drug overdose), and that the group was in disarray. After the McCartney–Epstein confessions, their image was tarnishing fast. All of which meant that they could now become targets in the war against drugs, with John Lennon being especially vulnerable for his outspoken views and 'outlandish' women.

Paradoxically, the new light in which the Beatles were seen also helped make drug use among rock stars an acceptable, if generally unspoken, fact. As so many times before and since, the moralistic outrage of the press ultimately served only to diminish the hold of its phoney puritanism. Magistrates and judges seemed more and more to regard drug use as a sort of occupational hazard, if not an unavoidable feature of the rock star's milieu. Accordingly, since the late sixties, while the police have opposed rock stars with some vigour, the courts have disposed of them with a sometimes surprising degree of leniency, based on the apparent assumption that the private use of drugs by rock stars is only to be expected.

When, for example, Jimi Hendrix was busted for heroin at Toronto Airport in 1969, his trial defence was that he had unwittingly accepted the drug as a casual gift from a generous fan. The court acquitted him

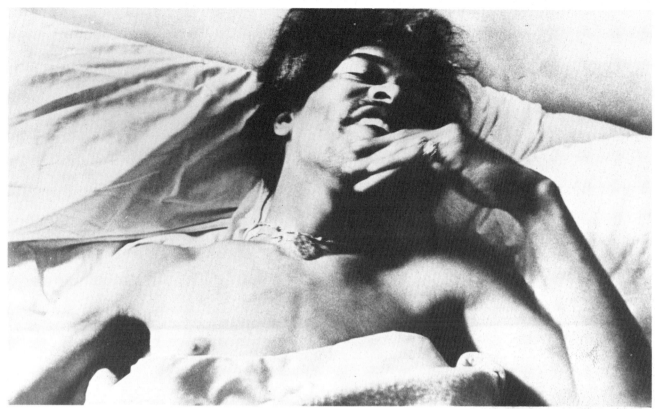

Jimi Hendrix died in bed on 18th September, 1970, choking on his own vomit after an overdose of pills. Hendrix was the personification of sex and drugs and rock'n'roll; 'he was the heaviest doper I ever met,' said Eric Burdon.

despite (or, perhaps, because of) his surprising confession to have taken LSD, pot and cocaine. Perhaps they believed him when he said he had outgrown drugs, as any number of rock stars seem to persist in falsely claiming. Jimi might have wanted to give up drugs but never did.

After ex-Animal Chas Chandler brought Seattle-born Hendrix to London in 1966, the guitarist's career rocketed. Hendrix's musicianship was stunning, and, of course, he had the added *caché* of black machismo, which he was quite capable of exploiting to the full. But his temper was fearsome and most of his personal relationships seemed unstable. Internal conflicts ensured the eventual break-up of his band, the Experience, after relations between himself and Noel Redding deteriorated completely, and in 1969, Hendrix split with Chas Chandler. On top of these problems, Hendrix's meteoric rise unleashed a hail of reissues and bootlegs. Everyone wanted to get in on the act, and by the end of the sixties, Hendrix was rapidly becoming entangled in a web of legal and business hassles.

Jimi made an attempt to control his own affairs but

After the death of Jimi Hendrix, West German skater Monika Danemann, suffering from shock, is helped from her hotel by a friend. Hendrix was discovered unconscious in her hotel suite, but was found to be dead on arrival at hospital.

British politician Jeremy Thorpe cops a lick from Jimi Hendrix backstage at London's Royal Albert Hall, in 1967. The strange meeting took place before a concert in aid of the Liberal Party, of which Thorpe was the leader before his disgrace and downfall in the seventies, following revelations of his relationship with a homosexual. In spite of this meeting, as far as we know Jimi never made a political speech in his life and Jeremy still can't play Purple Haze.

Keith Richard getting his teeth into the good things of life. Amazingly, for a man whose reputation is built largely on his consumption of dangerous drugs, Richard's appetite indicates that he is still alive. The same cannot necessarily be said for his playmate.

London's biggest evening sale

Evening News

LONDON WEDNESDAY MAY 19 1976

CITY PRICES
BEST TV GUIDE
—Centre Pages

Rolling Stone quizzed after M1 crash

KEITH RICHARD ARRESTED: DRUGS TEST

EVENING NEWS REPORTER

ROLLING STONE Keith Richard was arrested today on the eve of the group's sell-out concert at Earls Court.

His Bentley was involved in a crash on the M1 and police said later that they had taken away a substance found in the car.

It was on the . . . accident and police . . . Richard was asked . . .

A Transit van . . . arrived . . . away. Richard . . . got . . . arrested . . . . . . the . . . Richard . . .

One of . . . . . . certain . . .

ROLLING STONES STAR ARRESTED

The big ticket rip-off.

See Page SIX

MUGGERS ROB SISTERS AGED 91 AND 79

TWO elderly sisters were in hospital and penniless today after being mugged and robbed of their £700 life savings.

he was temperamentally unable to sort things out for himself. He formed an all-black group (the Band of Gypsies), and also became involved in a recording studio project. But he had neither the time nor the patience to make a success of either. Living in New York after the Toronto bust, he was harassed by the police. He was pulled one way and another by his contractual problems and his somewhat tentative desire to be associated with the mood of black pride. The pressures may have been too great for him, as his friend Eric Burdon suggested, or maybe his death was merely an accident. Whatever the truth, it seemed to occur just when the crest of Hendrix's wave had broken and something had to give.

On the night of 18th September, 1970, a year which had seen him in a downward spiral of lack-lustre performances and recordings, he took a handful of Vesperax sleeping pills, after an evening spent drinking white wine moderately, and smoking a little grass. He died choking on his own vomit as a result of the overdose of pills. The coroner declared an open verdict at the inquest, but Hendrix's death was probably just the result of a momentary desire for some temporary peace of mind.

Less than eight years after Jimi's acquittal in Toronto, Anita Pallenberg was arrested at the airport there while carrying drugs. She was in the company of Keith Richard who was himself arrested a few days later in his hotel room, almost ten years to the day after the Redlands raid. It was Richard's sixth arrest in four countries during the seventies alone – on a variety of

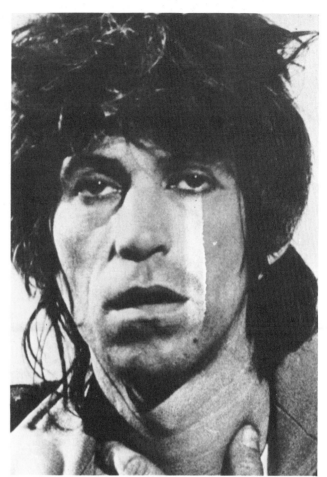

Keith Richard checks he's still alive, while facing the press in Toronto on 20th October 1978, after pleading guilty to the charges brought in 1977.

Accompanied by William Carter, the Stones' US attorney, Keith Richard arrives at the court in Toronto on 14th March, 1977, to face charges of possession of heroin 'with intent to traffic', and with possession of cocaine.

counts from possession of dangerous drugs to assault and weapons charges. Fears that the Canadian authorities' notorious severity on drugs matters would at last put an end to the Rolling Stones were, in the event, unwarranted. The really serious charge of trafficking in heroin was dropped and, to the chagrin of the state prosecutor, the court sentenced Richard to serve a term of probation and to play a benefit concert for the blind on lesser counts of possession. In 1981, Richard himself recalled the Toronto bust as the peak of two years of trouble with the law. 'I was so stoned throughout that whole period,' he commented about the arrests, 'that I just accepted it as part of doing what I was doing. I didn't even bother.'

Since the sixties the Stones have continued to be prime targets for the law and it's often hard to tell to what extent it is the product of their own carefully constructed 'outlaw' image. In Keith's case, we have his own testimony that he and Anita were indeed preoccupied with a variety of illegal substances for a long time, and, while Mick, Bill Wyman and Charlie Watts have remained in low profile, other Stones' associates seem to be at risk by virtue of their very association. In February 1980, Ron Wood and his girl-friend Josephine Karslake, were arrested in the West Indies on charges of possessing cocaine after the alleged suppliers had informed to the police. Even

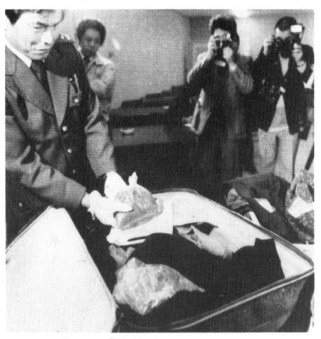

The 219 grams of marijuana found in baggage belonging to Paul McCartney by Japanese customs. 'Imagine smuggling half-a-pound of marijuana in an ordinary suitcase,' went a joke after the Tokyo bust. 'I always knew Lennon was the brains behind the Beatles.'

non-members of the group are at risk. In July 1972, for example, the group's chauffeur was arrested for possession during the US tour, and, in 1975, the year in which Ron Wood joined the Stones, his wife Krissie was busted for possession of cocaine and cannabis during a bizarre early morning raid when the police burst in on her in bed with a dress-maker friend, Audrey Burgon. They were later acquitted.

The war against drug use by rock stars continues, although evidently with a slightly different angle. When, in January 1980, Paul McCartney was arrested on his way into Japan for carrying half a pound of marijuana, at least one London paper was moved to comment that since McCartney had been busted three times for marijuana (in 1973, it was for actually growing the plant at his Scottish home in Campbelltown), the fact that he was a good father, an efficient businessman and a good husband demonstrated that marijuana was not a bad thing.

Even the Japanese – who, in 1973, had refused Mick Jagger a visa on the grounds of his 1967 conviction and in 1975 had banned McCartney, too – seemed less sure that severity was appropriate. McCartney, who was scheduled to play a series of concerts with Wings, had arrived at Narita Airport with Linda and their children. The Japanese customs were at first convinced that the marijuana was in one of Linda's suitcases, until Paul stepped forward to admit ownership. Paul spent nine days in jail, during which time questions were asked in the British Parliament about his treatment and the British Consulate in Japan made every effort to secure his release. Eventually, the Japanese authorities let McCartney go and dropped charges, although they banned him from re-entering Japan for a year. He had bought the marijuana for his
50

own use, they said, and had in any case suffered nine days in jail and the financial losses due to the cancellation of all his concerts. 'Imagine smuggling half a pound of marijuana in an ordinary suitcase,' went a joke of the time. 'I always knew Lennon was the brains behind the Beatles.'

The police response to *punk* drug use was less sanguine. In March 1980, Hugh Cornwell of the Stranglers was sentenced to (and served) two months imprisonment for possession of heroin, cocaine and marijuana – found in his car during a routine check. The sentence was surprisingly harsh, for a first offence and considering the small amount of drugs involved. The judge, however, echoing the wisdom of his colleagues across the years, told Cornwell that his term in jail would be 'an example to others'.

In fact, the favourite punk drug was often-lethal glue, for those who could afford nothing else, and amphetamine in sniffable powder form ('sulphate') for those who could. In 1978, Sid Vicious and Nancy Spungen were arrested for possessing the particularly powerful amphetamine, methedrine, in their room in a London hotel. Johnny Rotten's public denials that he took drugs did not prevent his flat being raided twice (to no effect). Police activity against punks maintained a particularly high level during the brief period of the music's popularity – and one was irresistibly reminded of the harassment of performers who had been thought equally threatening years ago.

By the mid-seventies, the rock establishment had become inseparably linked to the drug trade. Cocaine and marijuana had become staples of the industry – it was estimated that 90 per cent of all cocaine use in the US centred on the rock and film industries, while 10 per cent of the American population used cocaine and a considerably higher percentage used marijuana. Countries in Latin America producing these two drugs found their economies becoming grotesquely distorted by reliance on this illegal trade. The relationship between rock and drugs in the seventies encouraged law enforcement agencies to take a pragmatic view. In most cases, arrests were directed at clearing up a significant trade, but in only a few did rock stars or their associates suffer greatly.

In 1977, the Grateful Dead's manager Rock Scully was jailed for four months for conspiracy to smuggle marijuana, but he was something of an exception. Far more typical was the 1976 arrest and trial of John 'Scooter' Herring – Gregg Allman's personal roadie. Gregg was offered immunity from prosecution if he testified against Herring – the man who allegedly supplied Allman with the considerable amounts of cocaine he used. Allman accepted the deal, saying, 'I was scared to death to go in there and have them ask me these things, but it was either that or go to jail.' Allman's wife of twelve days, Cher Bono, had sued

Paul McCartney is dragged handcuffed and wearing compulsory sandals into Nakameguro Police Station, after his arrest at Narita Airport, Japan, in January 1980, when customs officers found a bag of marijuana in his suitcase. McCartney spent nine nights in jail before being deported without playing a note.

Blackballed by the Allman Brothers Band after testifying against his personal roadie, John 'Scooter' Herring, in a cocaine trial which brought the hapless Herring a sentence totalling more than 70 years, Greg Allman is seen in court answering reckless driving charges on 4th June, 1979.

him for divorce, she said, after finding out about his drug use, but his testimony in the Herring case helped convince her that he had licked his problem and she returned to him. Other members of the Allman Brothers Band were considerably less affectionate. 'There is no way we can work with Gregg again, ever,' said guitarist Dicky Betts, shocked at the coolness with which Allman betrayed the trust of a man who'd worked for him for two years and, apparently, saved his life twice. Herring had, according to the band, been doing no more than serving Gregg's requirements faithfully. He was sentenced to a total of 75 years (reduced on appeal) and the Allman Brothers Band effectively went out of business.

John Phillips, founder member of the Mamas and Papas, testified against an associate following his 1980 arrest on charges of being involved in a drug ring supplying pills and cocaine. After his arrest, Phillips – a highly successful songwriter and producer – and his daughter went on a lecture tour of the US to campaign against drug abuse. His six year jail sentence was suspended for all but 30 days, much of which had already been spent on remand.

Also in 1980, Fleetwood Mac's John McVie and his second wife Julie Ann were arrested on charges of possessing cocaine following a raid on their home in Hawaii, which also uncovered some pills, marijuana and seven guns. The cocaine charges against John McVie were dropped when his wife admitted possession, although he was convicted on lesser weapons charges. McVie, a resident alien in the US, could have faced deportation on the more serious charges. As it is, he will be able to pay his not inconsiderable US taxes for some time to come.

Once upon a time, drugs were seen as a route to a new form of musical expression. Today, with all the emphasis on 'recreational drugs' as new consumer commodities, drug-taking in quantity is all too often seen as the reward and proof of rock stardom. And between taking drugs to make music and making music to take drugs, the performers, the music and the fans have lost more than the law could ever take.

Syd Barrett, for example, was a founder member of Pink Floyd. He was apparently the first of the band to experiment with LSD, although as Floyd's Roger Waters once said, 'There was so much dope and acid around in those days that I don't think anyone can remember anything about anything.' Even so, it's clear that Syd overdid things. In no time at all, he had taken to a performance style which consisted of playing one chord all night. From then, it was only a matter of time before he learned to stand on stage and not play at all. Sometimes he didn't even appear. On a tour of America in late 1967, the Floyd played 'American Bandstand'. They were meant to mime to their second single, *See Emily Play*, but unfortunately Syd 'wasn't into moving his lips that day'. Two or three months later, Syd left the band and disappeared from view, only surfacing to cut two albums some years later and become the subject of a curious cult which considers him a genius. Meanwhile he has retired once more into obscurity.

Eric Burdon – who found initial success with the Animals – was another acid casualty. Always something of a rebel, Burdon started taking LSD in 1965, and didn't stop until the early seventies. In 1967, he and an Anglo-Indian model, Angie King, were married in London in a ceremony that was widely heralded as *the* 'flower power' wedding. Later Eric remarked that 'the ceremony was great; the marriage was dreadful'. When the Animals split, Eric followed the love generation to its source in San Francisco and recorded *San Francisco Nights* and *Good Times* – paeans to psychedelia. Singing the praises of LSD and meditation in 1968, he said mysteriously, 'I've done a complete circle. I am 21 days behind Bob Dylan.' By the end of that year he was planning to quit rock for a film career. He had suffered a nervous breakdown and the end of his marriage.

Living in Laurel Canyon in a house with his girlfriend, his road manager and a pick-up truck, he wrote elaborate treatments for movies (which no-one else could understand or wanted to buy), and talked about becoming a movie star. Meanwhile his girlfriend made pillow cases to sell for food. Eventually, a couple of management hot-shots informed him that if he wanted to be a movie star, first he had to become a rock star again. Eric attempted a comeback fronting a black group called War, but it was a disaster. He was still heavily into 'change and revolution' and War just wanted to be a funky band. 'The American black group

Eric Burdon abandoned the more exotic substances he once favoured for the mind-numbing effects of cheap Spanish plonk.

half-crazed notions of racial oppression, the exploitation of rock musicians and Hendrix's death. The idea eventually developed into a grandiose mixed-media package including a record and a film. But Burdon's sense of perspective seems to have been dissolved by acid, and his managers were not long in pulling the plug on what they saw as grotesque over-expenditure. A flurry of legal actions followed involving Burdon, his management company (Far Out Productions, would you believe) and his former record company, MGM. 'I lost about $6 million which the Animals earned,' he said in 1973 as a prelude to suing MGM for back royalties. By 1976, Far Out were suing him after he had spent, they claimed, $400,000 on *Mirage*. He was also sued for $17,000 as a result of a car accident, and while visiting Europe, his house in Palm Desert was seized by the State and sold by auction.

The upheaval of all this did have an effect of bringing reality back to his life. Despite being broke and effectively unable to work, Eric had become relatively content. In 1972, he had married a former topless go-go dancer called Rose who, he said, helped him get off drugs. And, with all his legal problems to cope with, the former love child was able to say, 'For the first time I hate somebody.' By 1977, the legal problems were sorted out, mostly in Burdon's favour, and the original Animals were able to record a 'get together' album, titled *Before We Were So Rudely Interrupted*. The next year, Eric was 'totally into music again', and in late 1981 he was planning to form a blues

I was looking for was not War,' said Eric. When Jimi Hendrix (a friend and profound influence) died in September 1970, Burdon appeared on British television and talked of their trips together, saying that Jimi 'used drugs to phase himself out of this life to go someplace else'. These comments caused a furore. 'I was stoned on MDA (another synthetic hallucinogen),' Burdon explained later, 'because Jimi Hendrix was the heaviest doper that I ever met . . . I felt I had something to say about Jimi . . . I wasn't going to walk on and say how great he was. He was a cunt! He was great, but he was a cunt. That's why I loved him.'

Burdon became obsessed with Hendrix and, during an English tour with War, he convinced himself that he was staying in the same room in a London hotel as Hendrix had once occupied. 'I was so low,' he said, 'and I'd caught pneumonia in Copenhagen.' He took MDA to get up for a gig and started hallucinating. The Hendrix track, *Angel (Came Down From Heaven Yesterday)*, was translated into a vision! This was, apparently, an infinitely more horrifying hallucination than his earlier LSD experiences of talking with Buddha, seeing the crucifixion of Christ, seeing himself aged 103 and, naturally, talking to God. None of it, however, was very funky, and War and Burdon spent the tour at each other's throats – the record company, according to Eric, encouraging the band to leave their front-man. In 1971, Eric and the band split up. 'I'm whoring myself to get to my end medium,' Eric said at around this time, 'which is motion pictures.'

The one picture he cherished was 'a Christ experience film' to be called *Mirage*, which tied up Burdon's

Joe Cocker faces life philosophically in spite of busts, and management troubles which started in the mid-sixties. Faced with a six-figure tax bill, what else is there to do but shrug?

band in America and star in a film in Los Angeles and Berlin to be called *Comeback* – about a rock singer, who is not Eric Burdon. 'I don't blame it on the drugs,' he once said. 'I just blame it on the mental stress of knowing you are being ripped off by record companies and everybody else and not being able to do anything about it.'

Joe Cocker was busted in December 1968, at the height of his meteoric career. He might have met with visa problems since a first tour of America was being arranged at the time of the bust. Luckily, Cocker's girlfriend, Eileen Webster, admitted the charge of possessing marijuana and the charge against Cocker was dropped. Cocker's legal problems continued, however, especially after his career began to decline. The Sheffield-born rocker had always been a heavy drinker, and in October 1972, he and six members of his tour party were convicted of drugs charges in Australia and ordered to leave the country. Before leaving Australia he managed to drink himself stupid, falling over during one of his final gigs and being evicted from his Melbourne hotel after a rowdy brawl involving his girlfriend, the hotel manager and the police. In 1973 he was busted again for marijuana back in Sheffield, and in 1977 he was deported from America on the grounds of illegal entry, none of which helped his career.

These victims of the drug culture have survived, after a fashion. Although drug-taking may only be a symptom of deeper problems, all too often they have lethal consequences. The list of drug-related deaths in rock'n'roll is depressingly long, reaching all the way from Elvis Presley to Sid Vicious and beyond, and taking in on the way those unfortunates like Janis and Brian Jones and Pigpen, whose sorry tales have already been chronicled. The main agents of destruction are drink, heroin, barbiturates and other depressants, taken either singly or in combination. (Nobody has yet died as a direct physiological result of taking LSD or marijuana and the incidence of death from chronic amphetamine or cocaine use is very small.)

The immediate causes of death vary from foolishness to neglect to suicide and, it has been surmised, murder. Tim Hardin got to the point of making records simply to pay for his habit until he overdosed. Mike Bloomfield – a rich boy who had been lauded in the sixties as America's greatest blues guitarist – spent some time in the seventies towards the end of his life scoring porn movies in San Francisco and recording background music for cremations before being found

Keith Moon holding forth at Paul and Linda, at the McCartneys' midnight matinee held in honour of Buddy Holly's birthday at London's Peppermint Park. The next morning, 7th September, 1978, Keith was dead, overdosed on tablets sometimes prescribed to help alcoholism.

dead himself in his car early in 1981. These two were both heroin overdoses; Bon Scott of AC/DC and John 'Bonzo' Bonham of Led Zeppelin both drank themselves to death like Pigpen. The coroner's report on Bonham estimated that he had the equivalent of 40 measures of vodka in his system at the time of his death. Like Jimi Hendrix, he died choking on his own vomit.

Bonzo's real tragedy was the evident emptiness of his life. He left £856,000 in his will. He had a wife of long standing and two children – Jason, born in 1966, and Zoe, born in 1975. Yet his life was coloured by 'speedballs' (a mixture of heroin and cocaine) and time passed only with the aid of sleepers mixed with booze. In June 1980, the 32-year-old drummer collapsed during a Zeppelin gig in Germany. He had suffered a suspected heart-attack. But he continued to abuse himself, and his last day alive was a desultory progress towards oblivion.

On 26th September, 1980, he began drinking at lunchtime at a pub near his home – four or five quadruple measures of vodka and orange. After lunch – a couple of cheese rolls in the pub – he was driven to Jimmy Page's house in Windsor for a rehearsal. He continued drinking in the rehearsal studio at the rate of two or three very large vodkas and orange an hour. At midnight, he fell asleep on the sofa, having eaten a pie and chips at Page's £900,000 home. He was carried to bed and laid sideways, braced with pillows: 'I'd had experience before of people being drunk,' said one of the men who put him to bed. At 2pm the next day, Bonham had still not stirred. When Zeppelin's road-manager looked into his room to wake him, he found Bonham dead.

Keith Moon died on the day after Buddy Holly's birthday (6th September) in 1978. 'Moon the Loon' did not, as one might have expected from his propensity for wild living, die while executing one impossible stunt too many, but from an overdose of Heminevrin tablets, a drug sometimes prescribed to help patients suffering from alcoholism. On the night of 6th September, Keith had taken a small amount of cocaine and gone out with his girlfriend, Annette Walter-Lax, to a midnight matinée of *The Buddy Holly Story*, followed by a party given by Paul McCartney to celebrate Buddy Holly Week. Back in his flat in Mayfair, Moon found difficulty sleeping. Early in the morning, he woke feeling hungry and consumed a steak in bed. He went back to sleep with the aid of 32 tablets of Heminevrin – more than double the lethal dose. At 3.40 in the afternoon, Annette woke to find Keith dead in bed beside her.

Robbie McIntosh of the Average White Band overdosed on heroin thinking it was cocaine. It was 1974 and the band had recently arrived in America where their white funk sound was being loudly applauded and they were introduced too rapidly into the high life. On 23rd September, they were guests at a plush party, where McIntosh indulged in what he took to be his favourite drug. An eye-witness recorded that the drummer 'turned blue', before gasping hoarsely for breath that somehow wouldn't come. In 1975, the man who supplied the drug to the unsuspecting McIntosh was arraigned for murder.

Tommy Bolin, who took Ritchie Blackmore's place in the hugely successful Deep Purple and played with them until they split in summer, 1976, was touring the US with a new band, Sailor, when he died in December of that year. His drug problem was severe and, clearly missing the adulation of Purple's audience, he had been hoping to make a comeback and straighten himself out. But that couldn't happen. After an all-night party in Miami Beach he was found dead from the inevitable overdose in his hotel room, by his girlfriend, Valoria Monzeglio. Similarly, Lowell George, who found considerable success with Little Feat, had split with the band – in part because of his heroin addiction. In 1979, while still trying hard to build a solo career for himself, George died of an 'accidental overdose', the details of which, curiously, were kept secret from everyone but his immediate family.

Such stories occur with numbing regularity. One of the saddest declines was Paul Kossoff's. His career peaked in 1970 when Free, his band, had a hit single, *All Right Now*, but it went downhill after that. Kossoff's father, David, is a moderately well-known

Tommy Bolin, after Deep Purple and before OD. Heroin consciousness equals a man in a frock with a plastic dog turd.

English character actor who, having carved something of a niche for himself with broadcast and recorded readings from the Old Testament, has struggled to keep his son's memory alive as a warning to all would-be drug users. Unfortunately, David Kossoff has not succeeded too well – partly because he has overlooked both the real problems his son had (which helped motivate him not only to take drugs, but to become a rock'n'roller in the first place) and the pressures under which Paul worked.

Through the early seventies, Free split, reformed and changed its members with disturbing unpredictability. The band's personnel suffered from destructive internal disputes – assisted by the presence of pop success on a group which had been, at first, an earnest blues band. Kossoff himself lived in the shadow of his father's renown and his instability was evident from an early age. In 1972, he left Free permanently and recorded a solo album, subsequently going into semi-retirement for two years in an effort to get off heroin. 'I have killed the drug habit,' said Kossoff in early 1975. His new band, Back Street Crawler, recorded an album for release in the fall and a promotional tour of Britain was arranged. Before the tour could begin, Paul Kossoff suffered a massive coronary and his heart stopped for several minutes. The tour was scrapped but the album release went ahead, and Paul was giving interviews barely six weeks after he had nearly died. His speech was slurred and incoherent, he seemed to be only semi-conscious. And, yet, he played three gigs with Back Street Crawler only three months after the heart attack. A new UK tour was organized for the spring of 1976, but, flying to New York, Kossoff suffered another coronary and died on the plane. Heroin had killed him at the age of 25.

At the age of sixteen, Jimmy McCulloch – a frail-looking Glaswegian guitarist who habitually hid behind dark glasses and enveloping shaggy cardigans – was picked up by Pete Townshend to play in a group he was forming called Thunderclap Newman (after its eccentric piano-player). In some ways the whole Thunderclap Newman concept was a move in a simmering war between Townshend and the Who's vocalist, Roger Daltrey. While Townshend sponsored his creation, Daltrey organized and produced a band called Bent Frame, which included McCulloch's brother Jack, on drums. Thunderclap Newman had one huge success in 1969 with *Something In The Air*, and the war hotted up. Bent Frame were pre-empted when a song recorded by them in demo form, *Accidents*, was released by Thunderclap Newman and became a moderate hit. Townshend subsequently persuaded Jack McCulloch to join his brother Jimmy's band for a planned tour. Meanwhile, Daltrey had persuaded one of the Who's back-up team to join Bent Frame. Not surprisingly, neither band survived this animosity and Jimmy McCulloch moved on to join John Mayall, Stone The Crows (stepping in after guitarist Les Harvey had died) and Blue, before joining Paul McCartney's Wings in 1974. McCulloch, then only 21, harboured a dream to be present at a Beatles reunion, which he fondly imagined might happen

56

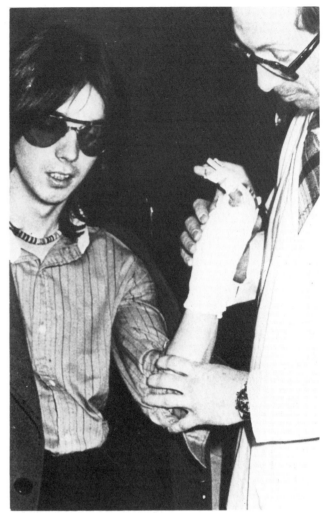

Unlike Jim Morrison's earlier experience in a bathtub, Jimmy McCulloch of Wings only fractured his hand in 1976 when he slipped in a bath in Paris. It wasn't until 1979 that he ODed on heroin, following Morrison to an early grave.

while he was with Wings. He also indulged in unhealthy quantities of drink and drugs – putting his 'weirdness' down to 'immaturity' and an inability to deal with people. He was, in some ways, a manipulated child. As a member of Wings, he was more or less an employee of Paul McCartney – despite McCartney's constant protestations that Wings was some sort of democracy. In 1977, after an extended period of quiescence, McCulloch and Wings' drummer, Joe English, left the band.

Jimmy was still drinking heavily, but even so received an invitation to join the newly reformed Small Faces. The Small Faces project was, unfortunately, short-lived and unspectacular. McCulloch left to form his own band, the Dukes – desperate to be part of a real, working group for the first time since he left Scotland. But a few days after announcing the formation of the Dukes, Jimmy went missing. Having failed to turn up at rehearsals, his brother Jack went anxiously round to his Maida Vale flat one morning in late September 1979, to see if he was there. Jimmy was dead on the floor, killed by an overdose of morphine on top of booze and pot. Curiously, the flat had been tidied and the police found no trace of alcohol or drugs or, for that matter, money. An open verdict was recorded by the coroner.

Gram Parsons – former Byrd and Flying Burrito Brother, and close friend of Keith Richard – died on 19th September, 1973, another victim of gross over-indulgence. There was a bizarre sequel to his death. His coffin was hi-jacked on its way back to burial in New Orleans by his friend and associate Phil Kaufman, and another man, who attempted to cremate the remains at the Joshua Tree National Monument. Parsons and Kaufman had once made a pact in which the survivor would ritually burn the body of whichever of them died first.

In spite of all this some have survived – if only just. The albino blues guitarist Johnny Winter came off heroin in the early seventies, as did Eric Clapton. Clapton reckoned to spend up to £1,000 per week on the drug at that time. Clapton, who moved in the sixties from an admired guitarist with the Yardbirds and then with John Mayall to superstardom in Cream, found it impossible to cope with his sudden elevation. The formation of Cream in 1966 was accompanied by a promotional campaign best remembered for the slogan, 'Clapton is God', which appeared as graffiti all over London. Clapton was the one for whom the term 'guitar hero' was invented.

The legend of his virtuosity on the instrument became a reality for fans who took to spraying the graffiti themselves and shouting at concerts 'We want more God.' Clapton, who argued that 'I'm just an unskilled labourer musician' who 'can't see how just being a guitarist is enough', rebelled against the reputation he had somehow achieved as 'the fastest guitar alive'. By 1967, he had discovered LSD and the love generation. He praised the lack of stages and admission fees at 'Be-Ins' in America and enthused over people 'having a gas time with people and not objects'. When Cream collapsed at the end of 1968, Clapton, reacting against the hype that had made him a celebrity, the egotism of the group as a whole and the evident lack of unity between the group and their record company, opted for a period of low-profile performance. He joined the short-lived 'supergroup', Blind Faith, went into tax exile in the Bahamas, moved on to Delaney and Bonnie, for whom he was virtually a sideman, and then started Derek and the Dominoes with a number of musicians from Delaney and Bonnie who allowed him to keep resolutely out of the limelight.

Unfortunately – and cornily – he also fell in love with his best friend's wife: the former model Patti Boyd, who had married George Harrison. (Clapton once claimed that his initial pursuit of Patti was revenge for George 'grabbing' one of his 'chicks'.) The combination of dissatisfaction with his career and the lack of reciprocation from Patti was apparently enough to guarantee addiction to heroin. When Derek and the Dominoes recorded the album *Layla And Other Assorted Love Songs* in 1971, few people realized that the record was a statement of Eric's love for Patti.

Layla is now recognized as a rock classic but, at the time, it went largely unheralded – despite the band's conviction that the album 'would go straight to number one'. Clapton found solace in addiction – rarely moving out of his Surrey home and converting virtually all his money into the deadly white powder for three years. He became known as 'Eric Claptout'. He sold his cars and, at one point he remembers, 'I told one of the roadies to sell the guitars for whatever price he could get. I couldn't get cash from anywhere.' Eventually, broke, unhappy and feeling that he 'didn't want to die', he made the effort to come off heroin. With the help of musician friends – especially Pete Townshend – he crawled his way back, taking a five week electronic acupuncture cure at a clinic run by Dr Margaret Patterson in Sussex (for whom he has played a number of benefits). The cure was 'pretty unpleasant' and cost £60 a day, but it was cheaper and more pleasant than continued addiction. 'Drug taking is escapism,' said Eric – although he managed to exclude booze from that dictum.

In 1975, he was jailed in Tulsa on a drinks charge. In 1976, he took to 'streaking' whenever he was drunk (which was quite often) – and in 1981, he ended up in hospital with a perforated ulcer before a planned US tour. Despite the fact that Patti and Eric finally married

Self-styled 'unskilled labourer musician', Eric Clapton hides his hangover behind dark glasses. The man for whom the phrase 'guitar hero' was coined had come off heroin by 1975, thanks to treatment with electronic acupuncture at a Sussex clinic.

Bloated and defeated, Jim Morrison leaves court on 30th October, 1970, in Miami, Florida, after being found guilty of profanity and indecent exposure. He was sentenced to six months in jail and fined $500, but remained free on $50,000 bond pending an appeal which he didn't live to hear. Eight months later he died in the bath in Paris, aged only 27.

in 1979 in a romantic ceremony in Tucson, he seemed no more able to handle the pressures of his life. After nearly a decade of association, he sacked bassist Carl Radle from his band in 1979. Radle was a heroin addict and died in June 1980, following a kidney infection. 'I couldn't believe it,' said Ron Wood. 'Carl was a lovely guy. He had nothing left in life after the Eric thing.'

The comforting thought for the fans, stunned by all this wasted talent and wasted years, is that all rock star drug addiction and its associated deaths are a form of suicide brought on by the intolerable pressures of stardom. In a way this is true, though self-destruction is more accurate than the deliberate taking of lives. Stardom tends to frustrate noble intentions and distort the stars' grip on reality and their view of themselves. Janis Joplin saw the futility of 'making love to 25,000 people on stage' and then going home alone. Jimi Hendrix complained he could never quite capture the sounds he heard in his head. Jim Morrison of the Doors, who perfectly captured the precise mix of sexual liberation, psychic exploration and political revolt which characterized sixties rock, found his vision clouded by complacent audiences who took him for the thing that he, like Janis, least wanted to be – a pop

Jim Morrison as he would like to be remembered; the Lizard King still plays the erotic politician to thousands of doting Doors fans.

star. He tried to shock and humiliate his audience out of their passivity. On stage he was, without doubt, magnetic – leather-clad, defiantly beautiful, play-acting the dying soldier or the doomed Oedipal lover in a sort of spotlit nether-world that focused all the audience's darkest hopes and fears onto his cathartic presence. The act, as many people have pointed out, was ritual enactment of chaos and anger.

But off-stage, Morrison was a drunken Lothario, a would-be poet cultivating a booze-soaked irresponsibility he might have learned from Baudelaire, Brendan Behan or Dylan Thomas, and finding an endless stream of women with whom he tried to play the 'erotic politician' (his own definition of himself) for real. He explained his fondness for the bottle over less legitimate drugs by saying that 'getting drunk . . . is a lot of small choices . . . I guess it's the difference between suicide and slow capitulation.' It was usually less romantic than that. On one occasion, at a friend's apartment in New York, he fell into a drunken stupor on a sofa and began urinating on the carpet; a large vase had to be held under his member to catch the flow – it was filled and emptied three times. Meanwhile

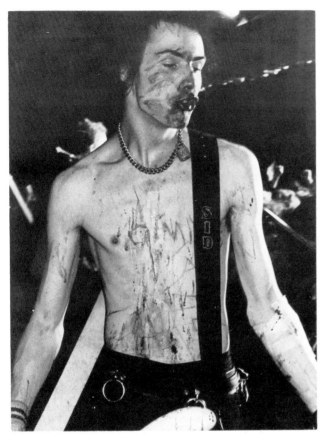

Sid Vicious playing bass with the Sex Pistols. His heroin tracks are bandaged, so Sid has taken to bleeding through some other orifice.

Morrison remained senseless.

Morrison seemed to be trying out the body and mind of the characters he became on stage in his private life, and the confusion between these personae began to intrude on both. He longed for the opportunity to galvanize an audience into action. At a concert at New Haven, Connecticut, in 1968, he introduced *Back Door Man* on stage by describing how a cop had 'maced' him backstage without realizing who he was. The crowd of course loved it – right up to and including the arrival of a cop on stage to arrest him for 'indecent and immoral exhibition', breach of the peace and resisting arrest. It would not be the last, nor the most serious occasion.

Jim Morrison was extremely impressed by the methods of the Living Theatre, a group of American performers whose techniques were based on psychodrama and the aggressive use of obscenity and violence directed at the audience. Their influence led directly to the famous incident at Miami in 1969 when, after a concert performance, Morrison was arrested for having allegedly exposed himself on stage. There are various versions of the event; one is that Morrison had it all planned and that he was wearing a large pair of boxer shorts under his leather trousers, so that when he took his trousers off, he would not actually expose himself. But fellow members of the band were also reported to have tried physically to restrain him as he began to unbuckle his belt. He was extremely drunk, slurring his words and apparently losing track of

things, so they could not predict how far he would actually go. But what is undoubtedly true is that the kids themselves, roused by Morrison's example, had divested themselves of plenty of clothing. One member of the Doors' entourage remembered that, in the concert hall afterwards, 'Every three or four feet there was another garment.'

Significantly, the concert took place on 1st March, 1969, the day after Morrison had seen the Living Theatre perform *Paradise Now*. The charges made against Morrison were not made until 5th March, long enough for the worthy citizens of Miami to have worked themselves into a lather of hindsighted indignation about the event.

The charges claimed that Morrison 'did lewdly and lasciviously expose his penis, place his hands upon his penis and shake it, and further the said defendant did simulate the acts of masturbation upon himself and oral copulation upon another.' Whether this was true or not, there is no argument that he verbally cajoled and assaulted the audience. During the trial it was alleged that he shouted at them, 'You're all a bunch of fucking idiots. Your faces are being pressed into the shit of the world. Take your fucking friend and love him. Do you want to see my cock?' This was the general tone of the evening – and it echoed the general tone of Living Theatre 'happenings' pretty faithfully as well. It couldn't pass without comment in Florida.

Morrison was found guilty of exposure and profanity, but not guilty of lewd behaviour and public drunkenness – an odd irony, since this latter was probably the one thing anybody could have been sure of on that occasion and one he himself admitted at the trial. Eventually, he quit the rock world in disgust and went to Paris to become a poet – apparently unaware that the poets had all left that city years ago. His body was already wrecked by drink at the age of 27; bearded and bloated, he tried to make a Door-less life for himself with his common-law wife, Pamela Courson, but his heart gave out and he died in the bath on 3rd July, 1971. Some say it was heroin, others booze; most agree it was inevitable – unless, of course, they don't believe that he died at all.

The theory that Morrison staged his own 'death' in order to escape his reputation and his past has gripped the imagination of his most devoted fans. It is put forward most cogently by one of Jim's greatest admirers, Jerry Hopkins, co-author of Morrison's biography, entitled, *No One Here Gets Out Alive*. The original manuscript went further even than the published book. Rather than put both sides of the argument together, Hopkins had written two different endings, one in which Morrison died, the other in which he disappeared to start a new life. In a note to prospective publishers, Jerry Hopkins stated: 'There are two "endings" for this book. The press run is to be split equally between them; if the print order is 10,000 copies, 5,000 will close with "End 1" and the other 5,000 will close with "End 2". The 10,000 copies are then to be "shuffled" and randomly distributed without any mention whatsoever of the two disparate endings.' The book remained unpublished for some time, and when it finally came out, Hopkins was persuaded to stick to a more conventional exposition. The book went on to become an international best seller.

The mystery surrounding Jim Morrison's sorry demise rests mainly on the fact that no-one considered sufficiently objective admits to seeing the body, and news didn't filter through to those who presumably thought they ought to be the first to know until nearly a week later. This is understandable given Pamela Courson's less-than-stable state of mind; she was equally a victim of Morrison's stardom and died three years later of a heroin overdose, having conducted a protracted battle to benefit from Morrison's estate. As she died intestate, her family and Morrison's share the still considerable royalties accruing from continued Doors' record sales.

Self-destruction or faked deaths alike are just excuses however. The unpleasant truth is that excessive drug use has become an essential part of the star system. Speed and coke are very common as 'working drugs', (providing, in the words of a Byrds song, 'artificial energy'), and as drugs to heighten sexual pleasure or delay orgasm. Many musicians resorted to heroin to ease their nerves or simply to get some sleep. It becomes easy, as Clapton has said, to 'rationalize it by saying that musicians live on a very intense emotional plane of necessity, and heroin is probably the strongest pain killer you can lay your hands on'. This is the sort of self-image that underlies Patti Smith's contention that there is something called 'heroin consciousness' that some stars have, whether

they use heroin or not, (Smith denies that she does). To use heroin (or to look like you do), according to this image, is to acquire artistic credentials, since no-one but a lunatic or a tortured genius would do such a dumb thing. And the aspiring rock musician of recent years often assumes that he or she needs to seem one part lunatic and one part tortured genius to have 'street credibility'. This assumption killed John Simon Ritchie when he came to believe that he was Sid Vicious, star, and not just a deluded kid that had hit lucky as part of rock'n'roll's most self-conscious satire to date. The sorry tale of Sid Vicious's short life and miserable death puts the lid on rock'n'roll drug deaths for all time, no rock star has followed such a futile career with such a violent and yet unsurprising death, and no-one is likely to in the future.

Recruited to the Sex Pistols because of his violent punk image, Sid Vicious fell for the hype completely. ('He believed his own publicity' said Johnny Rotten. 'He was called Vicious because he was such a wanker. He couldn't fight his way out of a crisp bag.') When the Pistols split up, he was just a celebrity with nothing to offer but the myth of his own empty stardom. Drifting aimlessly round London, he was latched onto by an American groupie, Nancy Spungen. Vicious, already a heroin addict, left for New York after she had been threatened with deportation following a brawl with

Goodbye Piccadilly! Nancy Spungen and Sid Vicious with Glen Matlock and Steve New (far right) of the Rich Kids, the night before Sid and Nancy flew off to New York in August 1978. Sid demanded fivers for all from the photographer to allow this happy snap to be taken, but was overruled by his management.

The body of 20-year-old Nancy Laura Spungen is carried out of New York's 'historic' Chelsea Hotel on 12th October, 1978. She had been stabbed to death.

some journalists. On landing in New York, Vicious had to be carried off the plane – 'Obviously under the influence of drugs or drink,' said the reports. Sid and Nancy moved into the notorious Chelsea Hotel where Nancy was subsequently found dead, stabbed several times in the stomach.

There were no witnesses to the killing, but evidence pointed to Sid, who was duly arrested on 12th October, 1978, and charged with her murder. Five days later he was released on $50,000 bail, put up by his record company, Virgin. Less than two months later he was back on remand again, this time in the tough Rykers Island prison, after being involved in a night-club fight with Todd Smith, Patti's brother. (So much for heroin consciousness.)

On 1st February, 1979, Sid's lawyers tried to get the charge of murder dismissed, but they failed. They then prepared to take the case into court on a 'Not Guilty' plea, so Sid was released yet again on 2nd February, once more on bail of $50,000. The story was beginning to sound like a game of legal ping-pong – except within 24 hours of Sid's release the ball was finally out of court. He was found dead by his mother and current girlfriend Michelle Robinson, in the latter's Greenwich Village flat. He died from an overdose, after consuming more heroin than his body

Slapped in the face by reality, John Simon Ritchie (a.k.a. Sid Vicious) is taken to be charged with the murder of Nancy Spungen.

Now its's Sid's turn to be bagged. Last act in the drama, Sid Vicious's body is removed from the Greenwich Village apartment where he died on 2nd February, 1979. He'd been out of jail for one day.

could stand following two months' enforced withdrawal in prison. He was 21 years old.

Back in the movies' golden age, Oscar Levant once said, 'Strip the phoney tinsel away from Hollywood and you'll find the real tinsel underneath.' In the rock world, the real tinsel can still be found in California. There is no illusion of angst among the select group of rock superstars whose success has converted the acid dream into their exclusive reality. Drugs offer not the power to change the world, but merely its paler shadow – the power to change *their* world by changing themselves. Heroin is becoming increasingly popular in the Californian rock community because it is now available in a form supposedly pure enough not to cause the user any danger. After a while, of course, it causes little else, apart from addiction. Cocaine too, has been subjected to refinement for the elite through 'free basing', an extremely dangerous procedure in which commercial cocaine (which is supplied as a chemical compound, cocaine hydrochloride) is dissolved in ether and heated to turn it into pure cocaine. It has a tendency to blow up in your face. Free basing is definitely a hobby for the wealthy alone, since a great deal of the already expensive drug is required to create the more potent 'free' cocaine, and the process also requires fairly sophisticated apparatus. Whichever it

is, heroin or cocaine (or both), the constant use of regulated and increasing doses of a highly expensive drug is surely the most convincing demonstration of wealth casually acquired and disposed of.

The Eagles, whose music is the very culmination of California rock, have grown up in the fickle atmosphere of a society devoted to 'changing its mind' by whatever means available. 'I'm not saying I'm an angel or a saint now,' said their drummer, Don Henley, when discussing cocaine in 1979, 'because I'm not. But I've slowed down quite a bit.' Even so, the Eagles are still proud enough of their capacity for alcohol to have invented their own generic term for drunken behaviour. They call it 'to monster'.

And in November 1980, Henley was arrested and charged with possession of cocaine, quaaludes and marijuana. A girl of sixteen was found in the house, naked and, by her own account, overdosed on cocaine and quaaludes. Henley pleaded 'no contest' to the charge of contributing to the delinquency of a minor. He was fined $2,500, given two years' probation, and required to take part in a two year drug diversion programme. Since then he has 'slowed down' even more.

Cass Elliott of the Mamas and Papas once said, 'Pop music is just long hours, hard work and lots of drugs . . .' In July 1974 she died in a London hotel room of gross obesity when her fatty heart gave out. It's been a long, hard trip to the place of definitions.

REBELS
WITHOUT A CAUSE

After all the ideals had been exploded in the late sixties, rock remained simply and solely an entertainment, and performances – once they had gravitated towards the mass arena – sought justification in outrageousness. At its best this was a cry against the distancing effects of stardom, at its worst it was part of a self-contained escalation of rock as spectacle. Since the cry generally went unheard, the worst case came to be the universal one – performances became increasingly outrageous because that was what was expected of them.

Outrage on stage was like a return to the time when rock'n'roll's appeal lay in its ability to express the forbidden. But it was a return with a difference – by the end of the sixties, audiences were better educated about the mysteries of the forbidden and more demanding about their thrills. And boy, did the rockers work hard to cater for them.

Excess became the watchword. It was partly in terms of mammoth amplification systems, gargantuan light-shows and a general tendency to deafening loudness. (It has been claimed by a colleague of Lemmy of Motorhead, that he is now so deaf that he once failed to notice when his guitar lead fell out of its amplifier; and Ted Nugent, boasting the title of world's loudest musician, wears earplugs on stage.) But it was also in terms of performance style. Mere histrionics were no longer enough. Hendrix burning his guitar and Keith Emerson taking stilettos to his organ keyboard pale into insignificance in the light of subsequent acts. The daddy of them all was of course Frank Zappa, whose 'atrocities' started it. Zappa cultivated outrage as a rock'n'roll style. Having neither the flashiness nor anger nor sexuality of earlier acts, it was a calculated product of his self-obsessive nihilism. You can see this in the names he's given his children – Dweezil, Moon Unit, Ahmet Rodin and Diva – and the recording of songs like the unforgettable *Yellow Snow*, a warning against the dangers of eating frozen dog's piss.

Zappa's background is instructive. The son of a history teacher who wanted him to be a chemist, he worked for a time as an art director in advertising and for a greetings card firm, helping to hone his sense of the absurd to a sharp point. Having made a few hundred dollars from work on a film, he bought up a sound studio in the small town of Cucamonga, California, shipped in a number of old film-sets that he bought up cheap and set about planning his first

movie – to have been called *Captain Beefheart versus the Grunt People*. With no money left and surviving on peanut butter, instant mash, coffee and honey, in 1963 he formed a 'blues' trio to play professional gigs locally. While playing in a Chicano club, Zappa was offered an apparently genuine offer to make training films for the San Bernardino vice squad. As he tells the story, he played a member of the force some of his tapes of friends, freaks, locals and girlfriends. Soon afterwards he was approached by a man claiming to be a used car salesman who wanted 'hot tapes' for a party. Zappa and his girlfriend obliged by grunting and groaning in front of a microphone. But no sooner had the tape been delivered than the studio was invaded by photographers and cops and Zappa was busted on a charge of publishing a pornographic record. A six-month jail sentence was reduced to three years probation, on condition that during that time he would not be in the presence of a woman under 21 without 'a competent adult' present. He served eleven days in jail and, as a result, was exempted from the draft.

The atrocities started more-or-less accidentally once Zappa's group, the Mothers of Invention, were well-established. When the anti-Vietnam movement was at its height, Zappa invited some uniformed US Marines on stage during a show. He gave them a life-size doll, saying, 'This is a gook baby, show us how we treat gooks in Vietnam.' The Marines, who rose to the occasion, tore the doll, stuffed limb from stuffed limb. 'After that,' says Zappa, 'we included props in all our shows. I call them visual aids.'

Zappa and the Mothers have had marriages performed in mid-show, cajoled members of their audience to make speeches and left the stage completely while up to 30 people from the audience performed and sang in their place. One of their favourite tricks has been to send objects down an overhead wire onto the stage: a spread-eagled doll, for example, followed by a suggestively shaped and well-aimed salami. One specially effective prop has been the 'soft giraffe' – a vast stuffed animal which squirts whipped cream out of its stiffened tail all over the front rows of the audience. 'Sometimes you can't write a chord ugly enough to say what you want to say,' he said in defence of these bizarre practices, 'so you have to rely on a giraffe filled with whipped cream.'

Despite Zappa's self-proclaimed seriousness, those in authority have often found him simply outrageous. Banned in London's Royal Albert Hall for obscenity in 1971 three days before he was due to perform, he took them to court in 1975. The

What most people prefer under plain wrappers, the Tubes turned into a rock'n'roll show in the seventies.

65

defendants contended that Zappa wrote 'filth for filth's sake' and Zappa, who would never deny that he wrote at great length about matters sexual, tried to prove that filth is in the ear of the beholder. The transcript of the case (which Zappa lost) reads at times like a subtle farce. 'Would you not say that any young woman who seeks to contact a member of a rock'n'roll group in order to procure sexual intercourse,' asks the Royal Albert Hall's barrister, 'that such a young woman is in a very sorry state?' Zappa (married to a woman he has described as a former groupie, 'and an excellent groupie, too'), replies: 'Er, no. I would not.' 'I don't think you can have heard the question,' says the barrister, who has plainly not heard the answer. 'I will repeat it . . .'

By the time the seventies had got under way, the hugely successful acts like the Stones, Led Zeppelin, the Who and subsequently, Rod Stewart, Pink Floyd, Elton John, David Bowie, the Eagles or Kiss, were little more than travelling circuses carting truckloads of equipment round the world, each vying for the title of 'world's most spectacular rock act' (sometimes misinterpreted as 'world's *greatest* rock act'). Jagger's inflatable phallus, the Floyd's light shows, Elton's 'Carmen Miranda' costumes, Kiss's smoke bombs and so tediously on, had become the kernel of their performance. The performers themselves became international jet-setters, flying from all corners of the world to come together for a tour or to lay down backing-tracks on a

Below: Two old troopers reliving past campaigns: Nico, once a member of the Velvet Underground, and Andy Warhol, who created the right atmosphere for them to work in.

Heroin consciousness for beginners: at Winterland, November 1974, Lou Reed gives an on-stage demonstration.

new album recorded in Munich, mixed in Jamaica, remixed in a chateau on the Loire and mastered in New York. They had become a whole new class of rich people maintaining houses or hotel rooms in three or four different locations, and hanging out in exclusive night-clubs, or else, like the Pink Floyd, maintaining a sturdy indifference to the fans and the glamour and emerging from their reclusive existences only for touring, recording or discussions about their investments.

This sort of rock'n'roll was increasingly soulless and mechanical, inspired only by the need to make money, fill the time and, just maybe, to reinject jaded lives with the frisson of adventure that touring brings. The sad conclusion of success saw the Stones (and entourage), once the bearers of progressive promise, as guests during their 1972 tour of America at the Chicago mansion of chief Playboy, Hugh Hefner. Hef wined and dined the boys in the manner to which they had become accustomed. And then, some years later, the group released an album called *Black And Blue* which was promoted with advertisements depicting a bruised woman, hands tied behind her head and legs spread, bearing the slogan 'I'm Black and Blue from the Rolling Stones and I love it'. Answering vociferous criticism of this promotion, the Stones – once held up as the great pop satirists of sexism – argued that some women liked that sort of thing.

Sexuality became the great playground of rock in the seventies. In fact, everything pointed in that direction: the permissiveness of the preceding decade, the sexual symbolism of performance itself, the need to exploit unconventional morality. Liberation became personal liberation, freedom from oppression became freedom from sexual repression, the democratic urge towards equality and freedom of association became an individualistic quest for guiltless promiscuity. Sex was the great leveller and the means by which the American Dream of power and achievement could be successfully pursued by everybody. Every nook and cranny of erotica was invaded by people in pursuit of the new holy grail. All 57 varieties of sexual experience could be found openly in almost every city throughout America and Northern Europe. It was taken as a sign of freedom and a new moral maturity, but in fact it was all rather joyless and perfunctory, a sort of orgasmic rat-race. It encouraged a notion of sex as a consumer good (even when it was not overtly paid for), the latest product of the 'leisure society'.

The Velvet Underground made much of the running. The band was formed in the late sixties by New York rock'n'roller Lou Reed (an *habitué* of the gay scene who once shocked his fans by announcing his impending marriage to a woman, but later reappeared, reassuringly, with a boy named Rachel in tow), and the classically trained Welsh violinist, John Cale. With the sponsorship of pop-art mastermind, Andy Warhol, and together with a smoky-voiced German chanteuse named Nico (who was the associate and friend of such stars as Bob Dylan, Leonard Cohen, Brian Jones and Jim Morrison), the band went out as a mixed-media event called 'The Exploding Plastic Inevitable'. Nico played the whip-toting Wanda in a song called *Venus In Furs* ('shiny, shiny boots of leather,' sang Lou in the role of Severin); she was, suggestively, a lesbian in *I'll Be Your Mirror*; Lou Reed played a white punk on heroin in *Heroin* and

67

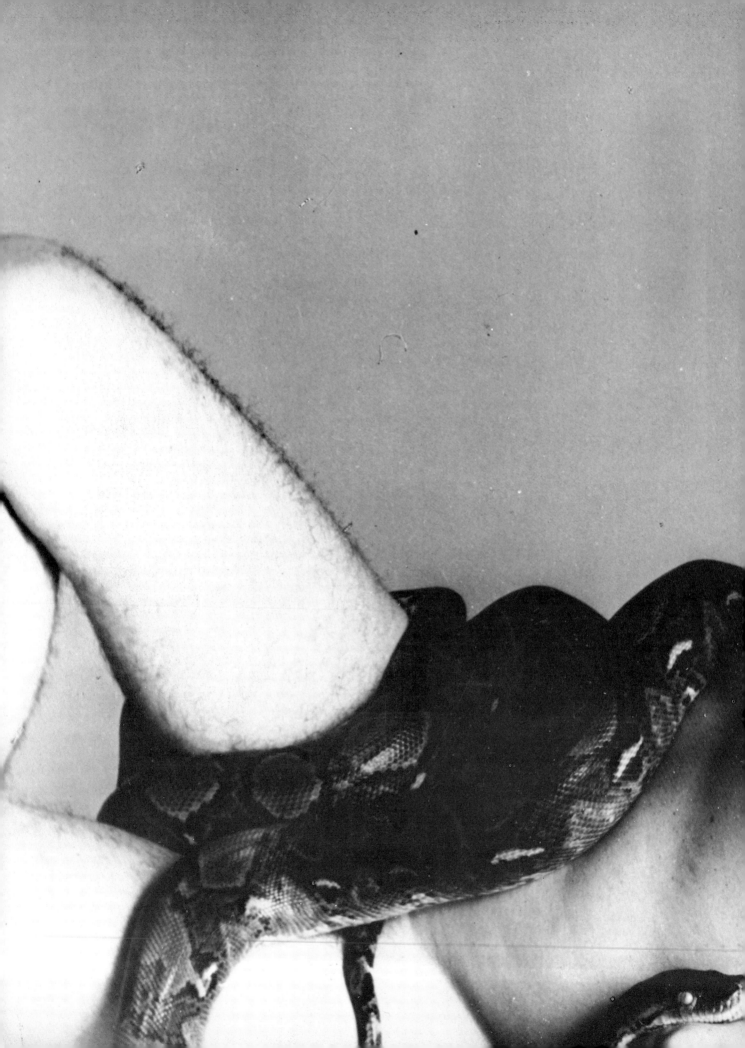

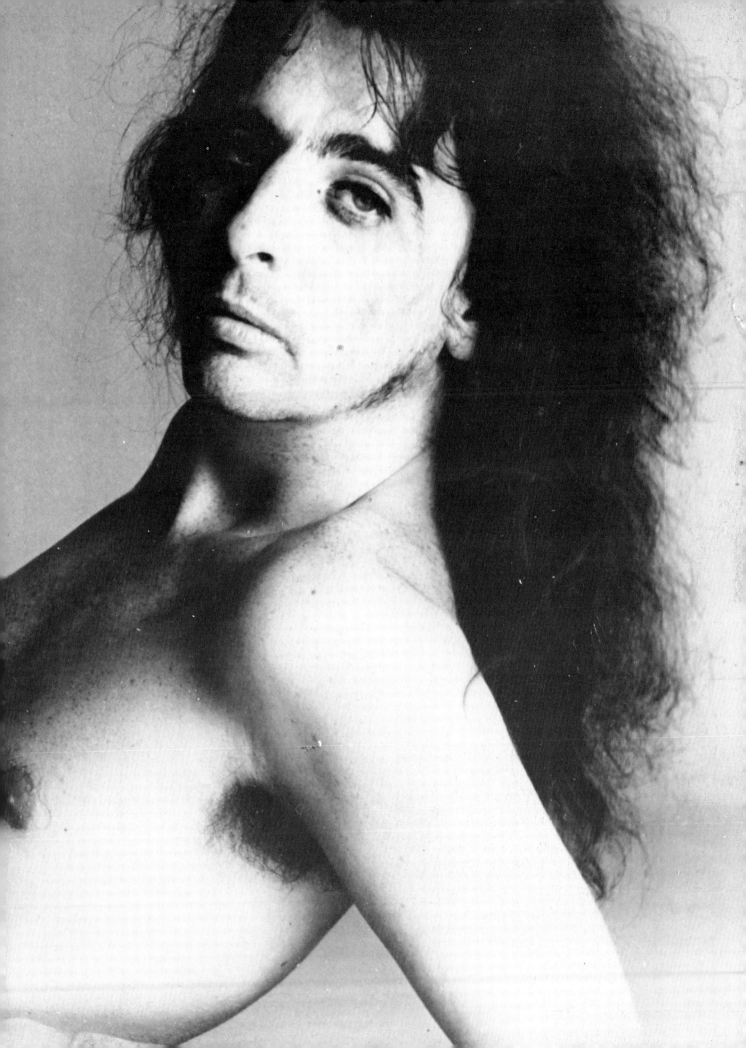

Waiting For My Man; John Cale played a nerve-jangling violin redolent of evil times, low-life and sexual pleasure-pain. The band as a whole was a startling visual and aural assault, virtually defining the seamy New York underworld – 42nd Street, Harlem, a life full of fixing, fucking and masturbatory fantasies in which the operative verb is 'to score': the gutter we all inhabit, as Oscar Wilde once said, from which some of us are looking at the stars.

Of course, the Velvets were no mere titillators, regardless of whether or not their audience got off on voyeurism. Their music was about enslavement, the complete destruction of freedom – but there was something quite thrilling about the extremity of the degradation they pictured and (they were not stupid), there was a reassuring certainty in the music which such a complete denial of freedom offered. Despite the Warhol association (and despite the fact that Lou Reed later recorded a song about Warhol's transvestite 'superstars' (*Take A Walk On The Wild Side*), they were not a Warhol package. But they represented something Warhol understood well – the fascination people have for the bizarre, the decadent, the degraded and the dangerous. They held up that old, old equation between sex and death, pleasure and pain, as a fundamental of rock'n'roll. Not even Jim Morrison learnt to do it as well. The Velvets were selling an image (like Warhol himself) and it was an image that captured the moment (before its time, it must be said) when rock's pursuit of a pastoral idyll would run slap up against the dreadful urban reality.

Throughout the seventies the idea of rock'n'roll representing images from the sexual sub-culture held sway. Former Zappa associate, Alice Cooper, built an entire career on a couple of good hard-rock songs and an act that even as early as 1971 he admitted was '60 per cent contrived'. Among Cooper's contrivances were the name itself (the band was all-male and Alice's real name is Vincent Furnier), whips, leather gear, dolls that were mutilated in the course of the act, a chicken that was 'killed' during the show amid a flurry of prepared feathers, a mock guillotining, even – at one point – the bizarre apparition of Alice dressed in his torn leotard and high boots brandishing a giant toothbrush and chasing a scantily-dressed woman disguised as a tube of toothpaste.

Alice, who had clearly made a study of his mentor, Frank Zappa, was hugely successful and inspired many a later punk rocker with his stage image of decadence refined to complete negativity. Zappa may have been a nihilist, but his sense of morality and humour cannot be doubted. The Alice persona was no more than a hollow shell which enabled the real Vincent Furnier to indulge his favourite activities of golf and drinking. This son of an Arizona preacher hit the green with the likes of Jack Nicklaus and Bing Crosby and hit the bottle with a will. In late 1977, he committed himself to a sanatorium to dry out and later

David and friend: a moment of harmony for David Bowie and Lou Reed, with Mick Jagger taking a back seat. Bisexuality, said Bowie, is 'fun'.

Who was that lady I saw you with last night? David Bowie plays Rosemary Clooney.

recorded an album, *From The Inside*, based on his experiences. 'I was drinking two quarts of whisky a day,' said Alice after his three month treatment, 'just to keep going! I was living at 100 miles an hour with alcohol for fuel.' In two-and-a-half-years, said Alice, he had *never* been sober. Even early on, the group used to boast of spending $250,000 a year on booze and Alice himself would regularly put away 40 cans of beer in one day. 'In the end,' said Alice, 'I was throwing up blood.' Alice's sado-masochistic stage twilight stood in evident contrast to Vincent Furnier's more straight-forward reality. After splitting with his lover, Cindy Lang, Vince married Sherryl Goddard in 1976. 'In two years of marriage,' he later said, 'she never saw me sober.' After committing himself to the sanatorium, Vince expected the worst. But Sherryl came through with flying colours. She declared that she always knew that her husband would straighten himself out one day, and she damn well intended to stay with him!

David Bowie's emergence in the early seventies was perhaps the single most important influence to the development of an explicit and outrageous sexual-ization of rock. The promotion of Bowie as bisexual superstar and mascot of the eroticists was a carefully calculated operation. It's no coincidence that Bowie and Lou Reed (one of Bowie's acknowledged influ-ences) were both signed by RCA in the same year: the man who signed them, lawyer Dennis Katz, was very keen to change RCA's image – tainted by association with the red-blooded defence industry and the heavily 'hetero' country music scene. Bowie's manager, Tony de Fries, was simultaneously eager to sign Bowie to a

company where he would be noticed. Bowie, already sporting shoulder-length tresses and wearing satin gowns, could hardly escape attention. The press coverage given to Bowie and his wife Angie's pro-fessed bisexuality and 'open marriage' gave credibility to the singer's musical claim to be a child of the future, at a time when 'free sexuality' was being passionately pursued as the most likely candidate to usher western, industrial society into a golden age. 'It's true – I am bisexual,' David said some time later. 'But I can't deny I've used the fact very well. I suppose it's the best thing that ever happened to me. Fun, too.' Well, that's as maybe – Bowie's cultivation of image ('I decided to adopt the masks so I didn't have the humiliation of going on stage and being myself') has shrouded his private life in a carefully concealing mist. But, regard-less of the testimony of one or two perennial rock starlets, like Dana Gillespie and Amanda Lear, that troilism and less mathematically complex activities were indeed practised in the Bowie household and ready gossip about David's singular and multiple activities in New York and Berlin, Bowie and his wife seem to have been rather less liberated than confused.

In 1974, Angie Bowie spoke approvingly of groupies – 'the people who make it all worthwhile,' she said. 'If you can't accept groupies,' she said, 'you

Angie and friend: Angie Bowie emerged emotionally bruised but still smil-ing from her celebrated open marriage with 'stud' David, thanks in part to the help of guitarist Keeth Paul, who saw her through a suicide attempt in January 1978.

shouldn't get married in the first place.' David was a stud, she said, and the two of them were happily married members of the gay culture.

Less than four years later, Angie and David were at each others' throats over their divorce and the issue of custody of their son, Zowie. The marriage may have started unconventionally enough, but it seems rapidly to have adapted to ploughing a familiar furrow. 'When we first met,' David was wont to recall, 'we were both laying the same bloke.' Angie seems to have been less sanguine. On their second night together, she had flung herself headfirst downstairs because David was going off to a rehearsal. Later, Zowie's birth left her with a cracked pelvis. Unable to cope with the problems and pain of motherhood, she ran off, leaving David literally holding the baby. In her simpering memoirs, entitled *Free Spirit*, Angie recalls that 'while I was in love with David and ready to share him with anyone he nominated, I still wanted to hold that privileged and treasured place as his wife'. She objected most of all to the way news of David's latest boy and girlfriends filtered through to her via the gossip columns.

Meanwhile, David was getting heavily into drugs. 'I used to try a new drug every time one came onto the market,' he said. 'I guess I've been near death a lot.' During 1975 and 1976 ('probably the worst year or year and a half of my life . . .'), Bowie's obsessive characterizations and mythologizing about himself (Ziggy Stardust, the Thin White Duke) became mixed up with the potent legends of a society in need of salvation. Helped along by over-exposure to cocaine and Los Angeles ('That fucking place should be wiped off the face of the earth,' said Bowie in 1980), he drifted towards the symbolism of Christianity, Arthurian myth and Hitlerism. In late 1975, he arrived at Victoria station in a black Mercedes flanked by blond outriders giving Nazi salutes. 'Britain would benefit from a period of fascism,' he said. 'I was in a haze of mythology,' he later explained. 'Mixed up too, of course, were my own fucking characters.' Bowie fled to Berlin where he was forced to face up to the reality of Nazism, not just its nightmare symbolism. Eventually, he 'came crashing down to earth', but by that time, the celebrated marriage was in a shambles and David was spending a great deal of time in the company of a young German waiter. 'It's been celibate for the past five years,' Angie confessed in 1979, about her relationship with 'stud' David. She had just recovered from a heavy dose of sedatives followed by an assault on her lover, Keeth Paul, and a couple of botched attempts at suicide.

'I never dreamed that the green-eyed monster called jealousy would get me – but it did,' said Angie. David, meanwhile, went to the custody hearings over Zowie with the claim that Angie was 'an unfit mother and a drug addict'. He got the child and she got a £30,000 divorce settlement. By 1980 she was living in apparently monogamous bliss with a certain Drew Blood (real name, Bogdan Andrzes Lipka) in a log cabin in California. Meanwhile David settled in Switzerland with his son. At home in Corsier-sur-

72

Vevey near Lake Geneva he struck up a friendship with his near neighbour Oona Chaplin, widow of a clown greater even than he.

Lou Reed, Alice Cooper and David Bowie opened the floodgates to a tide of performers more or less dedicated to rock'n'roll's pride of place in the sexual market. Glitter and glam-rock invaded the charts – a glaring expression of sexuality as packaging. Flamboyance reached new heights of camp elaboration, with performers like Bette Midler (whose act is liberally sprinkled with crudities), Elton John (who admitted his own bisexuality in interviews in 1976) and Labelle (who, for a variety of reasons, became mascots of a certain part of the gay and lesbian scene in America and Britain). The Tubes developed into one of the greatest and crudest rock parodies yet. Lead singer Fee Waybill would come on stage with a false prick and enormous stack heels as 'Quay Lewd', a totally zonked superstar, or in leather gear as 'Sado Man', and while TVs flickered on stage, he would strip and simulate sex with a female partner on a motor cycle. On one occasion, the Tubes held a talent contest in Los Angeles to find an opening act for their show. Among the competitors were Sister Marie de Sade, the stripping nun; Mr Penguin, who, dressed as the bird itself, sang 'Hello, I'm Mr Penguin/You do your thing and I'll do mine'; and – the winners – a group called the Fetus Brothers who sang 'He's no pansy, he's my lord', while crucifying a man dressed as a nun.

The Village People, artfully synthesized in New York, took the stereotypes of the macho gay world out of the closet and, in doing so, created a comedy act out of the deadly serious business of fist-fucking and male homosexual sadism. Even a dreadfully mundane group like Queen chose their name for its gay connotations, as lead singer Freddie Mercury once said, and cultivated an act and an image (in Mercury's case, at least) of such stunningly arch campness that people were either seduced by it or laughed out loud.

Such apparent sexual freedom was hardly liberating for women: it only made acceptable a wider range of male fantasy figures. Cute kids, vamps, virginal madonna figures and straightforward strumpets have now been joined by dominatrices and oh so glamorous lesbian types as stock characters for women to play. Someone like David Bowie is able to ride out the storms of his own confusion, even to translate it into a marketable commodity. Women performers are less able to do this. Their exploitation by the mainstream of rock has become, if anything, more subtle and insidious since the advent of rock'n'roll's overt sexuality. One all-woman group was named Fanny. Another – Birtha – had, according to their promotional material, 'balls'. The Runaways presented the studied personae of clawing, eyeball-scratching teenage bitch goddesses. Gaye Advert came on in a leather jacket and thick mascara. The Slits promised and sometimes offered a challenge to female stereotypes but appeared

'Sex sells,' says Debbie Harry of Blondie, plagiarizing the Monroe image.

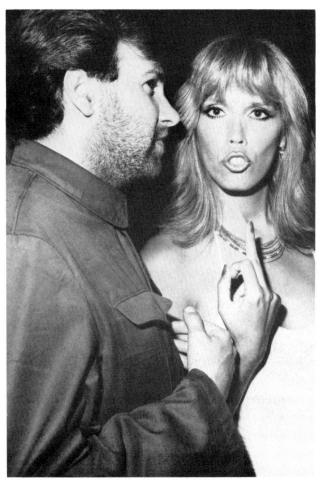

Former Raymond Revuebar showgirl, once known as Peki d'Oslo; writer of 'bullshit biographies'; calls herself a transsexual; Amanda Lear (seen here with Andy Mackay of Roxy Music) knows how to look after herself.

attempt to revive him after a particularly heavy night of 'fun'. They developed the glitter look into a studied cross-genderism: playing straightforward seventies R&B dressed in pancake make-up, bouffant hairstyles and high-heeled shoes, but usually with a couple of days' growth of beard showing through. The effect was rather like Danny La Rue singing the blues, and almost as offensive.

Wayne County – another influential figure on the New York rock scene – went one further. He was a gawky sort of gentleman who habitually wore a dress and fishnet tights with holes in them, *à la* Monroe in *Bus Stop*, and hair which looked like a bleached blonde fright wig. Wayne once appeared at a party dressed in a delightful frock made of inflated condoms. He also wrote an arch little tips and advice column, entitled 'Dear Wayne', in a New York rock gossip magazine, *Rock Scene.* Towards the end of the seventies he carried his image-building to its logical conclusion and was surgically converted into Jayne County, a move which had little or no outward effect. Wayne said before the final transformation, 'I figure I've lived half my life as a man, why not live the other half as a woman?'

What Jayne did for real, Amanda Lear pretended. This enterprising European disco semi-star made something of a stir in 1976 by claiming to be a transsexual. A distinctly smoky voice and a 'statuesque' figure helped further the titillating illusion. In fact, Amanda had been born a woman – although exactly where and quite how many years ago no-one can be sure – and had been persuaded by former lover David Bowie to play her masterstroke of a hoax. 'I learnt from him to make myself interesting,' she said. 'To stand out from all other girls.' Ten years previously, Amanda had been an undistinguished stripper at London's Raymond Revuebar, working under the name of 'Peki D'Oslo' while claiming to be French. In order to boost herself in the rock marketplace, she released a series of 'bullshit biographies', giving a wide range of exotic birthplaces and parentages. Amanda, who achieved more media coverage as Brian Ferry's girlfriend than she did as a recording artist, brazenly promoted the phoneyness of her image. In 1978, she happily demonstrated this with the immortal statement that 'Disco is the lowest form of music, but the quickest way to fame.'

Maybe all this is a product of popular sexual confusion. But, if so, the quality of rock's permissiveness is no less shabby. Heavy metal, the most consistently popular kind of rock since the early seventies, has made a virtue out of the most strident and offensive male posturing. Curiously the tradition which forms the basis of heavy metal fashions and attitudes most markedly, actually comes from gay male culture. The chained and studded leather outfits, tattooed bodies and 'bike boy' poses that are central to heavy metal style have all been lifted from the world of butch drag – nothing more or less than 'a nice bit of rough'. Not even the strutting cock-rockers like Led Zeppelin, Bad Company, Ted Nugent or Rush could be described as so masculinist as groups like Judas Priest, Saxon, Motorhead or Iron Maiden. In fact, the current crop of

on their first album cover tastefully nude and smeared with a light coating of mud. Deborah Harry, perpetually moaning in interviews about her 'cheesecake' presentation on album sleeves and in the press, has never yet been known to refuse to appear in a mini-skirt, off-the-shoulder dress, tight pants or whatever it takes. One of the early (British) ad campaigns for Blondie presented her in a tight black dress with her hair tied back, under the slogan, 'Wouldn't You Like To Rip Her To Shreds?' (the record was called *Rip Her To Shreds*). Patti Smith – the thinking person's sex object – proudly boasted not just that young boys masturbated over her picture but that she herself had 'jacked-off over the cover of *Easter*' (her second album).

But what is even more disturbing than such sexist stereotyping was in the way in which male performers, from Bowie onwards, co-opted women's images. The New York Dolls, for instance, were a major influence on the East Coast in the early seventies. They were suitably wasted. Two of them had major problems with heroin and bassist Arthur Kane was almost destroyed by booze. Drummer Billy Murcia died, during a visit to London in 1972, when his girlfriend poured coffee down his throat in a vain

Malcolm McLaren and the strong arm of the law. Top-dog in punk management, McLaren was among several revellers arrested after disturbances at a rowdy Thames riverboat party to celebrate the Queen's Silver Jubilee in June 1977.

heavy metal bands have gone beyond masculine exclusivity to outright woman-hating. It's hardly surprising to find among the repertoires of such groups songs extolling the virtues of violence against women, or attempts to elevate the notorious Yorkshire Ripper, Peter Sutcliffe, to the status of folk hero.

'If you want to find out how much freedom you have,' said Vivienne Westwood, 'make some kind of explicit sexual statement and wait for it all to crash down around you.' Vivienne, of course, was the partner in life and commerce of the Sex Pistols' manager, Malcolm McLaren. A fashion designer by training, she was instrumental in creating the whole punk style – an improvisation on themes of death, rape, sado-masochism and bondage. Through their shop in the King's Road, Chelsea, Vivienne and Malcolm promoted their 'provocative' and 'confrontational' theory of clothing. The resulting amalgam of leather, chains, straps, zips and rips made parts of London look like an explosion in a New York gay bar and its blast is still reverberating around the world. The Sex Pistols themselves were another 'explicit sexual statement', designed by McLaren, after his brief period managing the fading but influential New York Dolls. 'Rock'n'roll is not just music,' said McLaren. 'You're selling an attitude too.' The attitude for the late seventies, McLaren discovered, was the glorification of

Thieves and swindlers: the last act of McLaren's 'Great Rock'n'Roll Swindle' took the rump of the Sex Pistols flying down to Rio to record with runaway Train Robber Ronald Biggs in February 1978. L. to r.: Steve Jones, Jim Jetter in SS uniform, McLaren, Paul Cook and shy, fun-loving Ronald Biggs.

powerlessness, soulless despair and nihilistic perversity. McLaren already knew that to make any impact he had to say something that not even the 'progressive' rock world would feel happy to hear. In America in 1974, he had dressed the New York Dolls in red leather, stood them before a giant hammer-and-sickle Soviet flag and promoted them as 'Communist chic' – 'our "better-Red-than-dead" phase,' as Doll vocalist David Johansen said. The late seventies' version was, of course, the Sex Pistols.

After the Sex Pistols finally split-up (amid much acrimony), McLaren approached Adam and the Ants to star in a pornographic video film about a group of

75

kids who start a club to act out sex games, but the idea was axed by McLaren's lawyers and by Adam. Adam and Malcolm parted company after apparently exchanging musical ideas and Adam went off to form the remarkably successful Ants Mk II. Meanwhile, using the nucleus of the original Ants, Malcolm's masterplan produced Bow Wow Wow. Musically and visually, the two bands were remarkably similar – both cultivating a so-called 'tribal' music, which sounds like Gary Glitter's backing group playing in a paper bag, and appearing in heavy make-up and fancy costumes, now as pirates, now as American Indians, now as highwaymen. But Adam (real name Stuart Goddard) has shown greater admiration for the established values of showbiz than McLaren ever did – and he has in consequence seen far more commercial success than Bow Wow Wow.

McLaren, despite some possibly light-hearted claims that he took the pop world with a well-conceived grand strategy, (known as the 'great rock'n'roll swindle'), has always been motivated by a desire to be outrageous rather than anything subtler or better defined. Bow Wow Wow's singer was to be a fourteen-year-old girl called Annabella Lu Win (ostensibly of Burmese extraction, although her mother calls herself Mrs Dunn-Lewin). 'Why shouldn't Annabella be bait for lots of guys to get excited about?' asked McLaren, who planned to feature his new star in a sex magazine for pre-teens to be called *Chicken*. 'Underage sex,' said McLaren, 'is a very splendid thing.' Unfortunately, Bow Wow Wow's record company, EMI (no doubt trying to wipe some of the egg they had received from the Sex Pistols off their corporate face), didn't agree. They pulled out of *Chicken* after reportedly putting up £20,000. When Bow Wow Wow recorded a song advocating home taping of discs, at a time when EMI were vociferously engaged in a campaign against it, the company began politely to ignore the group – despite an investment of £55,000 (according to McLaren). The record (*C30, C60, C90, Go!*) flopped and, in an echo of earlier days with the Sex Pistols, the group ran riot in the EMI offices, throwing gold discs, hurling a clock out of a window, burning contracts and wrecking a revolving door. The group was dropped but, undaunted, McLaren found them another deal (with RCA) and the band went on to make an album which, McLaren thought, should feature a cover parodying Manet's famous painting, *Déjeuner Sur L'Herbe*, only with Annabella and not an artist's model in the nude. Annabella, at that time fifteen years old and still needing a special licence, a governess and a chaperone to perform in public, agreed to pose because she 'wasn't showing enough commitment to the band'. Annabella's mother threatened legal action, however, and RCA dropped the planned sleeve until Annabella was sixteen.

To date, therefore, McLaren's only significant success has been the Sex Pistols. They, at least, had all the right ingredients at just the right time. The Pistols emerged at the head of the punk movement which seemed implicitly to understand and accept what they stood for. McLaren's period managing the New York

Dolls had taught him something. With the Sex Pistols, McLaren was selling a label which advertised the ingredients necessary for the contemporary rock'n'roll mix – sex and violence. He may not have understood how the very explicitness of this touched a nerve of alienation and despair in the kids, but he did understand that the punk obsession with sex, and especially violent sex, was never more than a pose. There could have been few bands less sexy than the Sex Pistols (especially when Rotten started talking about cutting off his piles). But the important thing was not actually to be sexy or shocking, but to tell people you were, with all the gall of a street trader.

Johnny Rotten was the least musical of the Pistols, but he was the one who best understood the group's hollow image. Accordingly, he became their most celebrated and reviled member – attacked by Teddy Boys, harassed by the police, the person who, according to one writer at least, 'almost single-handedly defined punk rock'. His disagreements with McLaren, whom he accused of being a money-grubbing exploiter and who in turn fired him from the band at the end of their one and only US tour, helped to destroy the Sex Pistols. Sid Vicious, Paul Cook and Steve Jones carried gamely on – for a few months. The group, said Johnny Rotten (now using his actual name of John Lydon and in a new band, Public Image Limited), 'was a farce'. Legal action against McLaren revealed that most of the Sex Pistols' money had been dissipated. Not surprisingly, when subsequently questioned about PiL, Lydon said, 'No one in this band is a musician. We all hate the term. We're something close to factory workers. Machinists. Skilled operators.' His ambition for PiL, he said, was the same as it had been for the Pistols: 'To destroy rock'n'roll.'

Outrageous as it was, British punk remained essentially impotent – giving way in short order to only slightly more refined moves by the record industry to control the golden egg-laying goose of music. Despite that, it was seen as threatening by outsiders, and often resulted in actual violence and harassment. This was especially so in Britain's Jubilee Year of 1977, when the Sex Pistols released the distinctly unjoyous *God Save The Queen*, while others waved flags at street parties. Needless to say the record was banned from the airwaves – but it still reached number two in the charts.

Johnny Rotten and Sid Vicious were frisked by an over-eager policeman in June 1977; Rotten had been fined for possession of amphetamine sulphate in March; eleven people were arrested on a variety of charges when the Pistols' record company, Virgin, threw a rowdy party on a Thames river boat in June; Rotten and Paul Cook were violently attacked in separate incidents a fortnight later (Rotten suffered knife wounds while Cook was hit over the head with an iron bar); in May, Paul Cook had been fined for theft, and in July Vicious was fined on assault and weapons charges. The Clash, touted as the true revolutionaries of punk – were also harassed, but their harassment revealed the sad insignificance of their personal revolt. Joe Strummer was fined, in June 1977, for stealing

'All our songs are in praise of women,' say the Stranglers, seen here getting on down at an open-air concert in Battersea Park, London in the summer of 1978. Before the police stopped the show, bassist Jean-Jacques Burnel couldn't resist getting in on the act, adding a further appendage to the five-and-a-bit breasts visible.

pillows from a Holiday Inn, and earlier for spraying the band's name on a wall. Topper Headon was fined for stealing a hotel key. The next year, Headon and Paul Simonon were fined for shooting some racing pigeons, while Strummer and Simonon were fined in the wake of a riotous Glasgow gig.

The Jubilee Year also saw the Stranglers ordered off stage at London's Rainbow Theatre because Hugh Cornwell was wearing a T-shirt parodying the Ford Motors logo which actually read 'Truck', but which from a distance could have been read as 'Fuck'. Bob Geldof was attacked on stage at a London club. Kid Reed, singer with the punk group the Boys, was assaulted by Teddy Boys. Meanwhile, Leee Black Childers (manager of the New York group, the Heart-breakers) was attacked by punks because he looked like a Ted.

In Sweden, later in 1977, the Stranglers' show was disrupted by 200 neo-fascists and in the following year the same group was accused of causing a riot in Nice. But despite all the violence and brushes with the law, self-mutilation remains the most potent image of punk, and its ultimate expression was the deaths of Nancy Spungen and Sid Vicious. Perhaps the final comment should come from Malcolm McLaren. 'I didn't make the Pistols famous just for money,' he said in 1980. 'It was a great sexual turn-on too.'

Johnny Rotten dismissed sex as 'two minutes of slurping noises', and for many punks and post-punks

(reacting against the naïve optimism of the 'love generation'), the act itself seemed to have lost all meaning. Sex was an expensive commodity or, heaven forbid, something you had to take your clothes off to do. The late seventies even saw a brief period of trendy 'asexuality', when sex was touted as distinctly boring and, for some people, celibacy was promoted as a radical gesture. Sex was no longer about pleasure and people, but about power and objects. The S&M symbols cultivated by punk resolved sex into power games – and power games are what rock performers play on stage, and rock managers (like McLaren) play off it.

In America, where British punk's sense of irony and despair never had fertile soil in which to root, the 'new wave' picked up where the punk trinity of Lou Reed, Bowie and Alice Cooper left off. A group called the Dead Boys, lead by one Stiv Bators, caused a considerable stir by cultivating a stage act which made great use of S&M imagery. It was widely rumoured that Stiv and his colleagues enjoyed this sort of thing off stage too, although Bator's relationship with Bebe Buell indicated more conventional tastes. Iggy Pop, another of punk's godparents, made a vaunted comeback in 1979 in leather and lacerated flesh.

Not surprisingly, American women performers revealed most keenly the voyeuristic trend. Grace Jones, emerging from the New York gay/S&M disco scene, presented a wide variety of sexual diversions – now she would sing surrounded by a bevy of muscular men in leather jock-straps, now she recorded an album whose very title, *Warm Leatherette*, irresistibly evoked fetishism, now she appeared as a hi-tech androgyne with severely cropped hair. Cherry Vanilla, who once worked with David Bowie's management in New York, created an act of stunning vulgarity

making maximum suggestive use of the microphone. She once appeared at a party wearing a chiffon frock and parading a man in a leather mask around on a leash. Patti Smith ensured her own street-credibility by informing the press that, on what one can only presume were good nights, she would have an orgasm on stage.

Most stunning of all have been Wendy O. Williams and the Plasmatics – the ultimate sex-and-violence act to date. Sporting a Mohican haircut, Wendy might come on in a see-through body-stocking or tight black pants and some strategically placed sticky tape and clothes pins – sometimes, she would opt for no more than a couple of blobs of whipped cream to cover her nipples. The all-male Plasmatics looked no less bizarre and the music – if that's the right word – fitted the image. Songs like *Sex Junkie*, *Pig Is A Pig* and *Living Dead* were hammered out with all the subtlety of an

exploding elephant. Guitarist Richie Scott whacked himself over the head with his guitar. Wendy smashed televisions, took a chain saw to a plugged-in guitar and sliced it in two, and at the climax of the act, the group might demolish an entire motor car – talk about auto-destruction. This was the rock'n'roll equivalent of the super-gory exploitation movies of the seventies. 'Pornography rock' was how the Plasmatics described it. 'I've always been a kind of anarchist,' said Wendy. In London, the group were banned from performing before playing a single show of a 1980 tour because their car-demolition routine was considered too dangerous. In Milwaukee the following year, Wendy was dragged out of a concert hall by police. 'One of them grabbed my tits, another one grabbed my rear end. So I smacked them.' All charges were subsequently dropped, but Wendy commented that, 'I'd have gone along peacefully, but I was outraged intellectually.' Also in 1981, in Cleveland – the city, according to Wendy, with the third highest rape rate and the fifth highest murder rate in the US – she was charged with 'pandering obscenity'. After her acquittal, she emerged from the courthouse proclaiming her victory as 'a big thing for women's rights and the First Amendment'. 'I'm a rock'n'roll singer,' said Wendy. 'I should be able to do what I want.'

THE BLACK EXPERIENCE

When Frankie Lymon died as a result of his heroin habit in 1968, the tragedy was not just of wasted youth, the fault was not just the record industry's callousness or Frankie's impressionability and in-experience. Frankie Lymon, unlike all the white boys swallowed in and washed up by rock'n'roll success, was a victim of racism as much as he was a victim of a greedy industry or his own too rapid rise.

It was not that he was particularly exploited or ripped-off – although as a black teenager he was certainly a prime target for shady business practices – nor that he was any less able to cope with sudden success than dozens of other ill-educated, street-wise kids who stepped out of junior high school into the back seat of chauffeur-driven limousines. Lymon's tragedy had less to do with rock'n'roll as such than it had to do with being black in a white supremacist society. Not even a string of hit records could undermine the legacy of slavery and ghetto life. Rock'n'roll may have allowed blacks a degree of equality as entertainers (boasting that it broke down formerly rigid marketing distinctions between white and black musics) but rock'n'roll could not give *all* blacks pride, courage or insight into their own situation any more than it could rid the whole of white society of its prejudicial attitudes to blacks. Lymon, in other words, lived and died as a black first and as a rock'n'roll star second.

Like scores of others, the Teenagers (with Frankie Lymon) started as a street-corner vocal group, singing for pennies in Harlem. By the time Frankie was four-teen, the group had released half-a-dozen Top Ten singles – including the well-remembered *Why Do Fools Fall In Love?* and *I'm Not A Juvenile Delinquent.* Typically, black vocal groups have had anonymous members – a feature which not only makes their exploitation easier but also allows personnel to be moved around with impunity.

Frankie Lymon, however, emerged as a star from the Teenagers and left the group in 1956 to pursue a solo career. He was going on fifteen. While not unheard of, it was a brave move for a young black singer – even one whose status at the time was com-pared to that of Bill Haley, Chuck Berry and, at times, Elvis Presley. But his solo career flopped and Lymon became increasingly dependent on heroin. With the help and encouragement of his girlfriend, Lymon con-tinued to fight his addiction but the relationship didn't last and when the singer went into the Army he also

went back on heroin. After his discharge, Lymon went home to New York and a series of unsuccessful attempts to find and hold a steady job. In February 1968, aged 25, he died of an overdose on the floor of his grandmother's apartment – penniless and forgotten.

Lymon's story, with its combination of themes of golden youth, sudden riches, ambition, addiction, a slow descent back to grinding poverty and eventual death, has become legend – a moral tale capturing the essence of everything rotten about rock'n'roll (com-parable to Gene Vincent's sad history). But just as Vincent's tragedy is nothing without his poor white Southern background, so Lymon's resonates because he was black. Though, in the relatively enlightened world of rock'n'roll, the idea that blacks should keep their place may have been abandoned, nonetheless long-standing traditions of racism reverberate in their stories. And the black artists themselves feel this – they too understand the notion of the 'sassy nigger' sashaying through life in defiance of the old white conventions of black subservience.

Other black musicians, like Frankie Lymon, found failure a powerful stimulus to self-destruction. Guitar Slim, born Eddie Jones in Mississippi in 1926, topped the R&B charts in 1954 with a slow blues, *The Things I Used To Do* (featuring Ray Charles on piano). His spec-tacular act and playing style subsequently drew com-parison with Jimi Hendrix and perhaps he was ahead of his time. The respect and admiration of his profes-sional colleagues was clearly insufficient reward and, having failed to achieve long-term success, he fell victim to alcohol, dying in 1959.

Clyde McPhatter was another victim of early suc-cess. Born in North Carolina in 1933, he formed the original Drifters in 1953 and had a number of hits with them (*Money Honey* and *White Christmas*, for example), and as a solo performer (*Lucilla* and *Such a Night*) before being drafted in 1954. In 1956, he returned to the business and worked exclusively as a solo singer. He achieved a string of hits, including the unforget-table *A Lover's Question.* But from 1959 onwards, he started switching labels with alarming rapidity and, despite several notable hits (*Ta Ta, Lover Please* and *Little Bitty Pretty One*, for example), his career went into decline. He became an alcoholic and moved to London in the late sixties. Despite a strong personal following, he never achieved the sort of early success he had known. In fact, he walked his way through a series of recording disasters until finally people only put him in a studio out of pity or for the sake of old times. Jerry Wexler once called him 'the great, unique soul singer of all time', and Smokey Robinson said,

---

Mountain high: Tina Turner, queen of black female performers, is still knocking them dead on the wrong side of forty.

Little Frankie Lymon – only fourteen but already a star. He may have jumped for joy at the London Palladium, 1st April, 1957, but heroin finally got him eleven years later.

'He was the man'. But in June 1972, while visiting friends in the Bronx, Clyde died of an apparent heart attack, his liver, heart and kidneys all but destroyed by booze.

R&B star Johnny Ace shot himself through the head on Christmas Eve, 1954, during the interval of a show in Houston, Texas. On the point of breaking through into the mass market with his hit single, *Pledging My Love*, Ace apparently occupied his time backstage with a game of Russian Roulette – the perfect symbol of casual despair in the face of a capricious and hostile fate. In 1973, Paul Williams (one of the original Temptations but no longer with the group) was found, shot through the head, gun in hand and dressed only in his swimming trunks, sitting in his car. The inescapable verdict was suicide. Suicide was also the accepted verdict on Donny Hathaway – an ex-student preacher and gospel singer who had found international success duetting with Roberta Flack. The 33-year-old Hathaway had been recording in New York during January 1979, when, one Sunday morning, his broken body was found on a second-storey roof of his hotel, the Essex House. 'We suspect suicide

because the door of his room was locked and there was no evidence of foul play,' a police spokesperson said. Hathaway had either fallen or jumped from the window of his fifteenth-floor room shortly before midnight on the night before. The shock to many friends and critics was not assuaged by the news that the singer had suffered from frequent depressions. But perhaps the man who had once been billed as 'the nation's youngest gospel singer' found it difficult to cope with secular success.

It's not really surprising that many blacks should channel their general feeling of being society's outcasts into self-destructive outlawry. Despite the fact that drug abuse has always been as prevalent among white as black musicians, until the mid-sixties there were far more arrests of the latter on more serious charges and with greater attendant publicity. Louis Armstrong – Whitey's favourite jazz musician – was forced to forego his penchant for marijuana after a particularly harsh bust in the forties. Ray Charles – enormously influential on both soul and rock – was busted at Logan Airport, Boston, in 1964, on his return from a Canadian gig. Charles had been using heroin for seventeen years and this bust, for smack and grass, was his third. He decided to kick the habit. 'Kicking was something I felt I had to do,' he said in his autobiography. 'I didn't quit because the heroin was killing me – maybe it was, maybe it wasn't – but because it was going to bring down my family and maybe even cause me to rot away in some jail cell.'

As it turned out, he was able to avoid both outcomes – because he managed to kick the habit before his trial and because, as he himself says, 'I was blessed: I'd had the bread to buy decent junk, and then I had the bread to buy bail and a high grade of justice.' He was convicted, but was put on probation. Others haven't been so lucky. Blues singer Little Willie John died in jail after being incarcerated for theft. Drummer Buddy Miles – who had played in Jimi Hendrix's Band of Gypsies – was jailed for two years for the relatively minor offence of stealing a parked car (the British call it 'taking and driving away').

When not being attacked by the law, even successful black musicians find themselves entrapped by that negative institution of the law, organized crime. Larry Williams (who had several hits in the fifties and sixties with 'Little Richardesque' songs like *Bony Moronie* and *Slow Down*), ran a highly successful Hollywood prostitution ring. In 1979 he was shot dead – by his own hand, according to the police, by the mob, according to his family. 'King' Curtis Ousley – *the* fifties' and sixties' session saxophonist, virtuoso of the booting, yackety-sax style – was as successful as any black performer of the period. He was stabbed to death in New York in 1971 by a young Puerto Rican with whom Curtis had picked a fight, possibly because he thought the man was a burglar. Curtis came upon the man, 26-year-old Juan Montanez, sitting on the stoop of a brownstone apartment house, owned by the saxophonist on West 86th Street. It was late one Friday night in August, Friday the thirteenth as it happened. According to the police, the two men had a heated

Before the sixties, black musicians attracted more attention from narcotics investigators than whites. Blind Ray Charles sits helplessly as detectives examine drugs and paraphernalia, following his second arrest in Indianapolis, 4th November, 1961.

exchange; Curtis, a heavily-built six-footer, was notorious for his short temper and was known to fly off the handle with little provocation. This time however the Puerto Rican pulled a knife and stabbed the musician. Curtis grabbed the knife and stabbed Montanez four times in retaliation. Montanez managed to run off, but unluckily for him, collapsed later and was taken to the same hospital in which Curtis had by this time already died of his stab wounds. Montanez was then arraigned for the musician's murder.

This whole squalid incident may have been completely attributable to the unattractive side of Curtis's character, but it remains powerfully suggestive of the violence and criminality that surround black musicians. In another incident in 1974, singer Bobby Womack's brother, Harry, was stabbed to death by a woman at the door of Bobby's LA apartment. Harry, who had performed with his brother under the names of the Womack Brothers and the Valentinos, resem-bled Bobby closely, and it has been suggested that Bobby was the intended victim. The killer may have been exacting some curious revenge for Bobby's marriage to the wife of his former mentor, Sam Cooke, who was also killed in bizarre circumstances.

Not surprisingly for a people whose culture has been exploited, plundered and attacked as much as the black Americans', male black performers rely heavily on *machismo* as a mark of their identity, while many female black performers – Tina Turner, Ronnie Spector, Donna Summer for example – present themselves in a sexually obvious, not to say whorish, way. Of course, sexual stereotypes are one of the most obvious aspects of racism and, while most of the black female performers who have been popular with white audiences have depended on emphasizing their availability, male performers in a similar position have ironically compromised their macho image with emasculating touches (falsetto or high tenor voices, clownish costumes or stylized dance routines). Jimi Hendrix based much of his act on an *explicit* referral to black machismo, but his success was founded in

83

Britain, not America. Eric Clapton explained his appeal. 'Everybody and his brother in Britain still think spades have big dicks,' he said at the height of Hendrix's success. 'Jimi came over and exploited that to the limit, the fucking tee. Everybody fell for it. Shit.'

It's not surprising that the macho image displays an understandable confusion. Al Green, perhaps the leading gospel-influenced soul singer of the seventies, is a case in point. 'Green's style ... becomes the vehicle for a persona that is modest, even fragile, yet undeniably compelling,' gushed Robert Christgau after one performance. What he really meant was Green was sexy. In October 1974, Green was approached by a woman fan – 29-year-old Mary Woodson – who foolishly hoped to marry him. She discovered that Green did not match up to her fantasy image of him. Despite her persistence, she was rejected. Attempting to disfigure the reluctant lover, she tipped a pan of boiling grits down the Alabama-born Green's back. It ranks as an incomparable piece of poetic drama. She then took a gun and killed herself. The tragedy was not just one of unrequited love or burning sexual desire, but of black sexuality as it has been defined in public. Green may not have promoted a he-man version of black macho, *à la* James Brown, Wilson Pickett or Teddy Pendergrass, but his meaning

Courtroom blues: Ray Charles sits in an Indianapolis court on 9th January, 1962 to face charges made in the previous November. After Charles' third bust, at Boston's Logan Airport in 1964, he gave up drugs to save his family from distress and himself from destruction.

Al Green, one of the great black sex symbols of the seventies, preaching the gospel in Memphis, 26th January, 1980. After his experiences with a pan of boiling grits from an over-eager fan, it's not surprising he retreated into the ministry.

and his moans were intended to be just as clear.

Green's precursors included the far less restrained Jackie Wilson and Sam Cooke, both acknowledged architects of soul music's synthesis of spirituality and carnality. Like most soul performers, Jackie Wilson's recording career seemed shaky and uncertain – never quite sure of its direction, whether it was the Elvis pastiche of *Reet Petite*, night-club standards or high energy storm raisers like *(Your Love Keeps Lifting Me) Higher And Higher*. But on stage he was magnetic. Sexual hysteria could reach fever-pitch and engendered a violent intensity which white performers could rarely match at the time. Joe McEwan described a typical occasion at Boston's Back Bay Theatre. In the middle of *Shake! Shake! Shake!*, Wilson jumped into the willing arms of the women clustered round the edge of the stage and completely disappeared in the turmoil. Shirt shredded, he had to be escorted to safety by the police.

In July 1960, Wilson was arrested with six other black performers at a show in New Orleans. This time the police had tried to prevent the singer from 'mingling' with the audience at the all-black show. They only succeeded in creating a riot. The show was stopped and the anger of 5,000 disappointed fans had to be quelled by the riot squad.

On 15th February, 1961, Wilson returned home to his New York apartment at about four in the morning. Juanita Jones, a 28-year-old black woman, claiming to be a friend and fan, was waiting for him. As Wilson told it, she knocked on the door and asked him 'to pay her some attention'. When he refused, she threatened to shoot herself and pulled a .38 pistol from her belt. Wilson, a former boxer, said he grabbed the gun and was shot in the back and front during a brief struggle. He ran into the street, crying for help – his hysterical sexual persona turned back on itself. Juanita Jones, arrested for 'felonious assault', could only say, 'I've loved him ever since he cut *Lonely Teardrops.* I hope I haven't hurt him . . . I'm all mixed up.'

Wilson's career was as florid on the way down as it had been at its early sixties' peak. In 1967, he was arrested with a lorry driver for possession of heroin, hypodermic syringes and two loaded guns, after the police had stopped the two men's car in Catskill, New York State. Two years later, he was held as a material witness after an Atlanta waitress and former Playboy Bunny named Karen Lynn Calloway was murdered by her husband, shot five times. Wilson had just completed a six-day residency at the club where Karen worked. Her husband, a hand in a local carpet mill, claimed that he shot his wife because she had become infatuated with Jackie Wilson. Karen Lynn was a 21-year-old mother of two when she died.

Of course, the screaming had to stop sometime and Wilson declined into a parody of banal sentimentalism. He suffered a stroke while performing in New York in 1976 and spent much of the rest of his life in hospital. In February 1978 – a few months before his death – one newspaper recorded that in the course of his flamboyant career, the singer had sold 22 million records and generated around $200 million of revenue from record and concert ticket sales. Broke and unconscious following another stroke, Jackie Wilson had just passed his forty-third birthday, on which the former idol of millions received just six cards.

Wilson lived to see rock'n'roll change utterly from his halcyon days. Sam Cooke, however, was killed at the turning point. The most curious aspect of Cooke's death is the way that, even many years later, people find its manner in stark and worrying contradiction to his public image – invariably described as 'gentle', 'poised', 'graceful' and 'genial'. His death was a profound shock to his millions of fans – 200 people attended the Los Angeles Inquest, 200,000 filed past the body in Chicago and LA. Cooke remains for many whites just a man who composed and sang trite little pop songs like *Only Sixteen, Twisting The Night Away* and *What A Wonderful World,* but for blacks he was the embodiment of the drive towards black pride: a black capitalist with his own record company, management firm and publishing organization, a man who controlled his own destiny and could hold his own in the white world, and who openly allied himself with the cause of black liberation.

All this fuelled rumours that his death was not an accident – that he was the victim of some elaborate mob killing because, so it was said, his success made him too much of a threat to the white establishment. Much the same was said about the crash that killed Otis Redding some three years later, and similar rumours have circulated around Jimi Hendrix's death. In 1981, the French newspaper, *Le Monde,* actually carried an interview with an anonymous but self-confessed contract killer who, while denying he had been involved in Hendrix's death, claimed to have known the man who arranged it. As yet, the claim remains unsubstantiated. The evidence in all three cases is thin – but in Cooke's case at least, his death has acquired the resonance of myth. It is a sad fact, however, that the truth is probably as sordid as it seems and the reaction against it was the result of the poor light it shone on Sam Cooke.

The inquest testimony indicated that on the night of his death (10th–11th December, 1964), Cooke picked up 22-year-old Elisa Boyer at a small party at a Hollywood restaurant. Cooke was 33 at the time and married to his high-school sweetheart, Barbara Campbell. After offering to take Boyer home, Cooke drove to a motel in Los Angeles and registered (as 'Mr and Mrs Cooke') with Boyer apparently standing quietly by. 'He dragged me to that room,' Boyer told the inquest, 'and I again asked him to take me home. He turned the night latch, pushed me into bed and pinned me down. He kept saying, "We're just gonna talk" . . . He pulled my sweater off and ripped my dress. I knew he was going to rape.' Boyer picked up her clothes (together, it seems, with Cooke's) and ran out of the motel room. Cooke followed her to the motel office but she had gone to look for a telephone. The motel manageress, a black woman named Bertha Lee Franklin, told Cooke that Boyer was not with her but, after starting his car up, the singer returned to the office dressed only in an overcoat. According to Franklin, he persisted in asking 'Where is the girl?' and, after being told to get the police, he broke down the door of the motel office and attacked the manageress. She pushed Cooke away, grabbed a pistol and shot him three times. 'He said, "Lady, you shot me",' Bertha Franklin told the inquest. 'He ran at me again. I started fighting with a stick. The first time I hit him it broke.'

It was, by the witnesses' accounts, a bloody, brutal and unnecessary death. Sam Cooke's partner, J. W. Alexander, evidently hired a private detective 'to find out what the hell happened to my friend' – with no result. Alexander and his new partner, Barbara Cooke, fell out and Alexander eventually withdrew from the association. Soon afterwards, Barbara Cooke married Bobby Womack.

Naturally, RCA – Sam Cooke's record label at the time of his death – continued to release records by him. The first release after his death was the exhilarating ballad *A Change Is Gonna Come,* written by Cooke after he had heard Bob Dylan's *Blowin' In The Wind.* The song was Sam Cooke's own epitaph. Somewhere in

Sam Cooke, the suave, gentle soul singer of the early sixties, whose violent death belied the poise and geniality of his public image.

Sam Cooke's widow, Barbara, places a flower on her husband's casket. He died while out with another woman, who claimed at the inquest he had tried to rape her. Cooke's daughters, Tracey (4) and Linda (11) can be seen on either side of their mother.

200,000 people paid their respects to Sam Cooke's body after his death at the hands of a motel owner on 11th December, 1964. A further 5,000 people attended the funeral service at Mt. Sinai Baptist Church, Los Angeles on 20th December, many having to stand outside in the steady rain.

New York, Frankie Lymon may have been shooting himself full of heroin, but Cooke had known that for black and white alike the times were moving on.

Sam Cooke's hopes for the future of integrated popular music had already begun to bear fruit in the late fifties and early sixties when the formal and informal segregation of music started to break down. This earlier segregation had taken some curious forms. Until the fifties, the US had been a country operating an effective apartheid policy, at least below the Mason-Dixon line. Black musicians playing for white audiences were in many towns required to 'appear' behind a screen. Conversely, white performers on predominantly black tours were not allowed to play at all – one such tour which included Buddy Holly and the Crickets, Paul Anka and the Everly Brothers, found these white performers forbidden to appear in Chattanooga, Columbus (Georgia), Birmingham (Alabama), New Orleans and Memphis. These same integrated package tours, many put together by DJ Alan Freed, would often have to split up when the performers left the concert hall, even if they were actually allowed to play on the same stage, the whites going to one hotel and the blacks to other, inferior, accommodation. Many white performers refused to go along with this – Niki Sullivan, who toured with the Crickets in 1957 said that eventually they preferred to stay in black hotels, where, he observed, 'We were accepted'.

The record industry at that time operated a category of 'race music' (under whatever euphemism, usually Rhythm and Blues) which separated the recording, promotion, distribution and sale of records according to the performer's skin. There were black radio stations, black record shops and black record labels serving the black community but generally owned and controlled by whites. Rock'n'roll and British R&B began to change this; one early example involved Buddy Holly and the Crickets again, who, booked to appear 'sight unseen' at one venue, surprised the tour promoter mightily when he found out they were white.

Unfortunately, the de-segregation of musics and audiences made little difference to the practice of exploiting performers. White and black alike were ripped-off, because any inexperienced performer with an inadequate understanding of the business and inadequate advisers was a potential target for bad (or no) royalty deals, shark-like managers and agents, diabolical contracts and Faustian agreements. If blacks suffered more from this institutional cheating, it was because they tended to have less experience of business, less effective representation and perhaps even a lower level of aspiration. On top of that, the 'race' market was smaller and poorer than the white market which meant that deals were usually worse and the ultimate rewards invariably smaller.

The familiar practice of covering 'race' records for the white market was a particularly subtle form of exploitation stemming directly from the segregation of the market. Many white performers made their reputations on covering black records, many of which never sold in the white market at all. Pat Boone, for example, recorded successfully versions of Fats Domino's *Ain't That A Shame*, Little Richard's *Long Tall Sally* and *Tutti Frutti*, Ivory Joe Hunter's *I Almost Lost My Mind* and the Flamingos' *I'll Be Home*, in the middle years of the fifties. Clearly, every sale of one of Boone's anaemic versions reduced the sales of the original. Even where the original performer could expect a writer's royalty, such payments were often unforthcoming. The classic example is that of Arthur 'Big Boy' Crudup, whose *That's Alright Mama* and *My Baby Left Me* have been covered over the years by everyone from Elvis Presley to Rod Stewart and Elton John. But Crudup saw no royalties. 'The company paid my manager, but he didn't pay me,' Crudup said in the mid-seventies. 'I was to get 35 per cent of every dollar he received. Well, I failed to get it.' Crudup's Lester Melrose, died before his client received any money. Legal action resulted in an offer in settlement of $60,000 from the Melrose estate and Crudup's publisher. However, while waiting in New York for the cheque to be paid, Crudup was told that the offer had been withdrawn. The issue would have to go back to court, and Crudup himself died before any final decision was reached.

Similar experiences to Arthur Crudup's were, however, commonplace (and probably still are). They are worse among black musicians and writers but by no means restricted to them. Many of the popular black performers of the fifties and early sixties had to soften their blackness for white consumption. They were aware of the compromises they made. This awareness showed in their attitudes to the business. Sam Cooke and Chuck Berry, for instance, were both clearly motivated in large part by a desire not to be exploited. Cooke had his businesses; Berry had his by now notoriously rigid attitude to his contractual obligations. It's not surprising that someone like James Brown should fight and ultimately win the right to control the whole of his business interests, including management and record production. In the late sixties he risked the accusations of capitulation by black militants and of repetitiveness by rock and soul critics. But the Number One Soul Brother just ignored both; his answer to them has been to keep going in exactly the same, successful way, even at the approach of his fiftieth birthday.

If there was no specific move against racism or for black equality in the early days of rock'n'roll, there was a great deal of feeling that blacks should, at least, assert themselves and protect their own interests. The sixties consequently saw the growth of independent black record labels, song publishers, agencies and managements, and the prime example of this was Berry Gordy's Motown Company.

The Motown and Tamla labels were launched in Detroit in 1960 by Gordy, who had been one of America's most successful and prolific songwriters in the late fifties. With hits by Jackie Wilson, Marv Johnson and Etta James, among others, to his credit Gordy's move into distribution with his own label was – like the subsequent development of the publishing, management and film-making side of his business – motivated by the simple desire to maximize profit. Smokey Robinson, one of Gordy's early co-writers, leader of the Miracles (Tamla's first successful group) and later Motown's vice-president, explained that Motown started because black groups did feel they were being ripped off elsewhere. He said: 'Motown was just local and we decided since nobody was paying us for the national stuff anyway, why not see what the national market could do. So that's why we exist today.'

From the start, Motown was almost exclusively a black operation (unlike, say, the supposedly more 'authentic' black labels like Atlantic, Chess or later Stax/Volt). The company relied heavily on family loyalties – one of Gordy's first associates was his sister Gwen and two other sisters married Harvey Fuqua (of the Moonglows) and Marvin Gaye, both of whom were important members of the Motown team from the early days. Early Motown performers were treated like most of the other black performers scuffling around in the marketplace. Most effort was expended on groups: the Miracles, the Velvelettes, Martha and the Vandellas, the Four Tops, the Temptations, the Supremes were all patterned on the classic vocal group

Diana Ross as Billie Holiday in Lady Sings the Blues. *Once a nameless member of the Supremes, she was groomed for stardom by Motown boss Berry Gordy, who achieved his goal when she played the tragic Lady Day.*

format of much black music. Individual members were kept largely anonymous, which helped when the membership changed, as it frequently did.

The real Motown artists, throughout most of the sixties, were the writers, the arrangers and producers – the performers were moulded to a pattern and, in the end, tended to settle down with one or other team of composers and craftspeople whose conception they faithfully realized. Like the Platters, the Drifters, the Chiffons, the Ronettes or countless other earlier and later vocal groups, they were effectively faceless – it was the Motown *sound* that mattered. And this hard-nosed operation was also extremely paternalistic; Gordy obviously saw himself as some sort of patriarch, running his 'family' with an iron but gentle hand. 'We used to have a school at Motown Records called Artists' Development,' said Smokey Robinson, 'and in order to become a Motown recording artist – before you had been recorded and did any dates at all – you had to be at school. You had to go and you had to learn stage presence, choreography and the girls had to learn hygiene and stuff like that. You learned all about it before we presented you to anyone in the country.' The Supremes were told to finish their formal education before recording; Little Stevie Wonder's royalties were kept in trust until he came of age. Critics have accused Motown of manipulating its performers; Gordy and Robinson have always maintained that they cared for their artists, developing and nurturing

90

their talents. Motown has always aimed its music at the white market and the company tactic has been to understand the white market and supply what it wants. Successful though it has been, this tactic has not been without problems.

Gordy always seemed eager for his performers to move into the highly lucrative middle ground. His ambitions pointed to Las Vegas, the Copacabana and movies. By the early seventies, however, Motown finally achieved 'intellectual' respectability when the company's two most notable mavericks, Marvin Gaye and Stevie Wonder, produced albums that went against the Motown grain. Gaye's *What's Going On* and Wonder's *Music Of My Mind* were wordy and experimental and, although Gordy had never shied away from topicality or symbolism, Gaye was political and Wonder introspective. In addition, both performers gave themselves almost total responsibility for their albums. The Motown mould had been broken.

Motown's relations with its performers have frequently been criticized – most remarkably, by the performers themselves. As recently as 1981, Marvin Gaye complained that the company failed to treat him as 'an artist . . . a complete entity'. However, Gaye has stayed with Motown while many others have departed the fold, vociferous in their complaints – the Holland brothers and Lamont Dozier, Martha Reeves, David Ruffin and Eddie Kendricks among them.

The conflict which led to these departures is not so much between employer and employees but between the original idea of Motown's operations and the new attitude which began to take over in the sixties. Gordy's vision of a black company directing its product at the white market involved the cultivation of a corporate identity under which individual talent was buried. By the mid-sixties, a number of changes had occurred which overtook this vision. Black consciousness and the success of a handful of vanguard black performers like Sam Cooke were joined with a growing general acceptance that popular music could be an 'art' in the most traditional sense. Gordy and his 'employees' were well aware of these changes, but Gordy's response was to turn his company round from producing a corporate product to cultivating individual talent. Many of his protégées saw their future in terms of personal promotion and even stardom based on the recognition of their individual worth. Inevitably, many would feel that Motown was stifling their chances, while others, like Florence Ballard, would be left behind in the rush to build up the reputations of a handful of individuals.

Florence Ballard was one of the original Supremes (with Diana Ross and Mary Wilson). The three girls, all from the same poor quarter of Detroit, met at a church gospel meeting and sometime later decided to form a professional vocal group. Through Berry Gordy's patronage (and, as legend has it, after painstakingly sewing their own costumes), the Supremes became an immensely successful act. But then Gordy's design changed. In 1967, the Supremes were to become Diana Ross and the Supremes, and would start recording songs with what have been described as 'slightly more

Above: Florence Ballard in 1965, at the height of her success with the Supremes. By 1967, the group had become Diana Ross and the Supremes and Florence was on her way out.

Below: At Florence Ballard's funeral in Detroit, 18th February, 1976, Diana Ross (left) comforts Florence's daughter, Nicole Chapman, aged 7. Florence's husband, Tommy Chapman (right) cuddles twin daughter Michelle. Diana and Florence began life in the same Detroit housing project.

socially-conscious lyrics' (*Love Child* and *I'm Living In Shame*, for example). For Diana Ross, a career as an artist, actress and star stretched far ahead. Meanwhile, back in the sixties, Florence Ballard and Mary Wilson were pushed into the background.

Florence – whose contribution to the Supremes before 1967 had been as great as Diana Ross's, and who had recorded eight gold records with the group – did not readily accept such a fate. Despite the flashy accessories of a Cadillac Eldorado and a golden Fleetwood, she later claimed that she only received a weekly allowance through all those hits – a practice which may have been unfair, but was by no means illegal. It was put about that she quit because she couldn't stand the pace of world touring. She told the *Los Angeles Times* in 1975 that she had agreed to leave the group after being offered a million dollar settlement by Motown, but her $8.7 million dollar lawsuit against the company, the Supremes and her former attorney, was dismissed in 1971. By 1973 she was separated from her husband and had lost her home through foreclosure. She moved back to her childhood area and, with support from Aid to Dependent Children, moved into a two-family apartment with her three daughters, mother and sister, in the same Detroit housing project in which she had grown up.

In 1975, she told her story to the papers and received considerable publicity – and probably some much-needed remuneration. But a few months later, in February 1976, the 32-year-old singer was admitted to hospital complaining of pains in her arms and legs. She had apparently been drinking heavily at the same

Tammi Terrell emerged from convalescence to record this album with Motown heart-throb Marvin Gaye, but she died tragically of a brain tumour in March 1968, aged only 24.

Just walking in the rain. Marvin Gaye, enfant terrible of the Motown stable, contemplates the difficulties of combining artistic integrity with good commercial sense.

time as taking drugs to help her lose weight and reduce her blood pressure. She died shortly afterwards.

The accepted myth has always been that Florence Ballard died in poverty. But her sister Pat subsequently claimed that Florence had in fact received an 'unexplained legal settlement' shortly before her death. Indeed, at the time of her death, Florence had been reconciled with her husband and had bought a new home for herself and her family, as well as another Cadillac. The manner of her death may well be a clue to her original problems with Motown and the Supremes – heavy drinking could have made her a liability, hence the excuse that she left because of 'the pressure of touring'. But whatever the reason, Florence never made her dreamed-of comeback, and if she had ever been an embarrassment to Motown and its most successful female star, Diana Ross, the hapless Florence was no longer.

Stevie Wonder stayed with Motown because when he came of age the company released the $1 million they had held in trust for him. Having satisfied himself that Motown had handled his finances fairly, he signed with them again after securing a high royalty rate and the right to publish his own material. One wonders

how long he will remain, since even Berry Gordy's 'Trilby', Diana Ross, has left Motown for RCA's pastures, greener it is rumoured, by as much as $20 million.

Marvin Gaye has stayed as well, even though he's fared less well. His marriage to Anna Gordy kept him going through what was a disturbing period. In March 1968, Gaye's current singing partner, Tammi Terrell, collapsed in his arms of a brain haemorrhage and died some time later, aged only 24. Gaye was of course greatly upset. More than a decade later, he spoke of the internal problems of the company at the time. Gordy and Motown were getting backlash from some sections of the record business because of the success they were achieving among radio stations and distributors. Gaye found the combination of personal and professional pressure difficult and went into virtual retirement. 'I'd become such a creep basically,' he admitted. 'I'd made Berry very angry. I wasn't on the best terms with my wife. There was the Vietnam war still going on.' Eventually, he decided he had to come back, and he recorded *What's Going On*, but despite the appearance of having won a personal and artistic victory, things did not improve. By the end of the seventies, Gaye had demonstrated his artistic worth beyond doubt, but he had gone through two divorces and a bankruptcy following a tax bill of more than $2 million. Unlike Stevie Wonder, he has to keep struggling with more than just his art – he gained a reputation for unpredictability which is still current – but unlike many other graduates of Motown, he is still there struggling, and proving that the struggle can be worth it.

Bob Marley, the first Third World superstar, dedicated many of his perform-ances to Rastafarianism and the cult of the late Emperor Haile Selassie of Ethiopia.

The upsurge of black popular music in the sixties showed the world that it was as wide-ranging in its approach as anything white rock'n'roll could produce. In that respect it paved the way for the growing accep-tance of reggae as more than just an exotic dance rhythm from Jamaica. Unlike some other forms of black music, however, reggae has never felt impelled to enter the white market. If whites want to accept it, that's their business; for some Rastafarian reggae artists, in fact, the white acceptance of reggae has been resisted and is seen as an encroachment by Babylon (the Rastas' general term for the whole of the white dominated western world).

Reggae is a fundamental part of Jamaican society's political process – which is not true of black music in the US. While James Brown could sing, 'Say it loud, I'm black and I'm proud', *and* endorse Richard Nixon's presidential campaign, Bob Marley recorded *Get Up, Stand Up!*, supported the socialist Prime Minister of Jamaica, Michael Manley and, in 1976, was shot and wounded for his pains. A different level of commit-

Marley waits to be treated in the hospital, 4th December, 1976, after being shot by politically inspired gunmen who broke into his house in Kingston, Jamaica. Marley was a vocal supporter of Jamaica's leftist premier, Michael Manley. Marley survived this murderous attempt, but succumbed on 11th May, 1981, to the ravages of lung cancer.

ment is involved.

Marley's death from cancer in 1981 revealed just how important reggae and Rastafarianism had become in Jamaica. It wasn't just the crowds who turned out for his funeral, or the orations given by Jamaica's leading politicians. More significant by far was the attention paid by countries and commentators outside the West Indies who were unanimous in recognizing Marley as the first 'Third World Superstar', an accolade that had already been bestowed on him implicitly when he was invited to play at the 1980 Independence celebrations in Zimbabwe. Through reggae and its association with Rastafarianism – a belief that holds the late Emperor Haile Selassie of Ethiopia to be a god, uses marijuana (*ganja*) as a sacrament and preaches the eventual return of all blacks to Africa – Marley represented the unity of the Third World countries against the rest.

Bob Marley was also a crucial figure in Britain, giving young, disaffected blacks a focus – many of whom had never set foot in Jamaica, let alone Africa. Some accused Marley of selling out when he came out in support of Manley's regime in Jamaica. But most saw white imperialism as the great enemy, rather than any particular political position. Even Marley's much reported love life – unrestrained by conventional notions of fidelity – and his equally widely publicized penchant for *ganja*, did not dissuade most blacks from the essential rightness of his position. If Whitey paid the piper – as Whitey paid Marley – then Whitey was the only loser.

If black attitudes to reggae were equivocal, that is no more than can be said for white attitudes. After 25 years, the experiences of the mixed American tours of the fifties were being depressingly repeated in England, but in a much more unofficial way. Reggae attracted the attention of neo-Nazi groups in Britain when this style of music, along with its West Indian influenced predecessors, Ska and Blue Beat, were adopted by a variety of black, white and mixed bands in the early eighties. The punk explosion threw a new ingredient into the usual mix of rock audiences. The disaffected youth who coagulated around punk have always been a prime target for fascist and racist organizations, and in short order such organizations were openly trying to impose their version of rock'n'roll on the new wave. Things came to a head in July 1979, when the arch-populists of punk, Sham 69, played at London's Rainbow Theatre amidst Hitler salutes and in the face of a running battle in the auditorium. The stage was invaded by neo-Nazi kids (mostly skinheads), and the band was forced to retreat, convinced that they had been betrayed by their fans. Sham's singer, Jimmy Pursey, proposed a 'music strike' until the kids realized that such demonstrations were not on. Unfortunately, Pursey's ambitions tended towards punk-without-politics, while all around him Rock Against Racism, the organization formed to fight racist attitudes from within the rock industry, and the two main neo-Nazi organizations, the National Front

Marley taking (or toking) the sacrament of ganja, the rastaman's word for marijuana.

Bob Marley's family watch his coffin being carried into the National Stadium in Kingston, Jamaica, for the public funeral on 21st May, 1981, following a private family service earlier in the day. Thousands of people turned out to watch Marley being buried in a specially constructed grave near his birthplace of Nine Miles in St Ann's.

and the British Movement, were busy demonstrating the opposite.

Jealous of RAR's success, the extreme right-wing National Front started a woe-begone organization called Rock Against Communism, which put on one gig (headlined by a lamentably bad group called White Boss), before collapsing with hardly a murmur. Meanwhile, the new breed of skinheads latched onto the two-tone dance bands like the Specials, the Beat and Madness. A tour by Madness in 1980 was called off because the band realized the rowdy element it was attracting was not merely composed of 'skins' having a good time, but included substantial numbers of mindlessly violent neo-Nazi thugs. For similar reasons, the Specials resolved not to play live again.

Deserted, as they saw it, by bands like Sham 69 and Madness, the 'skins' looked for an alternative – a raucous, rowdy style of music which was dubbed, by Gary Bushell of *Sounds*, with the unaesthetic, highly descriptive and totally artificial generic term, 'Oi'. His paper encouraged the music throughout early 1981 as some sort of grass roots phenomenon, as punk had once been. In fact, Oi seems to have been more a media invention than anything else. On the other hand, a number of the groups and fans connected with it were the very same neo-Nazis who had earlier disrupted punk and two-tone gigs, who were only too glad of the

unaccustomed publicity they were being given. Criticism of Oi's supporters in the media (issuing, in the wake of a riot in the London borough of Southall, most notably from the London *Daily Mail* and the *New Musical Express*), led the editor of *Sounds* and Gary Bushell to institute libel proceedings. Against accusations of incipient or aggressive fascism, they countered with the argument that Oi was and remained a genuine expression of the despair and disaffection of working class kids and, as such (and only as such), they supported it.

While reggae developed its curious, millenarian and mystical political stance, much North American black music developed into the sterile repetition of disco. On the floor of ultra-exclusive clubs like New York's Club 54 (money was not enough to gain admission, you had to have a face too), the ultimate irony was worked out. Black music had arrived through its various phases of struggle and reached the arsehole of respectability.

Disco is black music as a parody of itself. There was no longer any sense of a struggle, only the exploitation of the tired old myth of 'natural black rhythm'. The whole orgasmic thrust of disco stars like Grace Jones or Donna Summer played on the assumption of black women's availability to men – as it always had done. The male counterpart tends to suggest sexual blockage and, once again, the image of most of these performers echoed the necessary personae of black male performers twenty years ago and more – clownish, macho, faceless, romantic.

Daily Mirror

MON APR. 18 1960

2½

No. 17,522

'ROCK' STAR DIES IN CRASH

● PICTURED ABOVE. Singer Eddie Coch
LEFT: The wreckage of the car after the c
which killed him.

By NED GRANT

AMERICAN rock 'n' roll singing star Eddie Cochran, 21, died yesterday after a car taking him to London Airport crashed.

Among the three other passengers in the car when it crashed at Chippenham, Wilts, on Saturday night were two Americans— "rock" singer Gene Vincent, 25, and girl song writer Sharon Sheeley, 20.

Last night Miss Sheeley— she wrote the hit song " Poor Little Fool " when she was seventeen — was in " fair " condition with a fractured pelvis in hospital at Bath, Somerset.

Her mother, Mrs. Mary Sheeley, sobbed in Hollywood last night when she heard of the crash.

The news was broken to Mrs. Sheeley by the mother of Ritchie Valens—the " rock " star who was killed at the age of sixteen last year in an air crash soon after recording one of Sharon's songs.

Mrs. Sheeley said: " Eddie Cochran and Sharon had been

Sharon Sheeley

going steady since they met two years ago.

" Eddie was the first and only boy friend Sharon ever had. They were terribly in love, and were planning to marry. They were unofficially engaged."

The car's driver, George Martin, of Hartcliffe, Bristol, was unhurt.

Cochran—with Sharon, Gene Vincent and the fourth passenger, Camberwell theatrical agent Patrick Thomkins. 29—was taken to hospital.

America-bound

Just after four o'clock yesterday afternoon, Cochran died.

Cochran—his record hits have included " Summertime Blues " and " C'mon Everybody "—was travelling from Bristol, where he was starring in variety, to catch an America-bound plane at London Airport.

He had been in Britain since January, appearing on the stage and in T V shows—including I T V's " Boy Meets Girls."

Gene Vincent, whose first big song hit was " Be-Bop-a-Lula," planned to fly with Cochran.

He said in hospital last night: " I hope to be out in two or three days."

Cochran's last record will be issued according to schedule in the next few days, his British impresario, Larry Parnes, announced yesterday. It is called " Three Steps to Heaven."

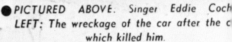

The toll: 33 dea 632 injured so fa

AT least thirty-three people have been killed and 632 injured on the roads since the Easter Holiday started on Good Friday.

And last night the Automobile Association made an urgent Bank Holiday appeal for safety on the roads.

First reports of YESTERDAY'S ACCIDENTS showed that twelve people were killed and sixteen injured.

Provisional figures for GOOD FRIDAY and SATURDAY announced by the Automobile Association were: Twenty-one dead and 616 injured.

Last year's figures for the same two days were: Fifteen dead and 460 injured.

In their appeal last night, the A A said :

● These figures tell their own sorry story, but they do not reflect the grief and misery in thousands of homes. An all-out effort will be

required by everyo the toll on the roa not to be greater last Easter.

Bank Holiday mot conditions call for bit of concentration the part of dr cyclists and pedestr

A second's careles could mean ano lost life.

The margin of allowed by com roads and heavy t is so small that ne can afford the slightest mistake.

● BUMPER "PAR TO THE SEA Back Page.

ROAD FEVER, STAGE FRIGHT

The Eagles' guitarist, Joe Walsh, had a motto to tide him over the long weeks of touring. You could often find it scratched into the furnishings of the hotel the group has just left. It read: PARTY TIL YA PUKE. When on tour, the group always set aside a large suite at the hotel for post-gig parties. They called it 'the Third Encore' and it was invariably changed utterly after the group, their friends and their entourage had all taken their bows. The group's manager, Irving Azoff, bought Joe Walsh a chain-saw one Christmas. The guitarist took it with him on the road – just in case something begged to be rapidly and completely destroyed. (The opportunity has not yet arisen.) Similarly Ian MacLagan, the former Faces' keyboard player, always carried an axe about on tour to dispose of any concert-hall pianos that didn't meet the stipulations of the group's contract. Nothing but the best for the big boys – and then some. It's a case of conspicuous destruction, of knowing, as the Eagles' road manager said, that 'we're going go pay for everything'. The Eagles called it 'life in the fast lane'. Everybody else knows it as 'road fever'.

Road fever takes many different forms – partying, practical joking, physical assaults, the sort of obsessive gambling that Buddy Holly, for example, used to indulge in to while away the hours between shows, or the apparently senseless activities of the likes of country rock star Waylon Jennings and his band, who once barricaded themselves in their hotel room all night for no apparent reason other than to play 'Fort Apache' or 'Beau Geste'. Usually it is fuelled by plenty of drinking and not a little drug taking. It can be the result of boredom, exuberance, frustration or plain annoyance, but it is always about the routine of the road, the sweat, the long and anti-social hours, the pent-up emotion of most performances, the isolation of rock stars and their entourages in unfriendly hotel rooms, on unfriendly stages, in claustrophobic trains and planes and limousines with black-tinted windows.

The pressures of touring have been a central part of the rock scene since its very beginning. More than any other kind of popular music or entertainment, rock'n'roll has always involved getting the message across to the most people in the shortest time. 'In this business it's not so much making it as fast as you can,' said Led Zeppelin's bassist, John Paul Jones, 'but making it *while* you can . . . The touring makes you into a different person. I realize that when I get home. It takes me weeks to recover after living like an animal for so long.'

Sometimes the pace can be literally killing, because most tours are organized into tight and exhausting schedules in order to cover what may be thousands of miles of travelling as quickly as possible. The deaths of Buddy Holly, the Big Bopper and Richie Valens in 1959 certainly indicate the dangers of constant touring. Had Holly not wanted to get to the next gig as quickly in order to make some last minute arrangements, organize some clean laundry and get a good night's sleep, neither he nor his companions would have bothered with the fatal plane journey. Talking in 1980, Buddy's widow, Maria Elena, recalled that the singer had never wanted to go on that tour at all. He was broke at the time, however, having recently split from the other Crickets. Perhaps more importantly, Maria Elena was pregnant after six months of marriage. 'He was unprepared,' she said, 'and everything was organized at the last minute. But we needed the money.' There was a further tragic twist to the story – the shock of her husband's death caused Maria Elena to suffer a miscarriage.

Many others have met with similar accidents – to a degree probably consistent with the uncommon mileage covered by rock musicians. Carl Perkins wasn't the only rocker to have his career interrupted by a road accident. 21-year-old Eddie Cochran, hugely popular in Britain, started a twelve-week tour of the country in January, 1960. The tour was so successful that it was extended for a further ten weeks. Cochran, Gene Vincent (appearing on the same bill) and Cochran's fiancée, Sharon Sheeley, were travelling to London Airport for a break between the first and second halves of the extended tour. Vincent was scheduled to play some dates in Paris, while Eddie and Sharon intended to fly back to America to get married. Twenty miles outside Bristol, travelling in a chauffeur-driven car after a show at the Bristol Hippodrome, a tyre blew out and the car skidded backwards into a lamp-post. It was just after midnight on April 17th. Cochran was flung from the car, amid confetti, photographs and his own guitar. He died the following afternoon at a hospital in Bath. Sharon Sheeley and Gene Vincent were both injured, and in Vincent's case the effect was to worsen considerably his earlier leg wound. Sharon, who had crawled around in the wreckage of the car, crying 'Where's Eddie?', seems never to have quite recovered from the trauma. She had only been visiting England for a week. Ironically, Eddie's next scheduled release was a medium-paced love song called *Three Steps To Heaven*. Immediately after his death, it shot into the British Top Ten and stayed there for two months.

Buddy Holly's last tour ended early in the morning of 3rd February, 1959, when the single-engine plane carrying him, Ritchie Valens (whose body lies in the foreground) and the Big Bopper, crashed in a snowy meadow near Fargo, North Dakota.

Four members of the Lynyrd Skynyrd entourage, the pilot and co-pilot were killed outright when their private plane crashed *en route* to a gig in 1977 (two roadies later died in hospital from their injuries). Apparently the plane – a Corvair 240 prop – ran out of fuel 200 yards from an open field near Gillsburg, Mississippi, where the pilot intended to land. On an earlier flight, one engine had nearly burst into flames, and several members of the band had planned to vote on whether to continue using it. Singer Cassie Gaines had been talked out of travelling in the equipment truck that day. The band and their entourage (amounting to about twenty people) were all close friends, whose tours more often resembled wild private parties than business trips. Both Cassie and her brother Steve died, along with the band's leading light, Ronnie Van Zandt, and their road manager, Dean Kilpatrick.

In December 1967, Otis Redding and five teenage members of his backing group, the Bar-Kays, died in similar circumstances when Otis's brand new private plane crashed into an icy lake just four miles from its destination. Clarence White, brilliant guitarist with

Left: The second step to heaven? Eddie Cochran, bridging the gap between fifties rock'n'roll and eighties new wave, died on 17th April, 1960 on his way to London Airport with his fiancée, Sharon Sheeley, who survived the accident. His latest release, Three Steps To Heaven, climbed to the top of the charts within two months of his death.

the Byrds for a time, was the victim of a hit-and-run accident while loading a van with equipment after a concert. And there have been many other fatal and near-fatal accidents. Bob Dylan crashed his motorcycle on a road near his Woodstock home in July 1966, breaking his neck and dropping out of circulation for some eighteen months. The crash and Dylan's subsequent silence only served to deepen his mystery for many fans. Many of them speculated that it was an attempted suicide, brought on by the heavy intake of drugs Dylan relied on to keep him going during his heavy touring schedule in the sixties.

Stevie Wonder's car collided with a logging-truck in North Carolina in August, 1973, four days after the release of the enormously popular *Innervisions* album. Stevie received head injuries which were happily less serious than had at first been feared, and he was back on stage by September. Phil Spector, whose eccentricities were already becoming legendary, apparently suffered burns and multiple head injuries in a car crash somewhere between Los Angeles and Phoenix in early February 1974. Rumours that Spector had faked the crash in order to 'get away from it all' (or even to undergo a furtive hair transplant) were fuelled by the lack of information about it and by Spector's subsequent behaviour – he became reclusive to the point of paranoia. Of course, the crash itself could have been

A rescue worker finds a publicity photo of Lynyrd Skynyrd among the tattered remains of their baggage. Three members of the band died when their Corvair 240 crashed into woods near McComb, Mississippi, on 21st October, 1977, while on a tour of the States.

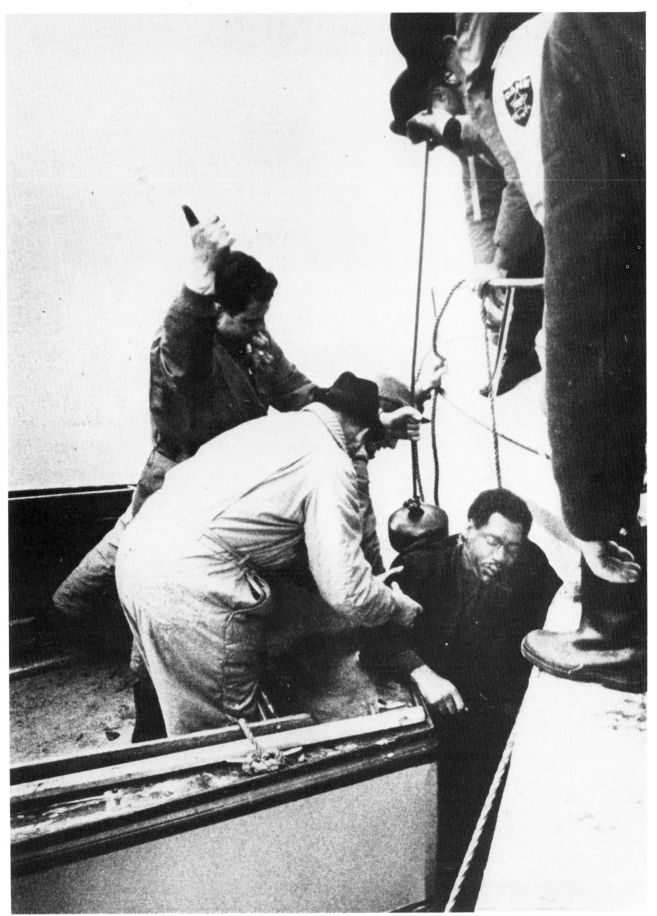

A physical wreck even before his fatal car crash in September, 1977, Marc Bolan's youthful glitter image belied the killing effects of the rock life-style. Even the teeth were false.

responsible for just those symptoms – but Spector, like Dylan, is the stuff of myth.

Later stars have fared no better. Robert Plant of Led Zeppelin, and his wife Maureen, were both seriously injured on the island of Rhodes in 1975. Their car left the road, plunged down a precipice and was caught in a tree. Among other Zeppelin disasters, John Bonham was involved in a car crash, breaking three ribs, in 1977. Eric Clapton, too, suffered a car crash in 1975. On his return from an exhausting tour of Australia and New Zealand he climbed into his silver Ferrari for the first time in weeks, only to crash into a lorry in a narrow lane near his home in Ewhurst, Surrey. The car was a write-off and, though uninjured, it took firemen twenty minutes to cut Clapton out of the wreckage.

In 1976, *en route* from a gig in Stafford, Keith Richards' Bentley ploughed through a motorway barrier at five in the morning. The car was carrying Keith, Anita Pallenberg and their son Marlon – but the only victim was Keith himself, who was busted by the police when they discovered cocaine and marijuana in the car on arriving at the scene of the accident.

Yet others were not so fortunate as to escape with their lives. Fairport Convention's Martin Lamble and clothes designer 'Genie the Tailor' (for whom Jack Bruce recorded the album, *Songs For A Tailor*) were

Otis Redding's body lifted from the icey water of the lake near Madison, Wisconsin, where his plane crashed, 10th December, 1967. Ironically, his posthumous hit was titled Dock Of The Bay.

killed when their car crashed in June, 1969. Duane Allman, whose talent for the guitar was matched only by his drug consumption, crashed his motorcycle in Macon, Georgia, swerving to avoid a truck. It was October, 1971, and Allman had just left bassist Berry Oakley's home. Just over a year later, Oakley himself crashed his bike along the same stretch of road. He smashed into a city bus and, having steadfastly refused hospital treatment, died of a brain haemorrhage

The car in which Marc Bolan (real name Mark Feld) died on 16th September, 1977. It was being driven by his girlfriend Gloria Jones, who suffered face injuries when the Mini ploughed into a tree on Barnes Common. Bolan was killed outright.

in November 1972. Allman and Oakley are buried side by side in the Rose Hill Cemetery in Macon – a place that inspired many early Allman songs.

Marc Bolan, returning home from a club with his girlfriend Gloria Jones at the wheel, was killed when the car they were in wrapped itself round a tree in September, 1977. Gloria, only slightly injured, was later charged with drunken driving.

It's fascinating to note that transport accidents (planes, cars and motorcycles especially) cause as many, if not more, deaths and serious injuries among the rock fellowship as drugs and alcohol. While some are the result of straightforward occupational hazards – fatigue and tight schedules – other accidents may be put down to a fatal fascination with speed (both sorts) which attracts so many musicians, dissolving caution and persuading them to chase that extra buzz of adrenalin in their implacable desire to live life in the fast lane.

Road fever is not just the product of the wearisome schedules that have plagued performers since those early days of the fifties, when rock'n'roll package tours first snaked their way across continents. Even so, road fever proper belongs to the era of mammoth tours by single acts, from the mid-sixties to the pre-punk seventies. If today there are hotels and local worthies who go out of their way to court rock musicians (a sign in the reception area of the Continental Hyatt House hotel in Los Angeles shows a typical 'long-hair' with the caption underneath: 'Be courteous to him, he may just have sold a million records'), things were different then. Nowadays wanton destruction may be part of the image, and hotel owners know that it will be paid for (plus). The time was, however, when road fever was less a rich man's hobby and more a sort of hooliganism, inspired by the absence of friends and the friendlessness of those who are present.

'You've been standing around an airport, had some accommodation problem because someone's hair's too long, or you've been on some vehicle for hours without sleep and have only three hours till you go on stage,' Grace Slick said, pointing out the hassles of performing under such circumstances. 'People in the group start getting uptight, and music's an emotional thing too, you know, so everybody's backstage yelling and screaming ... People get really strange getting on and off buses and talking to a lot of different people all the time.'

The feeling of strangeness is a product of the musician's very peculiar circumstances on tour. A tour offers freedom from the constraints of normal domestic routine combined with a sometimes threatening sense of unfamiliarity and isolation. But the musician on tour is also working – often very hard. Even worse, musicians on tour are working to a mirror-image of most people's daily time-tables. No wonder the experience of touring is disorienting and no wonder musicians fall back on their own company, or the company of other musicians and on the sense of bonhomie and solidarity associated with childish

102

pranks. No wonder, either, that some musicians on tour are driven to protest their curious situation in the most physical ways possible – fighting, fucking or wrecking.

When the so-called 'British Invasion' brought a tidal wave of musicians over from Britain to America, they found themselves in stranger situations than Grace Slick could imagine. They were, after all, not just hippies, Easterners or long-haired moral degenerates to those who disliked them – they were aliens and, as such, loved and hated, freer and more constrained than their American equivalents. Passions were higher, tensions greater, isolation more acutely felt. 'We usually take a party of four road managers, a production manager, a booking man, there's usually ten Englishmen going round in the States,' the Who's John Entwistle said in 1971. 'Americans have a different sense of humour, their whole way of life is different. If they're not in your business or if they don't come to your concerts they're boring. They're aliens and you're aliens to them and you can't mix with that sort of person, so you're thrown together and you spend a lot of time in hotel rooms and so on.'

The Who were one of the first groups to get a reputation as hotel wreckers – no doubt connected with the unprecedentedly violent nature of their stage act. 'The Who on tour is a very difficult trip,' said Pete Townshend in 1968. Aware of the implications of all this violence on their private lives, the Who tended to channel it into zany humour. 'If we were serious,' said Townshend, 'we'd admit that we don't like each other. But because we're not serious, we don't have to admit it.' The Who were by no means the only group to have a reputation for 'insanity' (as Townshend termed it) on the road. The Beach Boys were particularly wild, as were the Rolling Stones and, until they retired from touring in 1966, the Beatles. But thanks to Keith Moon (known universally as Moon the Loon), the Who will probably hold in perpetuity the title of 'Most Disruptive Rock Group On Tour'.

It all started back in 1967 when the group spent weeks of arduous touring in America trying to hit the big time. In the process they lost huge amounts of money and a substantial portion of their sanity, proving conclusively Townshend's dictum that the way to 'stop taking life seriously is to go out on the road'.

The group's first tour of the US set the pattern for the future. Moon discovered Cherry Bombs – a particularly explosive variety of firework – and began a long and fruitful association with havoc. As a younger man, Moon had been content to take out his destructive urges on a drum-kit. But a growing intake of booze and pills and the infectious insanity of road life soon expanded his horizons. In no time at all, he was blowing out hotel room doors with Cherry Bombs, pitching

Backstage hi-jinx with shock-rocker Alice Cooper, friends, and Stacia from the Heavy Metal band, Hawkwind. The Cooper band once boasted of spending $300,000 a year on booze. This sizeable drinks' bill may be partly explained by the curious use for a bottle of beer devised on this occasion. Alice Cooper eventually committed himself to a sanatorium to overcome alcoholism.

Who's who? Keith Moon and Pete Townshend (right) keep the good times going on board a Rally Escort. Life on the road isn't always so comfortable.

televisions out of windows onto the street below and blowing up toilet bowls ('This Cherry Bomb was about to go off in my hand,' he explained once, 'so I threw it down the bog to put it out').

During the 1967 tour, the Who found themselves in the Gorham Hotel in New York – a popular hang-out for visiting groups. In the middle of the night the hotel residents were disturbed by the sound of police tramping through the corridors and sirens wailing outside. Townshend woke up thinking that one of the Who's party had been busted for pot. While taking the elevator to the appropriate floor, he heard the last of what must have been a number of explosions. The elevator stopped and the doors opened. The corridor outside was filled with smoke, so Townshend got back in to resume his journey. As the elevator doors were closing, Moon walked past, his mission accomplished. He had just blown up the hotel manager's wife's room.

Latterly, Moon took to destroying hotel rooms artistically. With little or no noise he would methodically take apart the furniture and rearrange the room to look as if it had been wrecked. Sometimes, he would

John Entwistle – the one member of the Who you don't usually hear about. But he's suffered his share of road fever, too. John (below) was arrested in Houston, Texas for disorderly conduct at a party marking the start of the Who's 1975 tour of the US on 20th November, 1975.

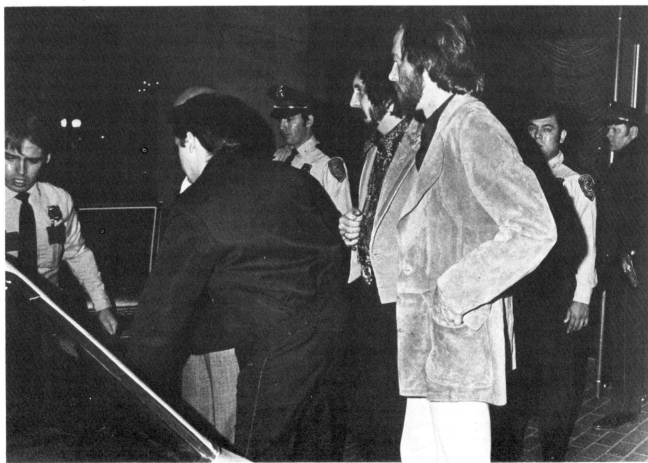

Harmless loon or unpleasant buffoon? The tasteless Keith Moon arrives at a Los Angeles premiere dressed as Field Marshall Rommel giving a Nazi salute, 12th November, 1976. He once enraged the Jewish community of London's Golders Green by parading in similar gear down the high street on a Saturday.

pour tomato ketchup in the bath and stick a pair of plastic legs in it. At other times, he would disturb other members of the Who or their entourage (or complete strangers) with itching powder, stink bombs, smoke bombs, plastic insects or whatever loathsome device he could find in the local joke-shop. Moon considered no town complete without such a shop. On one occasion, after playing a pier-end concert hall in Asbury Park, New Jersey, Moon decided he wanted the company of a groupie on the band bus. Everybody else said 'no' – earlier in the tour some girls had spirited away a few thousand dollars petty cash in the course of a stoned hotel room party, and the band wanted no repetition of that event. But Moon insisted and the band's dressing room – which happened to swing out over the sea – echoed to the aggressive sounds of yet another post-gig Who fight. Moon could be deadly serious about some things if he wanted to be, and it was scary to watch him then because you could see a genuine malice in his eyes, even though he often tried to defuse the situation with a joke. He was serious this time. 'She comes with me or I jump!' he shouted, leaping to the windowsill and, without further ado, he jumped. They searched for hours, they sent for the Coastguard and the cops, they called out to him. But Moon was nowhere to be found. When at last all hope had been abandoned and the group were

preparing to face the future without their drummer, a tiny voice wafted up from the pier rafters below. 'Thought I'd never do it, did you?' It was Moon.

If Keith was an obsessive practical joker with a fondness for shocking that sometimes plumbed the depths of tastelessness (as when he and Vivian Stanshall dressed up as Nazis and paraded up and down Golders Green in London, deeply offending the Jewish population there), he was also a maniac for transport. At his home in Chertsey he kept about a dozen vehicles from Rolls-Royces to a personal hover-craft. He thought nothing of driving an expensive Rolls into a swimming pool. Tragically, his chauffeur, Neil Bolland, was run over and killed by Keith's Rolls when the drummer, desperate to escape a rowdy crowd outside a disco in Hertfordshire, backed the car out in too much of a hurry. Moon was charged with drunken driving.

Moon was the soul of the Who's live performances. The other three always had other interests and shifting views on whether they liked the road or not. For Moon, rock'n'roll *was* the road – he was always on the move, the homeless one, the one who was constantly searching for something else to satisfy his roving soul. For him, the Who were live performance and live performance was loud. So, one day in a hotel in Los Angeles (that 'meat market' as he called it), he was playing a tape of a Who album very loud – as it should be. The manager's attention was drawn, inevitably, to the disturbance. He complained to Moon. 'It's a noise,' said the manager, instructing the drummer to turn down the volume. Keith obeyed, but a short time later the hotel was shaken by an explosion that blew the

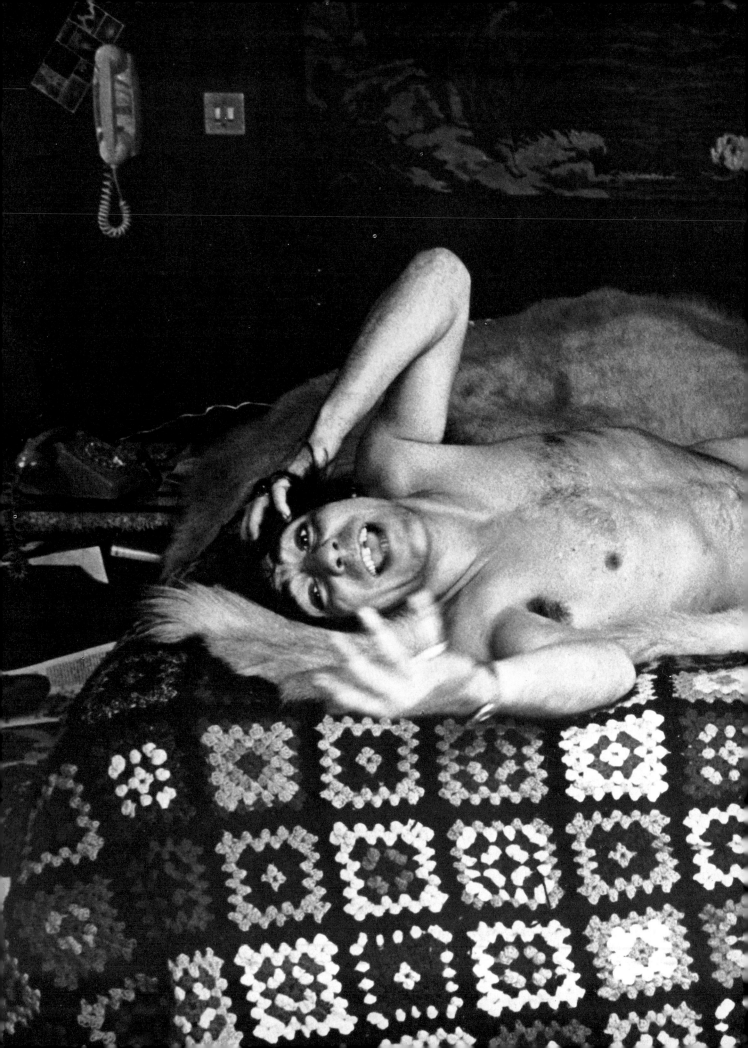

Rod Stewart woz 'ere ... the first-class lounge on Stewart's flight to London, 23rd December, 1977, after he and his party had finished pouring drinks on the carpet, smearing seats with jam and butter and dumping gourmet dinners in the aisle.

door of Moon's suite off its hinges. Seeking the by now enraged manager, Moon explained: 'That was a noise. What you heard before was the Who.'

Officiousness and bad service have inspired some awesome moments of road fever. Boredom, too. 'Sitting in a hotel room for a week is no picnic,' said Jimmy Page. 'That's when the road fever starts and that's when the breakages start.' Writer John Pidgeon kept a diary of the Faces' 1972 tour of Britain – a tour which was crucial to the band's success. Pidgeon was an acting roadie on the tour – it is often the roadies, who do most of the work for the least glory, who are hardest hit by road fever in their odd hours of relaxation. Pidgeon tells of how the band and entourage booked into an appalling Blackpool hotel.

'The lights on the second floor corridor had fused, the room phones were out of order ... the bedside lights wouldn't turn on, neither would the heating, and there were pubic hairs in the bath. We couldn't eat in the restaurant without a tie and we were only allowed into the informal, ghastly Cabaret Grill on the say-so of a receptionist.' After a pleasant night drinking a local bar dry of brandy, two of the Faces' senior roadies decided to make some 'alterations' to the

'Don't give me any of your lip.' After falling over on stage during a San Francisco concert, Rod Stewart, with stitched lip, flew to London for his traditional Christmas shows, 23rd December, 1977. Clutching a glass of brandy, Rod arrived singing, 'I'd walk a million miles for one of your legs.'

hotel's fixtures and fittings. During the show the next night, fans invaded the orchestra pit and the police were called. Rod Stewart himself talked them out of stopping the show. Back at the hotel later 'some further alterations' were made – despite a snarling guard-dog. Next morning, one of the roadies drove the band's truck away. 'He meant to nudge the concrete ball off the gatepost,' Pidgeon recorded, 'but we whapped the pillar so hard it collapsed, bringing ten feet of brick wall down with it.'

This kind of deliberate destruction is a revenge for not having a good time laid on. In fact, there is little to tell between the good and bad times on tour – under the pressure of touring everything seems to take on a curiously joyless and perfunctory air, as if good times offstage were just another part of the job.

'We had another party planned after the show in Sheffield,' said Pidgeon. 'By the time we'd finished packing the truck, the girls we'd lined up had left and the mood at the hotel was drab.' They recovered their party spirits however and 'decided the Warner Brothers' man's room was as good a place as any to celebrate. Woody (Ron Wood), Mac and Rod thought so too, although our host didn't. He had eyes for two girls and was nervous they would be lured or, more likely, frightened away. He was right. Woody and Rod hauled one of them into a wardrobe. When she escaped she ran right out of the room, so they treated us to a closet cabaret routine of songs, jokes, even dancing, mostly from inside. Mac gave a practical demonstration of how to dismantle a cheap armchair, lecturing us on its construction faults as he did so.'

Pidgeon continued: 'Everyone had a *smashing* time. Except the Warner Brothers man, who grew increasingly frantic as he tried to figure out how he could explain away his room bill as a business expense.' He needn't have worried – as is always the case after these bouts of road fever, remorse set in the morning after, and the group took care of the bill.

And so it goes, from one dreadful hotel room to the next, from one disappointing gig to the next, from one grey town to the next, from one tour to the next. Some groups, or at least certain members of them, seemed to thrive on the high pitch of excitement which characterizes and surrounds rock performance and life on the road. Until, that is, the concert tour routine began to become more and more elaborate as the seventies progressed. Then the whole basis of road fever began subtly to change. The tours themselves became big money operations, like military manoeuvres organized by teams of expert managers.

During the 'Diamond Dogs' tour of 1974, David Bowie used an entire theatrical set – scaffolding hung with painted flats to show an expressionist version of a modern city, an enormous lighting rig, towers to carry loudspeakers, a moveable bridge and chair attached to a motorized steel beam which could raise and lower Bowie on the stage or up to 30 feet into the auditorium. There was also a giant mirrored perspex egg called the Diamond Module, with a motor and wheels to transport Bowie about the stage, opening up to display the artist in all his finery. All this added some $200,000 to the cost of the tour. A travelling road crew of fifteen was housed in a bus complete with bunks, a stereo, colour TV and bathroom. They, and a local crew of about two dozen, spent up to nineteen hours a working day (discounting travel time) erecting, supervising, dismantling, loading and unloading equipment. Whatever Bowie and the musicians were doing, the crew had little time to party. 'After five or six days,' said one of them, 'a large shipment of cocaine arrived, which initially cut the working day to fourteen hours, but no-one got any more sleep than before, because we were all wired and sat up babbling; after a couple of days, the working day drifted back to 21 hours and remained that way. Fortunately, I have forgotten what it felt like to be that tired but everyone was in a constant state of near-psychosis and hallucination.'

Through all this, the rock stars themselves became increasingly pampered. The private jets that had once seemed such a luxury were now *de rigueur*. By 1973, Led Zeppelin were in a position to have $180,000 in cash stolen from their hotel safe at the end of the tour – money that had apparently been earmarked to pay for hotel rooms, a film crew and the hire of an airplane. By 1978, the Rolling Stones were playing to a total of 760,000 people on one tour, taking more than one million dollars gross at some shows, and paying out a minimum of around $25,000 in expenses for even the smallest show (a gate of about 2,500). The Stones' hotel bill for a few nights in Texas came to $17,000, food and drink for *one* show to more than $2,000.

At these exalted heights, the rock star on tour is insulated from the hostility and disappointment that might once have greeted him. In fact, he is insulated from almost everything. 'It's a real hassle to go out,' said Keith Richard. 'You got all you needed from room service, sent out for it . . . You're getting really cut off.' Entertainment can be bought, and even the opportunity to run riot comes quite cheap. 'It's strange how success and room-wrecking seem to go together,' ELO's Bev Bevan remarked. 'For years we never destroyed so much as a toothbrush holder and it was only when we were playing every night to sell-out crowds of anything from 20,000 to 72,000 did we get trouble.'

This kind of conspicuous destruction reached its peak with Led Zeppelin. 'From the shit holes to the classiest hotels,' said Robert Plant, 'it's all been fun.' But even Plant grew jaded. Seven years after the group's first American tour, he looked back with something approaching yearning. 'It's been a long time,' he said. 'Nowadays we're more into staying in our rooms and reading Nietzsche. There was good fun to be had, you know, it's just that in those days there were more people to have good fun with than there are now.'

'There were a lot of fun-loving people to crash into,' Plant continued. 'People were genuinely welcoming us to the country and we started out on a path of positive enjoyment. Throwing eggs from floor to floor and really silly water battles that a nineteen-year-old boy should have. It was just the first steps of learning how to be crazy.'

110

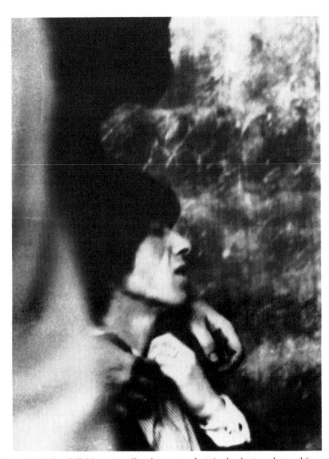

Stage fright: Bill Wyman suffered a severe electric shock at a rehearsal for a Stones concert in Oclense, Denmark, 27th March, 1965. Wyman, Mick Jagger and Brian Jones were all affected when a 'live' microphone shot 220 volts through them. Bill Wyman was unconscious for several minutes.

Increasingly, boredom is cited as the major reason for the callous destructiveness that rock superstars seem to rely on to lighten the load of performance. But destruction is also a status symbol, demonstrating their ability to disregard material values, to acquire the most exotic toys that money can buy. Rock stars can realize their fantasies. But when a fantasy becomes real it also becomes subject to the tedium of everyday life. And more exciting fantasies just become harder and harder to think up.

Performance itself remains the arena of rock's most potent fantasy – the fantasy that audience and performer can become one. 'We all share the simultaneous experience of forgetting who we are at a rock concert,' said Pete Townshend, 'losing ourselves completely. When the music gets so good . . . everybody for a second forgets completely who they are and where they are . . . If you have experienced that enough times, it starts to become something that you strive for, because it is so sweet.' Yet the undercurrent of pain and aggravation in the Who's stage shows has led to aggressive outbursts on stage that show the act of striving itself can be most bitter. Townshend

Patti Smith's acrobatics led to serious injury when she fell off stage in Tampa, Florida in 1977. 'All I know is that in some moment every night, I'm so committed that I piss myself or I come on stage,' said Patti – seen here with her head in the air.

whacked 'youth revolutionary' Abbie Hoffman over the head with his guitar when Hoffman's acid dream led him to take the stage at Woodstock, interrupting the beginning of the Who's set. Hoffman, half-crazed, demanded that the half-million strong audience march down to free the jailed John Sinclair and Townshend couldn't take it. I have seen Townshend leap off stage and half throttle a kid whose only crime has been to keep requesting a song.

But Pete Townshend has an answer to this too. 'There is a particular attitude I call the "tour armour",' he told Greil Marcus in 1980. 'When you go on the road you throw up an armour around yourself, you almost go into a trance. . . . When I say armour, I mean armour that actually *allows* you to be more abandoned, and freer, that allows you to be tougher, harder . . . I'm not trying to glamorize it and it's not something I'm necessarily proud of.'

Tour armour does not however save the performer from the dangers of actually performing on stage, many of which result from a too-hurried setting up or too eager exit. Stone the Crows' guitarist, Les Harvey, was killed in front of 1500 fans when his guitar electrocuted him on stage at the Top Rank ballroom in Swansea, in May 1972. He had done no more than start to play. In a rush to set up the gear, nobody had bothered to check whether the guitars and microphones were safely connected and Harvey's guitar became live. In October 1974, Uriah Heep bassist, Gary Thain, was similarly electrocuted on stage in Dallas. He was ordered to rest for two weeks, but the effects of the accident, combined with heavy drug use, made him increasingly unreliable. He was sacked from the band and in February 1976, he was found by his Japanese girlfriend dead from an overdose, in his bath at home. Even the Rolling Stones have suffered electrocution, once causing Bill Wyman to spend several minutes unconscious. Tom Petty is another performer who suffered an admittedly minor shock on stage. But with so many electrical connections to come adrift during a stage show, it is surprising that so few of these accidents occur.

Needless to say, the suicidal possibilities of the electric guitar have also been explored. Keith Relf, focus of the Yardbirds, whose career floundered after that group mutated into Led Zeppelin, was found dead in his West London house in May 1976, holding a live electric guitar. An open verdict was recorded on John Rostill, who had joined the Shadows to replace bassist Brian Locking in 1963. He joined the Shadows as a complete unknown after an audition, and remained a background figure until the Shadows effectively disbanded in 1968. In November 1973, Rostill was found apparently electrocuted by his own guitar. His death remains a mystery, because it occurred shortly before a planned reunion of the Shadows. In the event, the reunion went ahead without him and led to a resurgence of their popularity.

The stage itself is, of course, responsible for numerous minor injuries. Serious injuries (when not the result of missiles accurately aimed by members of the audience) are less common. In 1971, Frank Zappa was hurled from the stage of the Rainbow in London by an irate fan jealous of his girlfriend's enthusiasm for the American star. Zappa fell into the orchestra pit and broke his leg so badly that he had to perform wearing a steel brace for a year. Now he has an ex-policeman as a permanent bodyguard. 'You get a lot of very strange people at any rock concert,' he says, 'and the drugs people use at the moment increase the risk of a crazy, violent attack.' In 1977 Patti Smith – whose extrovert performances inevitably skirt major injury – broke her neck and needed 22 stitches after spinning on stage until she got so dizzy that she tripped over a monitor and was pitched head-first towards the audience at the Curtis Nixon Hall in Tampa, Florida. Typically, Patti denied that she had been on any drugs at the time – although the performance commenced with a vitriolic and gratuitous diatribe against Florida and its people. She claimed to be high on rock'n'roll. 'Performance,' as she says, 'is the drug'.

Performance can call forth complex emotions, leaving the musician floating somewhere between ecstasy and despair. It is always a sort of failure, because it is always temporary. Yet every performer is aware of the power they have, even if it is only half-formed. Performance is, after all, a surrogate sex act, and for some the very act of getting on stage in front of an audience is its own self-contained road fever.

'You were at school and you were pimply and no-one wanted to know you,' Eric Clapton explained. 'Yet get into a group and you've got thousands of chicks there. And there you are with thousands of little girls screaming their heads off. Man, it's power.'

For some, the power itself is both awesome and frightening – not least because when it fails to work (or works too well) audiences have been known to riot and individuals to assault performers. Jimi Hendrix's last, sad performance in America suggests something of what was behind his prodigious partying, his violent arguments with associates and his general tendency to road fever. (After one particularly vicious row with Noel Redding in a Swedish hotel room, Hendrix landed himself in jail – and it had taken three policemen to get him there.) Hendrix's last show was in Seattle, his home town. The guitarist played badly but eager fans rushed to the stage all the same, desperate for their magic moment. Hendrix was reduced to swearing at the audience. 'Fuck you! Fuck you!' he shouted, despite which people began to chant, 'We love you, Jimi!' At the end of the show he flung his guitar down and walked off the stage, only to return dejectedly to the microphone a few minutes later and ask if there was anyone in the audience from his old school. The shouts of 'Yeah' met with a desultory comment from Jimi. 'Far out', he said.

Jim Morrison, too, felt increasingly aggressive towards his audiences. At first he said, 'Concerts are great but it gets into a crowd phenomenon that really hasn't that much to do with music.' As the crowds got greater and eager for more thrills, and as Morrison failed adequately to harness his own stardom, the risk of losing control became greater. Morrison's ambivalence eventually and effectively destroyed the music and turned his concerts into freak shows. And Iggy Pop, who ironically took to exposing himself on stage like Morrison (but without the same legal consequences), remembered at the time of his late seventies comeback how he 'hated the audience, at times, for the things they made you do. They're cunts,' he said. 'Why did they come and see me?' Iggy, of course, used to assault both his audience and himself. He would dive into them, provoke fights, daub them with peanut butter. He ripped his own body with broken glass and invited audiences to invade the stage. He played the sound of amplified toilets. But he was addicted to heroin at that time, and was sometimes unable to perform without a massive shot of methedrine beforehand. (He remembers how, on one memorable occasion, a gorilla walked on to the stage and held him in the air while he was singing – he was heavily dosed with speed. 'I was out of my mind with fear,' he says – but the gorilla turned out to be Elton John in an ape-suit paying a friendly, if rather mistimed, surprise visit.)

'When I'm on the road, you know, it means I'm away from somebody I love,' said Patti Smith. 'It might

mean I'm alone for the night, it might mean I'm not gonna be making love for a month, and so I have to get that shot on stage ... All I know is that in some moment every night I'm so committed that I piss myself or I come on stage – once I even shat myself on stage, I was pulling in so much to try and hit a note or try to hit a sensation or hit a word that I just lost control of myself.'

Smith sees the rock star's role as a mirror for the audience. 'You give them a lot of fantastic energy and they eat it and spit it out,' she announced. 'They're like loving vampires or something.'

Patti Smith is a performer committed to herself as a performer. Her moment of fever is on stage. Mick Jagger knows the same power she does, but he is too cynical, possibly less pretentious and certainly too distant from his audiences to accept performance as anything more than an imperfect imitation of life. 'I don't understand the connection between music and violence,' he has said – a trifle disingenuously. 'I just know that I get very aroused by music, but that it doesn't arouse me violently. I never went to a rock'n'roll show and wanted to smash windows or beat anybody up afterwards. I feel more sexual than actually physically violent.' Maybe the feeling only lasts five minutes as Jagger says it does – but it is still a strange sensation. The road is long for people prey to such volatile and strident emotions and, like snow-blindness to the Antarctic explorer, road fever is the malady they develop as a result.

'It's big,' said one authoritative source, 'but not that big.' Mick Jagger once said, 'I get very aroused by music', but is his sexual image just so much hot air?

STAGE-DOOR SEX

Somewhere at the heart of rock'n'roll's magic is the groupie – whether nameless fan or glamorous socialite – who converts music into the currency of the orgasm and spends freely. She (it is almost invariably a woman) is a central character in the myths and legends of rock – proof to fans and observers that rock stars have found the modern holy grail of guiltless promiscuity, evidence that people's dreams of release, refuge and reward can be made real. But to rock stars, groupies are little better than a demonstration of power, expressed through sexuality – success symbols. 'You won't make much money,' Ronnie Hawkins promised Robbie Robertson when recruiting him to his band, 'but you'll get more pussy than Frank Sinatry;' a promise which puts the groupie on about the same level as a free meal.

Backstage or in hotel rooms, the Beatles lived at the centre of a hive of grotesque sexual hyper-activity. John Lennon told Jann Wenner: 'Derek's (Derek Taylor) and Neil's (Neil Aspinall) rooms were always full of fuck knows what, and policemen and everything. *Satyricon*! We had to do something, and what do you do when the pill doesn't wear off . . . If we couldn't get groupies we would have whores and everything, whatever was going.'

Chrissie Shrimpton – model Jean's little sister – gained fame for a while as Mick Jagger's girlfriend, a title later bestowed on the hapless Marianne Faithfull. Chrissie delighted in telling the press that she knew from experience that the Stones were not homosexuals. Marianne Faithfull remembered her determination to have 'a Rolling Stone as a boyfriend'. 'I slept with three and then decided the lead singer was the best bet.' But she fell in love with the lead singer, this nice upper-class, convent girl who believed, like so many others, in the myth that rock'n'roll would lead her to liberation. Her liberation, it turned out, was the freedom to become captivated by Mick Jagger's lusty image. She followed him around like a lap-dog, they made love in the changing room of an exclusive clothes shop, her name – kept out of the trial following the Redlands raid – was dragged through the gutterminds of randy young boys obsessed by the sexual riches at Jagger's disposal. She and Jagger had been caught at Redlands *in flagrante delecto*, it was whispered rather loudly, having discovered a novel use for Mars Bars as an accessory to cunnilingus. Assuming

this curious rumour was invented (and it surfaced in America with minor but significant changes – the place was Woodstock in upstate New York, the chocolate bar was an acid-infused Baby Ruth), it still defined Marianne as a horny fantasy figure: the whore with the looks of a virgin (even an angel): the willing victim.

But Marianne was learning to suffer. 'Once you start to care about anything or anybody,' she said, 'it always fucks ambition up.' Four hit records had crystallized her ambition. Mick shattered it. 'He had me on a pin,' she recalled, 'and he was watching me flail and writhe, but it was something that fascinated him as an artist.' Marianne became hooked on heroin, overdosed in Australia in 1969, once walked into a plate glass window and later miscarried Mick's child. She broke with him, and after ducking the rock limelight into acting married another musician, Ben Brierley (the Bride Wore Scarlet', said one press report), and re-emerged quite successfully as a recording artist again in the late seventies.

There can be little doubt that the image of Marianne hanging over from those heady days is still potent enough for her to exploit to her own advantage. In 1977, tentatively cast to play Sid Vicious's incestuous mother in a fictional Sex Pistols film, she described a planned nude scene with Sid as 'pretty disgusting', while admitting that 'basically, I suppose I'm still a dirty little girl'. On the other hand, she has struggled to come to terms with her own complex emotions, recording a song about sexual jealousy on her 1977 album, *Broken English*, which was explicit enough to invoke the displeasure of the BBC. About Mick Jagger she says that 'no-one was deserted. My relationship . . . just came to a natural end.' And, insisting that she 'was never a victim', she said in 1981 that 'perhaps I can get hurt easily, but on other levels I'm very strong.'

She rejected promiscuity ('People tried all that in the sixties and seventies,' she says, 'and it didn't work'), and tried, less successfully, to renounce heroin on several occasions. Her addiction led to her losing the custody of her child, Nicholas, to his father, John Dunbar. She was busted as recently as early 1981 for possession of fifteen milligrams of heroin and was fined £100, after claiming that 'a friend called Nicky' left it in her bedside cabinet.

'I've got over the drug problem,' she said, 'but even now I get tempted, especially when I'm down, or on my own.' The past itself is perhaps the most potent drug and, even today, Marianne is still 'the former girl-friend of Rolling Stone Mick Jagger' to the world's press.

Bare hug. Once hailed as the world's highest paid model, former Vogue *cover-girl Jerry Hall, naked but for her jewels, shows her love for Mick Jagger.*

Above: Marianne Faithfull confirming her public image as the whore with the looks of a virgin (even an angel): every adolescent's horny fantasy figure.

Above right: The beautiful and the damned. Mick and Marianne arrive at Sydney Airport, 6th July, 1969, for the filming of Ned Kelly. For Marianne, who had endured two years of reflected glory and legal hassles in the company of the Stones, it was nearly the last landing.

Below: The tears gone by. Marianne Faithful in intensive care in a Sydney hospital, following an overdose of 150 sodium amytal tablets on 8th July, 1969. Her heroin addiction, the death of Brian Jones five days earlier and a troubled relationship with Mick, had resulted in an attempted suicide. Marianne had seemed the epitome of the swinging sixties, but as that decade ended, its glossy veneer cracking, Marianne arrived at death's door and almost entered.

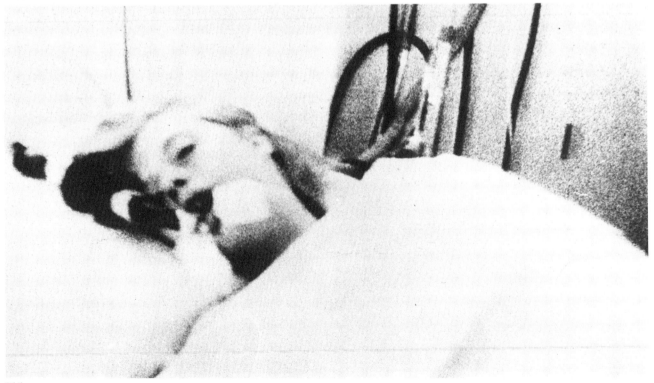

Miss X riding high. The Redlands raid and her role in Girl on a Motor-cycle *(1967) with Alain Delon (shown here) killed off Marianne Faithfull's virginal image.*

Although the word 'groupie' is relatively new, similar camp followers have existed for centuries. Fame itself is not necessarily the magnet, but the sort of renown associated with those men whose lives carry some sort of risk, threatening to be short and therefore (so the theory goes) lived at a high pitch of excitement. The sexual activities of such women can be called acts of generosity, services to the lonely, tired and tragic, whose relationships are always tenuous and usually short, shots at vicarious excitement and fame, or simply whoring. In a sense, all these descriptions demonstrate the same underlying motivation – the desire to flirt with death and life, taking the dangerous chance that a temporary sexual association will turn into a permanent emotional attachment. For the women, such associations are pale shadows of the

Older and wiser? Marianne re-emerged in 1979 as a singer with a voice that showed her age and pain.

self-defining experiences of their men. Often, that is all they can hope for.

Among musicians, camp followers have been known as 'band chicks', 'starfuckers', 'snuff queens' (in country music) and, since the sixties, 'groupies'. The big difference between rock groupies and their predecessors and fellows is their infatuation with groups. The Beatles, of course, set the pattern. They were not just stars, they were an exclusive band of brothers, to which people so much wanted to *belong*. Sometimes, the sex came later. The girls hung around stage doors, waiting for a glimpse. If a roadie came out to procure for the Fab Four, it was easy to offer yourself – and, once made, the offer was rarely refused. Later on, perhaps, roadies and concert promoters and local DJs would arrange back-stage passes in return for services rendered. What else could a poor girl-fan do?

It was easy to slip from fan to groupie in the early sixties. The whole atmosphere of rock'n'roll concerts was charged with adolescent sexual electricity. Against the backcloth of fumbled experiences with untutored and ungainly boyfriends, the worldly

Reach for the stars. The nearest most groupies ever came to stardom was to feature in a magazine article or, as here, a film. The shot comes from Groupies – *a semi-documentary of 1972.*

118

image of the love-toting pop or rock musician was truly seductive. The girl who once stood outside a stage-door and found herself ushered into the holy of holies to minister to the needs of some lust-gripped musician often found the experience worth repeating. The sexual act itself was little more than symbolic. It was a demonstration that the barrier between audience and performer had come down for her, setting her above the crowd. Sex was the show carried on backstage – no longer a surrogate, but the act itself.

Although the groupies quickly developed favourite performers or formed into a hierarchy reflecting the hierarchy of rock stars, their common motivation was more important. This depended on an idea of the exclusivity and alien character of group life, so that while any group might attract groupies, the phenomenon really mushroomed with the so-called British Invasion of America in the mid-sixties.

Young girls from nice middle-class homes quickly latched on to the idea of becoming groupies. They were 'often well-heeled, living on Daddy's money, a solid educational background', the Electric Light Orchestra's Bev Bevan remembered. Many British groupies were inspired by the fuss that was made about Chrissie Shrimpton, Marianne Faithfull, Jane Asher (Paul McCartney's girl-friend for a time in the sixties) or Patti Boyd (the model who became first George Harrison's wife and then Eric Clapton's). Others were content to enjoy what the moment seemed to offer. 'You get to ball the prettiest boys, smoke the best dope and meet all the most far out people,' said one girl known as Patti Cakes. 'You're there three or four days, waited on hand and foot, and there's just all the dope and food you can eat,' said Anna, from San Francisco, 'and all the people paying attention to you and your lover. It's very beautiful.'

Whatever a groupie was after, her sexual services were clearly a marketable commodity – even if the price she was paid was often insultingly low. Sherry, a Los Angeles groupie (now retired), would cruise Sunset Strip looking for long-haired boys on hotel room balconies. She would shout up and ask them their room numbers. She also had engraved visiting cards printed with messages like 'I want you' or, more circumspectly, 'Let's get it on'. Another groupie from Cleveland spent many a night chasing likely looking limousines. One hopeful wrote Mick Jagger a note beginning, 'Can you move your prick/As well as you kick/When you dance, Mick?' and signed it with her name, address and phone number. Less artistic efforts have included hiring a helicopter to buzz a house where the Beatles were staying, sending a pair of panties to ELP drummer Carl Palmer accompanied by a telephone message suggesting 'a personal demonstration', plain lying and, of course, setting a sexual sprat to catch a mackerel.

Anybody with the right sort of connection would do. For example, there is the story of the sixteen-year-old New York groupie who climbed out onto the ledge below a sixth-floor hotel room occupied by a journalist travelling with the Rolling Stones. Having entered the room through a window and ascertaining that she was indeed dealing with a friend of Mick and the boys, she stripped and got into bed. In Robert Greenfield's account of the Stones' 1972 US tour, *Stones Touring Party*, we are introduced to Renée, a 'fresh-faced' nineteen-year-old secretarial student who lies her way backstage at a Philadelphia show, into the beds of a roadie or two and onto film as a featured player in Robert Frank's unreleased documentary about the tour, *Cocksucker Blues*. In this she agreed to let herself be filmed with her fresh-face stuffed with the genitalia of Stones' associates. Renée was not a top groupie – as she herself said, 'The Stones should have had the Butter Queen, Suzy Creamcheese or Cherry Vanilla there' – but she understood her role well enough. 'I think a tour makes it easy on a chick,' she said after the tour was over. 'She doesn't have to bother putting the make on anyone. She's there just to say yes.' It's a comment worthy of Jagger himself, for whom 'there's really no reason to have women on a tour unless they've got a job to do; the only other reason is to screw'.

'Girls come round and pose like starlets, teasing and acting haughty,' Led Zeppelin's Jimmy Page once complained. 'If you humiliate them a bit they tend to come on all right after that.' A groupie's job was to serve, to be available – and it is in the nature of her availability and service that she will be humiliated. This is one reason why fellatio ('blow jobs', 'giving head', 'cocksucking') is the preferred mode of backstage and hotel room sex (another is a not unrealistic fear of venereal disease). By itself, the act is the epitome of sexual servility.

Bev Bevan tells of a strange encounter with four groupies in the bar of a Holiday Inn in Salem, Oregon. It was 9.30pm and the group retired there after playing the opening set at a Wishbone Ash concert. Apart from themselves, a bored barman and a piano trio playing a medley of show tunes, the bar was empty. Four girls, dressed in best Basin Street brothel finery, strode in purposefully. They were very self-assured. Their leader, Penny ('double for a young Mae West' according to Bev) introduced them. 'We call ourselves the Flying Garter Girls and, honey, I run the finest academy for oral sex on this side of the Rockies.'

Soon, in the interests of 'laying it on you', as Penny assured them, she and 'Miss Memphis' were dancing with two members of the group, while the other girls (Cheryl and Cindy-Lou, would you believe), were making love to each other on the floor of the bar. 'We're AC/DC,' Penny is said to have explained. 'We like each other's company as well.'

Voyeurism, group sex and a little bit of mild sadism are all important parts of the groupie scene. The rock stars maintain the proper distance of a discerning consumer, while the groupies maintain the high standard and wide range of services one might expect of a good department store, an ice cream parlour – or a brothel. Breaching the etiquette runs the risk in extreme cases of fathering unwanted children. Brian Jones is said to have managed six in his time (two admittedly before he was a star); Jimi Hendrix (who coined the derisive term 'Band Aids' for groupies) is supposed to have left

119

Marianne had a miscarriage, Bianca had Jade. Marsha Hunt, squeezed between the two in Mick Jagger's affections, found time to have Karis in 1970, and settled paternity with him out of court.

a trail of children and threatened paternity suits across Europe and America; in 1980 a Berlin woman, Erica Huebers, claimed that her seventeen-year-old daughter is Paul McCartney's child, the result of a supposed liaison during the Beatles' night-club days in Hamburg ('Paul has no recollection of this lady,' said his publicist); Marsha Hunt settled with Mick Jagger out of court over the contested paternity of her child, while he admitted fathering the child that Marianne Faithfull miscarried.

'You look for certain things in certain towns,' said Jimmy Page. 'Chicago, for instance, is notorious for sort of two things at once. Balling two chicks, or three, in combination acts.' When *Rolling Stone* ran a groupies' issue in 1969, there was some criticism that they hadn't written about New York groupies, who were, it was said 'a different breed'. According to Jimmy Page, San Francisco groupies are 'like friends', while New Yorkers and Angelenos 'make a religion out of how many pop stars they can fuck'. Eric Clapton remembered playing the *Murray the K Show* with the Who in New York, 1967. 'There were just tons of them around then,' he told Steve Turner. 'I mean, pretty ugly ones but some fair ones, too. There were both ends, really – horrible spotty scrubbers and really nice looking middle-class chicks. Or just nice chicks who didn't realize they were making themselves into groupies – they were pretty innocent.'

Little Jimi, aged six, pictured with his mother, Eva Sundkvist, six years after Jimi Hendrix's death. The Swedish courts supported her claim that he was Hendrix's son.

The callous classification of women has been something that groupies themselves have always done – at least, since the idea became current that being a groupie could be a full-time occupation. Jenny Fabian, who used her experiences with a number of English groups as background material for her novel *Groupie* (co-written with Johnnie Byrne), suggests how competitive the groupie scene was.

At the bottom of the groupie heap were those who were totally disposable. They received no payment, no thanks and no second chance. They were room service or 'in-flight entertainment' – ready and willing to be used or abused as fancy dictates. 'We're the ugliest band ever born,' claimed Bobby Colomby, drummer with Blood, Sweat and Tears. 'We have the funniest groupies in the world – real bottom-of-the-barrel stuff.' Led Zeppelin were plagued by two particularly unattractive but persistent Detroit groupies. Members of the group once conceived the idea of taking them to one of the group's motel rooms and pelting them with cream-filled doughnuts. In the event, Robert Plant couldn't find an open doughnut shop so it never happened. Then there was Renée again, doing her stuff on board the Stones' plane. The guy she was with wouldn't come and Renée was naked and hot and tired. Another member of the entourage came up to her with a drink in his hand and Renée asked for a sip. 'Not after what you been doin', man,' he said. Eventually, he magnanimously handed her his empty glass. Moments before, he had been watching two other groupies performing and shouting, 'Get me some orange juice. Get me something wet I can throw!'

But at the top of the pile are the groupies whose attentions are prized. Some of them may not even consider themselves groupies, since they are treated rather like wives or high-class prostitutes, (but without the legal protection of either). 'It doesn't matter what their motivation is,' Country Joe MacDonald said in the sixties. 'There are times when they come around after something and you're after something, too, so you get it together and everybody's happy. Groupies are beautiful. They come to hear you play, they throw flowers and underpants, they give you kisses and love, they come to bed with you. They're beautiful.' Living in Topanga County in 1968, Neil Young had observed that 'there are about eight girls who go around, keeping house, cooking food, and making love to everyone.' It was, he agreed, 'beautiful'.

'As a rule, they're the most incredibly warm people,' said Eric Clapton about groupies in the early days. 'If making love to you was going to make you happy, they'd make love. If you were tired and didn't want to make it, they'd cook you a meal and make you feel at home. They really were ports of call.' Hendrix said much the same thing. 'Instead of saying, "We're part of the love scene", they're actually doing it,' he once remarked. 'They take you around, they wash your socks and try to make you feel nice while you're in town because they know they can't have you forever.'

Behind this romantic fiction lies the brutal reality of male chauvinism. Hendrix's 'love scene' consisted of

this: 'He had an incredible sexual appetite and would often sleep with three or four girls in the same night,' said Kathy Etchingham, one of Jimi's long-term companions. His casual attitude was legendary – the only surprising thing being how readily it was accepted, by colleagues, friends, fans and lovers alike. 'One night after a concert in Manchester,' said Kathy, 'I even found him in the ladies' loo with a chick. She meant nothing to him, and it meant nothing to me – apart from the fact that I had to tell him to hurry up or we would miss the train back to London.'

Jimi, apparently, was as over-indulgent with women as he was with drinks, drugs and music. And, like most men, he enjoyed a double standard. 'When we first started living together I was very young and kind of wild,' Kathy recalled, almost apologetically. Eventually, Hendrix locked her in the bedroom as a punishment, and spent 'many hours of patient explaining' how she was 'supposed to act', according to Kathy, 'both as a woman and when I was living with someone I love.'

In fact, the gallant Jimi often relied on a more basic teaching method. One night in the Bag O'Nails, a London nightclub, Kathy left Jimi at his table to go upstairs and phone a friend. After a while – longer

Exits, bold as love. Hendrix associate Alan Clark comforts New York supergroupie Devon as they leave the Seattle funeral home where Jimi Hendrix's body awaits burial on 18th September, 1970. Devon was more than just a groupie to Hendrix, and she only survived him by two years, overdosing in 1972.

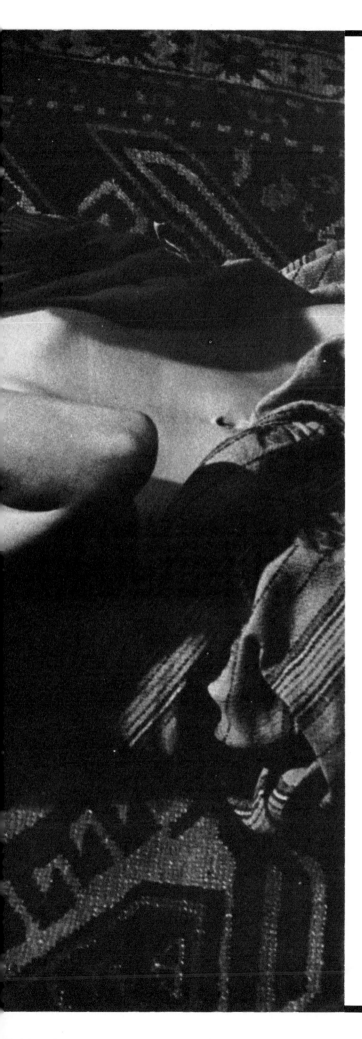

than Hendrix approved of – he came upstairs and, assuming she was talking to some male competitor (she wasn't), he grabbed the phone out of her hand and started beating her about the head with it. Kathy was screaming when, luckily for her, those two well-known tunesmiths, Lennon and McCartney, happened to be passing and pulled the gallant Jimi off his lover. 'That may have been the first of our many fights,' said Kathy. On one occasion her nose was broken in three places by a well-aimed kick from Hendrix.

'Jimi Hendrix was a genius,' said one of his most intimate associates, Eric Burdon, in 1976. 'But one minute he's on stage singing about the mass of under-dogs in America and the next he's kicking the hell out of some poor chick in a back alley.' Perhaps Jimi Hendrix's best-known companion was the New York 'supergroupie', Devon. She was, said writer Al Aronowitz, 'the closest thing Jimi had to an old lady ... one of the most beautiful and sensuous of the groupies and one of the most successful.' In the late sixties there were (according to Devon's friend, Pat Hartley) 'four or five sort of famous groupies and Devon was one of them, but she never lasted long with anybody. She didn't want to live with anybody, it was just a real status thing ...' Devon was a rock star's favourite. She went through Brian Jones, Mick Jagger, Jimi Hendrix. 'Whenever a rock star came to New York,' wrote Al Aronowitz, 'chances are you'd find Devon in his hotel room.' Her services were recommended. Jagger phoned her up after getting her number from a friend and invited her to go to Philadelphia with him for a concert. 'After the Philadelphia gig,' she remembered, 'we spent the week together in New York. Six beautiful days and nights ... If I wanted to go to Boston with him, I could. Or I'd wait for him to come back. I just felt beautiful ... I'd get calls from my friends who'd congratulate me and say "Hey, you did it!" Like *heavy* score, right?'

The congratulations had something to do with the fact that Devon was black. She was also Jimi's girl – she even wanted to marry him. And she provided the extra service of pimping half-a-dozen other girls for Hendrix. Pat Hartley recalled 'all kinds of weird shit going on and telephones ringing and girls being kicked downstairs and all kinds of nonsense ... very late night acid trips and things like that ...' Jimi, said Pat Hartley, 'was shy, but that doesn't mean he wasn't going to beat you up if you took too much of a liberty with him ... some of it was an absolute horror.'

As for Devon, she was happy to be wanted. But it was all somehow so sad and empty. She lived for the next date, to get her photograph in the papers, to have journalists like Al Aronowitz write columns about her. Truly bereaved after Hendrix's death, she killed herself with an overdose less than two years later.

Chris used to be another top-flight groupie. But she actually fell in love with Lynyrd Skynyrd's road manager Dean Kilpatrick, who died tragically in the Skynyrd air-crash in 1977. She'd been through some

Soft surfaces and hard edges. Anita Pallenberg shows her form.

shit even before that, though. 'Woodstock was the first time I was away from home with the licence to be totally free,' she told writer Michael Segell. 'I was very drunk, very high all week,' she recalled. 'I had smoked some before but had never tried heavier stuff. And I made it with a lot of people. I can't even remember who.' When her boyfriend arrived, he didn't like what he saw. Chris walked off with another man – a performer at the festival. When they got to the Chelsea Hotel in New York, the week's intake of drugs and drink (including Woodstock's notorious acid-spiked punch) was taking its toll. Her companion was having none of her explanation of fatigue and sickness. He tried to rape her and beat her so badly that she had to be hospitalized.

Yet she continued as a groupie for a while, even through further brutalization by other musicians. Eventually, she won the demeaning accolade of being voted Cleveland's top attraction. 'I always imagined I had some great purpose in life,' she told Segell, 'to fulfill someone's dreams or help someone or do some segment of mankind a great deal of good ... In retrospect it didn't have much purpose. I just learnt a great deal about life.' When Kilpatrick was killed, she gave

'Would you let your daughter go with a Rolling Stone?' Right: Anita Pallenberg with Brian Jones in 1966 – the ice princess. Far right: Anita holding Marlon, her first child by Keith Richard – maternal but insecure. Italian-born Anita was told by the British authorities in 1969 'Marry or Leave,' so she flew off to America. She and Keith never married. Below: Anita passes a joint to Mick Jagger on the set of Performance. *Her seduction of Jagger during a shooting break made her Stones score equal with Marianne Faithfull's.*

up the rock world for ever, and went to work as a receptionist in a law office, returning home each evening to live quietly with her parents.

The enhanced status of the 'rock'n'roll old lady' is an illusory triumph. She may win her way into the holy of holies, but she always does it as a sacrifice. Marianne Faithfull found that out – in time, perhaps, to save her life. Anita Pallenberg, too, has found it difficult after her long association with the Rolling Stones. Anita, a teutonic beauty as a young woman, first entered their lives as Brian Jones's girlfriend, in the mid-sixties. The couple's relationship was stormy, to say the least. Brian would beat the hell out of Anita; Anita would support Brian in his paranoid fantasies. She joined him on his trips. On one occasion, Brian dressed up in a Nazi uniform and had his photograph taken grinding a doll into the ground with his jackboot – Anita suggested he send the picture to the newspapers, telling them it was 'an anti-Nazi protest'.

In 1967, Anita left Brian for Keith Richard. While on a drive to Morocco, Brian fell ill and was left behind in hospital by the rest of the vacationing group. Keith and Anita got together in Valencia, but kept it a secret from Brian. 'He was becoming increasingly vicious,' Keith explained later. Joining them in Morocco, Brian paid a trip to a local brothel, brought back two prostitutes and demanded a scene with them and Anita. Keith, in a sudden fit of revulsion at all this excess, threw Anita into a car and drove off. 'I was disgusted with the way Brian treated her,' he said.

But Anita herself was no angel. She was at one time dependent on drugs, notably heroin, although she

eventually managed to kick it. She developed, like so many in the rock world, a preoccupation with the occult. While acting in the Nicolas Roeg film, *Performance*, she purloined a variety of props with occult associations. In the late seventies, she professed to being a member of a witches' coven – although her lawyer later denied it on her behalf.

In July 1979, in Keith Richard's twelve-room mansion in South Salem, New York, the body of seventeen-year-old Scott Cantrell was found on Anita's unmade bed. He had evidently shot himself through the head with a stolen Smith and Wesson .38 revolver that had been in the house. The oak double bed was propped up in one corner of the room by an old chair. The bedclothes were soaked in blood. Anita had been in another room when the boy shot himself, blowing off the back of his head, but her clothes had become blooded when she went to investigate the noise of shooting and she had turned Scott over onto his front. Anita said that she had heard a click, then a shot. When examined, the .38 was found to contain three bullets – one discharged and two live, one of them nicked as though it had been hit with the firing pin. The boy had, according to Anita, been discussing Russian Roulette earlier – he was depressed, didn't get along with his father and felt considerable remorse about his mother's death which had occurred some six months earlier. The two of them, Anita said, had been drinking white wine all day and Scott had been smoking a lot of marijuana.

Scott's father, Robert Cantrell, said that Anita was desperately in love with his son and had seduced him. But it was also pointed out that some time earlier a police patrolman had reported the noise of chanting from bushes not far from the house. The police report of the incident said that the patrolman was jumped on by a robed and hooded man, resembling Scott Cantrell in height and weight. Was he involved in occult practices with or without Anita? Inside the house, police noted a hangman's noose – holding up a hammock – and a 'voodoo style doll depicting Elvis Presley' on the mantelpiece. It is not surprising that Anita Pallenberg was cleared of any part in Scott Cantrell's death, although she was charged with the possession of one stolen gun (the .38) and with criminal possession of an unregistered automatic, also found in the house.

Whatever the truth of Anita's bizarre life, her tragedy seems much more straightforward. As a rock'n'roll girlfriend, she had been prey to the gross enlargement of conventional insecurities. Her sexuality had become, for a time, the essential prop in her life.

How far Anita's condition at the time of Cantrell's shooting was attributable to the state of her relationship with Keith Richard can only be surmised. However, Richard's constant companion through most of 1979 was the Swedish model Lil Wenglas Green, who had lived with him in Paris for a year. But Richard's publicist, commenting about Keith and Anita at the end of 1979, said that 'Keith's position was that they never parted. Only the press said they did.' Indeed, within a few months of the shooting, Keith was back

125

Life with the Stones can seriously damage your health. After the Scott Cantrell shooting, when Anita left court in Lewisboro, N.Y. on 24th July, 1979, charged with illegal possession of a gun, she looked bloated and vacant.

with Anita. But, as one of his friends has commented, 'The person Keith really loves is their son Marlon.'

The Stones of course have attracted the most distinguished of all followers. Margaret Trudeau, then wife of Canadian prime minister, Pierre Trudeau, was one of them. Just after Keith and Anita were busted in Toronto for heroin in the summer of 1977, 'Madcap' Margaret (as the press knew her) became entangled in their magic. 'I didn't encourage or dissuade her,' said Mick Jagger after she had spent some time pursuing the group to New York. 'It would have been difficult to kick her out. She had six security men with two guns each. No, thank you. She was a very determined young lady – er, older woman. I think she was just a very sick girl in search of something. She found it, but not with me. I wouldn't go near her,' he added, 'with a barge pole.'

Evidently the 27-year-old cement millionaire's daughter was going through a bad patch in her six year marriage to 56-year-old Pierre. After meeting the Stones, she followed them to New York, booked herself into their hotel and attached herself to their party. She returned to Canada some time later with a black eye, the last chapter of her 'modern girl' autobiography, *Beyond Reason*, and an extraordinarily contradictory testimonial from the Satanic Majesty himself (who was, at the time, separating from his own wife, Bianca). 'I have no relationship with Margaret Trudeau,' said Jagger, 'just a passing acquaintance for two nights.'

The women who best survive in the male-dominated rock world are not groupies at all. Jenny Fabian, for example, said Family's vocalist Roger Chapman who knew her well, 'was just a part of that whole underground scene'. Deborah Harry spent the late sixties in a flower power group called Wind In The Willows and always harboured a desire to be a performer. For a while she worked as a Playboy bunny although waiting on table at Max's Kansas City in New York was more rewarding, allowing her to hang out with musicians and nurture her own talent. While she would admit, in 1981, 'that sex sells and I do exploit my sexuality', she could also argue, with an eye to her own position, that 'women are going to be the new Elvises. That's the only place for rock'n'roll to go. The only people who can express anything new in rock are girls, and gays.'

For Linda Eastman, photography was both an occupation in its own right (she worked for *Eye* Magazine in New York) and a means of access to musicians. The two things were never, of course, entirely separate, but when she met and married Paul

What's up, Deb? Harry as bunny – but where's the carrot?

Photography brought them together, but Paul and Linda sometimes prefer photography to leave them alone.

McCartney in 1969, the rapidity with which she gave up professional photography for a place in McCartney's new group, Wings, suggested a certain lack of application at the time. 'We met in a club in London called the Bag O'Nails,' Linda recalled three years into marriage. 'It was a real pick-up job. Georgie Fame was playing and I saw Paul and I just felt I had to meet him. So I managed to get talking to him and afterwards we went to another club called the Speakeasy with Keith Moon and Roger Daltrey from the Who . . . We considered living together, but it wasn't really on, so we got married.'

If Linda's description sounds rather like the perennial approach of the groupie, it must be emphasized that her marriage to Paul has been successful. Having already had one child, her daughter Heather, by a previous and brief marriage when she was still a student, Linda once remarked thoughtfully, that 'you've got to love someone a heck of a lot to stay married.'

Britt Ekland, a Swedish starlet, moved from Peter Sellers to Lou Adler to Rod Stewart. With Sellers, she recalled, there was no love in the marriage, and despite the fact that he fathered her daughter Victoria, she has said that she only learned to love him after they had separated. Lou Adler, the emperor of the West Coast rock scene, fathered her son Nicolai. But Britt's greatest love appears to have been Rod Stewart. After they split, he said ruefully of her memoirs, *True Britt*, 'The book made me feel sorry for her because she's a born loser. She's always the one that's jilted and always the bridesmaid.'

While Rod and Britt were together, he once claimed to have fathered a child in 1963, only to confess later

that he had made it all up 'on the spur of the moment'. 'Sometimes I don't think he is very truthful,' said Britt, disingenuously. 'But it's not because he means to lie. It's because he wants either to confuse people or to please them.' Quite which member of the Britt and Rod team was living in the other's fantasy world is not clear, but, apparently, morality and judgement were infrequent visitors to the couple's glamorous household.

Britt claimed that Rod was excessively mean with money. However, seasoned commentators of the rock scene have long remarked on Britt's obsessive love of shopping. Rod's former girlfriend Dee Harrington, and his present wife, Alana Hamilton, have both leapt to his defence. But despite their protestations, Rod himself has shown that where Britt was concerned, he'd spent as little as he could get away with. He even confessed to stealing a copy of *True Britt* from an airport bookstall. 'Well, I was damned if I was going to pay for it,' he said.

When it came to the separation, Britt claimed that Rod and she had a verbal agreement to pool their 'earnings and abilities', and as such she demanded some recompense. Everything, she said, should have been split down the middle and, considering how she had sacrificed her acting career to help Rod, she felt she deserved £6,000,000 – especially, she said, since Rod was about to sign a £13,000,000 deal when he left her. As an interim award, Britt asked for £2,750 a month while her claim was being assessed. But her arguments were rejected by the courts.

Rod, eventually, married Alana Hamilton, the former wife of the actor, George Hamilton, whose name had earlier been linked with Lyndon Johnson's daughter. Alana and Rod first met in 1977, after which he got his press officer to phone her up and ask for a date. 'I found him sensitive, witty, intelligent, sexy and shy,' said Alana. Apparently, on their first date, they sat up most of the night talking.

Flying between famous men, such women tend not even to be celebrities by virtue of their celebrity, but rather because of their men's. They are, as a result, the staple of gossip columns – that journalistic domain where all that matters is who was with whom and when. Living from star to star is the tedious routine of these lives. Bianca Perez Morena de Macias, a Nicaraguan model and former girlfriend of Michael Caine, looked promising when she told the press after her first meeting with Mick Jagger that 'I have no name'. Once she had been granted her husband's, however, she soon took up the regular sport with a vengeance. 'Bianca,' said Andy Warhol, 'is the greatest movie star who's never made a movie.' Towards the end of her marriage to Mick, she began to be seen in the company of numerous gossip column items – Ryan O'Neal, Princess Margaret's friend Roddy Llewellyn and a number of art dealers, oil tycoons and other businessmen. For a few weeks she ran the hectic

Do you think I'm sexy? Rod Stewart gropes his wife, Alana, during a 1980 post-gig party at London's Embassy Club. Having replaced Britt Ekland in Rod's affections, Alana soon replaced her in Rod's bed.

route of New York high-life revolving at the time mainly round the ultra-exclusive disco and haven for coke users, Studio 54.

Her split with Mick was hotly denied at the time (in 1977) and legally complex afterwards. Having married him and mothered his daughter, Jade, Bianca had a legitimate claim to alimony. She claimed $12.5 million – calculating Mick's earnings in their eight-year marriage at $25 million. After some haggling out of court, Mick sought to have the case heard in Britain, where divorce settlements are generally smaller than in the US. (Bianca's lawyer, Marvin Mitchelson, had already represented Marsha Hunt in her paternity suit against Jagger.) While this attempt was in process, Mick was ordered to pay Bianca over $3,000 a week in expenses (including $500 a week for transportation, $250 a week for entertainment and $1,000 a week for rent or mortgage repayments). Eventually, the courts decided the divorce case should be heard in London. An interim payment of some £25,000 was awarded to Bianca but the case dragged on even after a decree nisi had been granted. A year later, in November 1980, a judge in

Above: Sweet nothings and rich somebodies. Mick and Bianca celebrate the Hon. Colin Tennant's fiftieth birthday on Princess Margaret's hideaway isle of Mustique.

Left: Admitting no impediment to a marriage of true minds, Bianca Jagger struts her stuff at the reception to celebrate her wedding to Mick, 12th May, 1971.

Right: The price of Love? Specialist divorce lawyer Marvin Mitchelson suggesting to Bianca that it might be $12,000,000, outside the Los Angeles Superior Court, 8th May, 1979. The Jagger divorce was finally settled privately under British jurisdiction by a judge in chambers, for an alimony figure rumoured to be around £1,000,000.

chambers fixed the final amount of the settlement in private – a figure which has never been revealed but is estimated at £1,000,000.

Somehow, Bianca retained a certain degree of perspective – demonstrated in the early eighties by her efforts in support of her Nicaraguan compatriots, who had suffered enormously in the struggle to overthrow the oppressive Somoza regime and the battle to defend their new democracy. (She had already given much time and money in their aid back in 1978 when a severe earthquake devastated the country.) She has also spoken up for the freedom fighters in El Salvador. 'The rock business is like a secret society run by men,' she commented in 1981. 'Every woman is treated like a second-class citizen.' Women, she said, became their own worst enemies by virtue of the competitiveness with which they regarded each other – as she herself had proved when she declared her dislike for Mick Jagger's new companion, Texan model Jerry Hall.

Jerry Hall, six foot and a former *Vogue* cover girl, was once said to be the highest paid model in the world. Bryan Ferry, the elegant son of a Durham miner who fronted Roxy Music in the seventies, saw her on *Vogue* and used her for the sleeve of the Roxy album, *Siren.* Then he fell in love with her and the couple got engaged. He was, not unnaturally, hurt when Jerry went off with Mick Jagger in October 1977. After all, among Jerry's admirers could be counted the former Shah of Persia, and Bryan – who liked nothing better than to Christmas on shipping heir Takis Theodarakis's yacht or to holiday on Princess Margaret's hideaway island of Mustique – could aspire to nothing higher than a woman who was admired by the richest man in the world. 'I do not like being accused of going uptown,' said Ferry after recovering from the Hall affair. 'I like social exploration.' The trouble is that in the social stratosphere inhabited by the likes of Ferry, very little exploration is possible. In the end, what is the really significant difference between Jerry Hall and, say, Amanda Lear (another of Ferry's girlfriends), but the precise list of celebrity names appended to their's in the gossip columns – even their memoirs are tediously similar re-runs of the same sort of tittle-tattle. Perhaps concern for wealth and fame sets these people apart but (as Bianca suggested), to male rock stars all women are potential groupies.

Meanwhile, the dedicated groupie, following the dictum that 'if he doesn't strum a guitar and sing like a sex maniac, he's nobody,' concludes that doing those things qualifies almost everybody as a somebody. The dedicated groupie plays the field, collecting musicians and groups like other kids collect stamps or train numbers. The memorable Plaster-Casters of Chicago carried the collecting mania to the level of artistry. The Plaster-Casters – Cynthia, Dianne and Marilyn – made a unique collection of plaster models of the erect penises of rock stars. They started in late 1967 when Cynthia was about twenty. She had been 'chasing groups' since 1965, but 'wanted to stand out from the other groupies and get to meet the groups first'. The first group she met was the Stones. 'Since then,' she says, 'well just about everybody, I guess.'

132

The Plaster-Casters' technique was simple, direct and unashamed. They would approach a group with an unusual degree of openness. They carried their equipment in a briefcase marked 'Plaster-Casters of Chicago'. They took their casts around to show prospective 'clients'. They even had T-shirts and visiting cards printed up. A typical session would involve one of them as 'plater', one as mould-maker and plaster-caster and one as assistant. The operation would be recorded in a diary in almost clinical detail. 'He . . . kept his hard for the entire minute,' one entry reads. 'He got stuck, however, for about fifteen minutes (his hair did), but he was an excellent sport – didn't panic . . . he actually enjoyed it and balled the impression after it had set. In fact, I believe the reason we couldn't get his rig out was that it wouldn't get soft.'

The last gasp of the traditional groupie was blown on to the 'pretty boy' teenybopper idols of the seventies, like Marc Bolan and the Bay City Rollers. Even David Cassidy claims to have enjoyed the services of groupies. It gave him credibility as a rock musician. 'On the road there was always this one room where we'd corral a handpicked dozen of the most beautiful,' he said in 1977. 'After the show, I'd go up to this room, pick the one I wanted, and let the band divvy up the rest. I was an animal.' But even for him it palled. 'I was tired of strangers in my room, my bed; tired of girls climbing up the fire escape and hiding in my closets, in my shower.'

Today the rock scene attracts a wide variety of sexual opportunists of greater or lesser degree. The innocence of an earlier age, when sex with the stars was usually no more than harmless fun, has disappeared. There are would-be supergroupies who always seem to be at a loss for more famous names. There are male groupies and gay groupies. And for some, close association with rock stars has provided a launching pad or a welcome boost to a separate career. Bebe Buell, having become something of a celebrity as a friend of the stars, recorded an unmemorable album in an attempt to strike out on her own. Paula Yates (daughter of Jess Yates, one-time presenter of British TV's quasi-religious show *Stars On Sunday*, until a scandal with a divorcee lost him his job), latched on to Boomtown Rat Bob Geldof and rode his rocket to a hallowed place in the pop gossip columns. Her career as a celebrity columnist in the music press, Sunday papers and women's magazines was assured.

Of course, things have changed since Jimi Hendrix or Neil Young were able to talk of groupies as the practical exponents of hippy love. In the eighties, groupies and musicians alike know that starfucking is what it's all about. The people who have actually made it to the starry heights tend to find that the hassle of groupies now outweighs any possible benefits. Ten years ago the people who organized rock stars' lives – managers, agents, promoters – saw provision of groupies as part of the general paraphernalia of the concert or recording schedule. Nowadays, the priority is to protect stars from too much contact with the

Hey, hey Paula ... Yates, that is, then a 19-year-old 'professional punk' according to the press, girlfriend of Boomtown Rats' Bob Geldof, according to herself. Here she is revealing hidden qualities on a chilly July day in 1979.

outside world.

Rock music now means status and exclusivity. Today's big stars would never admit a need for groupies. But for those at the bottom of the heap, groupies are still a sign of some sort of stardom. On the way down, in Dallas, Sid Vicious left the Sex Pistols' dressing room to pick out a groupie. 'I don't want to fuck them all,' he screamed at the guards keeping the girls at bay. 'I just want to fuck one!' (This, from someone who described himself as a sexless monster.) He picked up with an American groupie – Nancy Spungen – when he left the Pistols. Nancy, whose father owned a paper company in Philadelphia, was – according to Malcolm McLaren – 'the first and only girl Sid went out with. Before meeting me' (said McLaren), 'he was a homosexual.' Like the nice American girls who get into sado-masochism because that's what punk groups are supposed to dig, Nancy just wanted to be noticed.

The trouble with being a groupie, one of them once said, is that people are always leaving you. In fact, they never have any intention of staying. It's the groupies who yearn for some permanence – perhaps a reassurance of their own desirability, even in the least promising circumstances. The story goes that Gram Parsons, the rich boy who joined the Byrds, hung out with the Stones and was desperate to be a star, collapsed in his motel room after a typical day of drinking and drugging. Parsons – who regularly ended up financing his unsuccessful musical ventures with his own private income – was himself a sort of groupie. He liked nothing better than to get doped up with Keith Richard. He was desperate for the recognition the Stones afforded him as perhaps *the* founder of sixties' country rock. He was loved by the singer Emmylou Harris and, indeed, recognized by those who knew what he had done. But that was not enough. Drugs, drink and groupies were what he craved – the palpable rewards of stardom.

On 19th September, 1973, Parsons was in the Joshua Tree Inn, California – where he often stayed on his frequent visits to the area, which had an obscure mystical significance to him. 'About ten, I just caught some weird vibes from over in his room,' recalls the motel owner's son. 'When I got there, there was this chick jerking him off, trying to revive him. She was probably in love with him.' Gram Parsons was dead. Three years later, in 1976, girls were still arriving from time to time at the motel. 'They ask if they can have the room Gram Parsons died in,' the owner said.

John Lennon's life & music in stories and pictures

Special 16-page Pullout

25¢

New York,
December 10, 1980

DAILY ⊚ NEWS
Tonight

LATEST STOCKS

TUESDAY NIGHT EDITION

Killer stalked him 3 days

Page 3

Lennon signing autograph for Mark Chapman, before the shooting.   **News photo by Paul Goresh** © Copyright 1980 New York News Inc.

EXCLUSIVE: Lennon & suspect

FAN DANCING

In rock'n'roll's Babylon, the stars occupy the upper storeys of the sacred ziggurat, frolicking desperately among the exotic foliage of their own hanging gardens. Meanwhile down on the street are the people who put them there: the fans. Fans buy their records, go to their concerts, collect their autographs, read their magazines; and above all they identify with their heroes.

The true aristocracy of fandom are the Elvis followers. These people think nothing of filling their houses with Elvis records and Elvis memorabilia. Otherwise apparently sensible, they might spend their last penny on a Nigerian copy of an Elvis Greatest Hits compilation or on a bottle of sweet white wine bearing Elvis's image and the name 'Always Elvis – (Blanc d'Oro)' – utterly regardless of the fact that they might have the same album in seventeen different sleeves already and unworried by the knowledge that Elvis never drank wine ('We feel that this is the kind of wine Elvis would have drunk if he did drink wine,' said a spokesperson for the company that markets 'Always Elvis'.) With Elvis interred – actually, or only spiritually within the walls of Graceland – the Elvis fans have lost all sense of Elvis as a real human being.

Elvis fans can be men and women of almost any age or class. Their obsession is a strange blend of hobby and quasi-religious devotion. They invariably speak of their trips to fan conventions, their holidays in Memphis to visit Elvis's mansion and their pursuit of Elvis live (when he was alive) or on film, as social events, excuses for a bit of fun and occasions to meet like-minded friends. They are often deeply concerned at the exploitative excesses of the Elvis memorabilia industry and yet they are all collectors and avid readers of the vast body of Elvis literature (most of it brazen-faced rubbish). Even so, their illusions about Elvis are treasured – so that, when Albert Goldman's scurrilous biography of the man was published in 1981, the British Elvis fan club boycotted it, presumably on the grounds that either Goldman's *Elvis* was a lie from start to finish, or it must have been a deliberate half-truth designed to tarnish the image of a great man.

Elvis fans talk a great deal about Elvis the man and Elvis the singer, they worry of the future of Elvis's daughter, Lisa-Marie, on his behalf (even donating money to her to help maintain Gracelands) and yet they often discuss him as if he were a candidate for canonization or even godhead, rather than the human being they all pretend to know. One English fan said he'd have given his life for an hour with Elvis – since Elvis was dead at the time, however, it was a pretty safe bet. Most bizarrely, there is a group of Elvis fans who believe that a child in North Carolina, christened Elvis Presley Patterson, is Elvis's reincarnation; there is at least one book, and one song, purporting to be dictated by Presley from beyond the grave, while a sensationalist American magazine about the supernatural ran a story some time after Elvis's death claiming that a half-formed clone of the singer had escaped from an institution where 'scientists' were attempting to control its murderous urges.

Elvis of course didn't have a monopoly on fan worship. There are plenty of other examples of obsessive devotion, bordering on lunacy. There are, for example, the Deadheads; the ninety thousand fans on the Grateful Dead's mailing list who trail around the world after their superheroes, tape-decks at the ready to record every note and nuance of the Dead's performances. Their language sometimes reaches new heights of obscurity as they try to describe their feelings for the band. It is difficult to believe that a fan who talks seriously about 'shifts into hyperspace', 'quantum chemistry', 'stretching the Taos' and similar distillations of psychobabble when talking about a rock group could also be a successful case lawyer, who, according to his wife Michelle, 'has argued final arguments – to juries – behind three nights of the Dead' and 'whose trip is so charged he wins cases'.

On the other hand is this any less weird than the one-man Bob Dylan fan club known as A. J. Weberman? Self-styled inventor of the science of 'garbology', Weberman coined that most useful of critical concepts, the CB (or current bag), for Weberman delights in the analysis of garbage – especially Bob Dylan's. At first, Dylan was amused, even captivated by A. J., but Weberman's desperation to find out the true meaning of the world's most mysterious rock star led him to spy on his subject's house at all hours, concentrating on rifling through Dylan's garbage cans for any clues to the elusive CB. Once, Dylan confronted A.J. and offered him a job as his chauffeur. However the conversation between the two great minds took such a curious turn that Dylan brought it to a close with a touch of typical enigmatic brilliance. 'I'm not Dylan, A.J.,' he pronounced, 'you are.' What greater accolade for the true fan?

'I read the news today, oh yeah.' The ultimate fan, Mark Chapman got John Lennon to sign his Double Fantasy *album a few days before returning to gun him down outside the Dakota Building where Lennon lived. 'Do you know what you just did?' said the appalled janitor. 'Yes,' said Chapman. 'I just shot John Lennon.'*

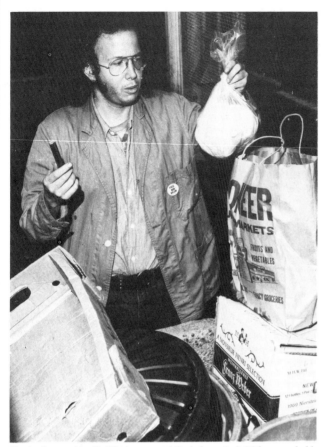

If only they could talk. The inventor of Garbology, A. J. Weberman, holds an unsmoked cigar and a bag full of diapers removed from the trash-can outside Bob Dylan's Manhattan home on 12th October, 1971. For the ultimate fan, garbage isn't rubbish.

London where his car hit a tree and killed him, and Duane Allman and Berry Oakley's adjacent graves in Macon, Georgia, have become a place of pilgrimage, where fans leave guitar picks and joints as offerings to appease the grim reaper.

In Lubbock, Texas, Buddy Holly's tomb is one of rock's holy places, as is Jimi Hendrix's grave in Seattle. Fans, unable to face the sordid facts of Jimi's death, cling to the curious fiction that Hendrix took his own life as a supreme artistic gesture ('phasing himself out onto another plane of being' as Eric Burdon once put it). Others try to ignore the fact of death altogether. Jim Morrison's acolytes have defended the theory that he staged his own 'death' but is actually still living somewhere under an assumed identity (unlikely, as fellow Door Ray Manzarek drily observed, since 'he hasn't called the accountant recently'.) Even hardened rock journalists fall into the trap. 'Four days after John Lennon was shot,' Greil Marcus wrote, 'I woke up to find Beatles music off the radio and the story off the front page . . . Does this mean, I thought, that it's over? That he's not dead any more?'

It's not really surprising that Lennon's death caused the most widespread trauma among fans, and it wasn't simply the shocking circumstances of the

A desert shrine to the memory of Gram Parsons, whose coffin was hi-jacked by his friend Phil Kaufman and burned near this spot at the Joshua Tree National Monument in September, 1973.

The herd instinct is strong in fans: there's safety in numbers. And there's the community spirit felt especially when a hero's life is cut brutally short. Early death destroys the possibility for ever of the fan and star meeting as equals, but it also has the advantage of enabling the star to be frozen for ever in his ideal image, rather than the often unsavoury reality. More prosaically, nobody has ever been able satisfactorily to explain the morbid curiosity of the general public when any media mogul dies in unusual circumstances. This magic combination of hero worship and morbidity explains why an estimated 1,500,000 people visited Elvis's grave in the year following his death; and why fans rededicated the site of Gram Parsons' illicit cremation at the Joshua Tree National Monument to the memory of the singer. At Joshua Tree, someone has scrawled the dedication, 'A bird flying high over the San Andreas fault' and, from time to time, flowers and other sacrificial items are laid there. Jim Morrison's grave at the St Pierre Lachaise cemetery in Paris is covered over in graffiti. Fans congregate there to leave small offerings, meditate and play music. There's 'Lizard King' graffiti, inscriptions reading 'I Want To Kill', drawings of Morrison scratched onto his tombstone, dedications to acid and, among others in French, the words *'Monstre de sensualité'* and *'Jim, tu les a libéré'*. A similar shrine has been dedicated to Marc Bolan at the spot on Barnes Common in

Stars are also fans: Patti Smith seeking inspiration at Jim Morrison's burial place in Paris. The grave may be unmarked, but fans have made sure that it doesn't go unnoticed.

shooting. Beatlemania was, after all, only the most extreme example of the all-consuming passion of fans to connect. At its simplest, it manifests itself as the sort of sexual frenzy at concerts that once inspired the old showbiz adage that a successful show means 'not a dry seat in the house'. From the days of Johnny Ray, Elvis and Fabian, up to the teenybop days of glitter rock, and right into the eighties' adulation for Adam and the Ants, the sound of pubescent girls screaming has been a constant accompaniment to rock'n'roll. It even came through the TV screen. 'In six minutes,' said Patti Smith of her first viewing of the Rolling Stones, 'five lusty images gave me my first glob of gooie in my virgin panties.' Adam Faith, remembering the girls of the late fifties who adored him, was being realistic when he said recently, 'I'm still that sort to let them wet their knickers on the seats. That's basically what it's all about for me.' Cliff Richard admitted that the first time girls screamed for him (at the Gaumont, Shepherd's Bush, in the late fifties), 'It was nice'. Tom Petty echoed this in the seventies. 'It's always good to have a few screaming girls in the front row,' he said. 'It makes it more rock'n'roll.' And Bill Wyman, the oldest teenager in the business, admitted the Stones' relief that the audiences at their 1981 concerts still contained sixteen and seventeen year old girls.

But the uninhibited sexual attraction that this implies can have disastrous results. The crush of girls trying to touch their idol led to 240 girls fainting at a

Leif Garrett show in 1979. These figures aren't exceptional, and can lead to real tragedy. In 1974, fourteen-year-old Bernadette Whelan died after being squashed against the stage at a David Cassidy concert. She had been trying to get close enough to take photographs of her idol; her camera survived the crush and the developed film shows how near she got; but she didn't live to see the results.

But if young female fans relate to their heroes as sexual objects, young male fans often feel no less pressing a need to get close to the star on stage. Predictably male fans tend to identify with the objects (usually male) of their admiration, rather than feel their idol worship in a sexual form. For instance, heavy metal fans don't just dress like their favourite bands, they often copy them to the point of playing along with songs by strumming along with imaginary or cardboard cutout guitars. Often the mimicking can be dangerous – especially when the act mimicked makes use of potentially dangerous props. In June 1974, at the height of Alice Cooper's mock-hanging act, a thirteen-year-old boy from Calgary, Canada, hung himself by the neck until he was dead at a copy-cat 'hanging party'. (Alice dropped the item from his act after this tragedy.) In November 1978, a male Kiss fan in Baltimore gave himself severe burns trying to copy his favourite band's fire-swallowing act. Disasters like this are, thankfully, rare.

The first time the press and general public became aware of the shocking power at the disposal of an uncontrolled rock audience was at Alan Freed's first concert promotion, on 21st March, 1952, at the Cleveland Arena. With 2.5 people after each seat, the music was all but inaudible. One stabbing and five arrests for drunkenness later, police and fire reinforcements were called in and the concert stopped.

When Bill Haley toured Europe in 1957, seats were smashed at concert halls across the continent and there was a virtual running battle at a show in Berlin. For the most part, the papers treated it all as good, clean fun but, on 5th February 1957, Haley arrived in London's Waterloo Station to be greeted by a near riot. 'You saw all around faces turned upwards, crumpled in fear by now, the ecstasy gone,' wrote George Gale in the *Daily Express*; 'angry faces trying to touch the car and see the face inside; faces bewildered like faces in the panic scenes of Russian films.'

The fans, wrote Gale, who witnessed the 'riot', were 'children tossed like jetsam in the swaying human tide'. Professing indifference to rock'n'roll and Haley, Gale described the scene as 'very nasty'. Next to his column, the paper printed a 'Warning' notice, telling its readers that 'preparations are being made to start a new trend' to replace rock'n'roll. Even something 'very nasty' could be tolerated if it was destined to be short-lived. But the fans knew what they wanted and, although often exaggerated in the press, the delinquent behaviour continued.

After Haley and the fifties came Beatlemania, a curious mixture of riotous assembly, political sycophancy and trendy exuberance in which almost everybody seemed to participate, from Prime

Ministers who knew a vote-catcher when they saw one, to society hostesses who knew what made cocktails go with a zing, to crippled teenagers whose earnest guardians persuaded the Beatles to meet their charges for a sort of laying-on of hands. Pop psychologists and sociologists explained that Beatlemania was a natural stage of adolescence; women's page journalists described how, even as jaded thirty-year-olds, they enjoyed a good scream. Almost everybody agreed that rock rioting was probably fun – they all had one reason or another to pretend to be fans.

Even doctors got into the act. Some declared that the Beatles 'were not sexy' – an analysis presumably meant to comfort the parents of teenage girls swept up by hysteria. Another declared that Beatlemania was like 'the frenzied dancing and shouting of voodoo worshippers', learnedly noting that 'beat music has a rhythmic stimulation on the brain' which induced behaviour rather like an epileptic fit. However, such distasteful analogies were not designed to prove that Beatlemania was harmful. On the contrary, sociologist J. B. Mays noted that while he couldn't say whether Beatlemania actually reduced the incidence of juvenile delinquency, 'it does syphon off a great deal of surplus juvenile energy into socially innocuous channels'. Thank heavens for that.

Meanwhile, the police were struggling to contain vast crowds at concerts and before concerts – in one case, taking almost an hour to restore order among fans queueing for Beatles' tickets in Newcastle-Upon-Tyne. An editorial in the *New Statesman* (written by Paul Johnson), described the 'menace of Beatlism' in much the same way as Bill Haley's Waterloo 'riot' had been written about a few years earlier. The Beatles themselves had, by the end of 1963, to travel with 35 guards in tow. Their popularity was such that within a week of revealing a taste for jelly babies, they had apparently received in the post over 100lbs of the confection – not counting the ones thrown to them on stage. As 1964 was about to begin, the owner of the Cavern Club announced that he was intending to break up the club stage and sell pieces of it for charity. 'This is the most sought after wood in the world,' he said, of an event echoed in the late seventies, when Bill Graham, owner of the Fillmore West, did exactly the same with that hall's considerably larger dance-floor.

The Beatles, for all the distaste they inspired in some people, were cultivated as relatively harmless symbols of new, jolly, swinging England. The Rolling Stones, who followed them, were a little less polite and, consequently, their fans were considered a little more dangerous. The Stones inspired riots across the world from Warsaw to Los Angeles and, with each one, a new shock headline. At first, the Stones were presented as part of the rhythm and blues scene, and Mick Jagger made this immortal comment about his potential fans: 'I hope they don't think we're a rock'n'roll group.' But the Stones' attachment to black music was in itself rather shocking, and the rapid abandonment of any group uniform, combined with hair that was noticeably longer than the Beatles' and an act that involved a certain amount of lascivious

Below: Beat music. Danish police use batons to quell a riot in Copenhage(n) following a showing of Rock Around The Clock, 8th August, 195(6). Rock'n'roll was an instant hit . . .

The New York (Times)

Four Young Singers Pay a Call on the Que(en)

138

Right: Baby, please don't go. A desperate fan tries for a glimpse of the Rolling Stones as they leave the Los Angeles Sports Arena after a show, th December, 1965.

STONE BONKERS!

Law and disorder. Beatlemania comes to Atlantic City, New Jersey, in December 1964.

nes. WEDNE!

Look What Happens

movement, especially from Jagger, soon won the Stones the undying hostility of many members of the press. Even the music press was uncertain whether to praise or to bury them. As early as the summer of 1963, one reviewer in the *New Musical Express* could be found comparing the group to 'long-haired dervishes' und in March 1964, the staid *Melody Maker* printed an article under the eye-catching title: 'Would You Let Your Daughter Go With A Rolling Stone?'

The non-rock press delighted in reporting all the bad news about the Stones – they were the ugliest group in the world, they didn't wash their hair, hate mail accused them of being filthy and vicars and country justices remarked on the decline of Britain's moral welfare, as though the Rolling Stones had brought it all about. It must be said that the Stones themselves encouraged much of this, not even displaying the mocking deference that marked the Beatles' early relations with the press and the authorities. As manager Andrew Oldham once said: 'For the Stones bad news is good news.'

The Stones toured the US in 1964 and, in the wake of Beatlemania, found themselves often playing behind a line of policemen. Much of the publicity in America had been generated by a taxing regime of photo-calls and TV appearances, which the Stones undertook with no evident discrimination. Dean Martin, hosting the show featuring the group, introduced them with a tedious series of studied insults. 'Their

hair is not that long,' he said, 'it's just they've got smaller foreheads and higher eyebrows.' He joked about a 'Hair-pulling contest with the Beatles' and introduced an acrobat on the show as the group's father. 'He's been trying to kill himself ever since,' said Martin. While Dino was playing up the neanderthal image beloved of the British press, others noted the group's sex appeal. 'To women, Jagger looks fascinating,' said *Vogue*, 'to men a scare.'

It was a combination designed to sell records, and engender fan worship. By the end of the US tour (which had started quietly enough), the group were greeted by a riot at Carnegie Hall. A month after their return to England, 50 fans had to be taken to hospital after a show in Blackpool. A grand piano was pushed off stage and destroyed and chandeliers were wrenched off the ceiling. It took a hundred men to quieten the crowd down. 'It wasn't more than twenty that really started it off,' said Jagger the next day, 'They sort of pushed their way to the front. I saw some girls being punched in the stomach and it was really violent and horrible.' The show had to be stopped and the Stones pulled off, leaving their instruments and

---

Death in Cincinnati. One of eleven people killed in rock's worst concert disaster to date. Thousands of fans, queueing in near-freezing conditions for a Who gig, stampeded into the Riverfront Coliseum on 2nd December, 1979. The fans thought they had heard the band start to play and trampled the victims to death in a mad rush to get a good position in the hall.

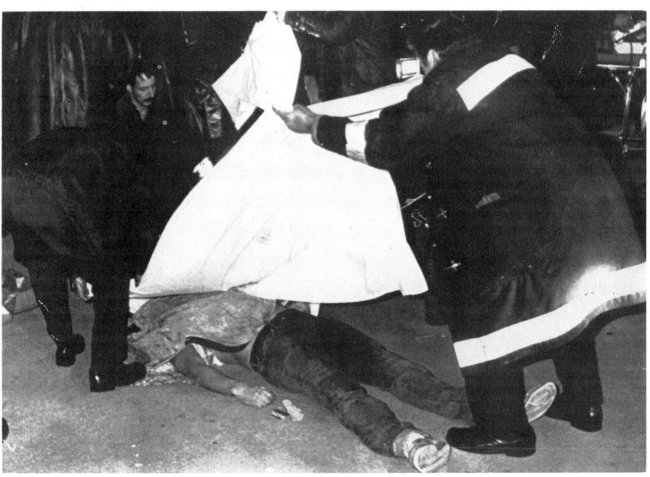

amplifiers at the mercy of the rampaging crowd. There were subsequent riots in Belfast and The Hague and near riots in Manchester and Jersey. In October 1964, 150 fans were arrested in Paris after a Stones concert at the Olympia, as the audience rampaged through the concert-hall foyer and into the streets. The next year, fans rioted when the Stones flew into Sydney, Australia. Twenty girls were crushed, two seriously, as the airport crowd burst through fences in an attempt to get closer to the group. By the time Jagger, Wyman and Brian Jones appeared in court in July, 1965, charged with insulting behaviour after pissing against a garage wall on their way back from a gig, the Stones were well on the way to becoming a fully-fledged 'public menace'.

Beatlemania and Stonesmania meant that rock rapidly acquired an elaborate paraphernalia of control – high stages, security guards, crowd barriers. These were anathema to fans and their very presence often turned the rush to the stage into the riots the security measures were supposed to prevent. The Beatles retired from live performances in 1966, but the paraphernalia surrounding their big venues has remained. So have the riots, which have become a regular feature of rock shows wherever they're held.

Between 500 and 1,000 Led Zeppelin fans – known for disorderly conduct – rioted at the Orange Bowl in Miami in the small hours of 17th April, 1977. On this occasion the fans feared the tickets for a Zep show in Tampa would be sold out before the official on-sale time, 8.30 in the morning. The rioters broke seats, windows, lawn-mowers and loud-speakers. They vandalized offices and left a trail of debris behind them. Just after 4am the police arrived, to be followed by a SWAT (Special Weapons and Tactics) team. About 200 people threw a hail of rocks on the police, who opened up with teargas to disperse the crowd. One rioter was arrested for allegedly pulling a .357 Magnum revolver on a policeman.

In May 1979, Elton John played Leningrad for the first time. Around 2,500 Russian fans, starved of rock music, paid up to £75 each to buy black market tickets. After a 2½ hour show, many of them clearly felt worked up enough to surge to the front of the stage. Had it not been for the fact that many of the audience were specially selected as stolid servants of the state who remained in their seats, the crush would have no doubt been considerably worse. As it was, the aisles were swamped with cheering, stamping fans demanding an encore from Elton. The star obliged with a rendition of *Back In The USSR*. 'I didn't plan to sing that song,' he said, 'it just came to me.'

Too often in recent years, as at the Miami Orange Bowl, crowd control has broken down before the fans even get inside the auditorium. Concerts run like military operations can expect at times to have casualties more appropriate to a small war. The worst incident to date took place on the evening of 3rd December 1979, just before a gig by the Who at the Cincinnati Riverfront Coliseum. Over 18,000 tickets had been sold within 90 minutes of the box office opening. They were mostly for 'festival seating', which meant that the

Festivals seemed fun. A girl indulges her fantasies of freedom at the Isle of Wight Festival, August 1969, which drew 150,000 people to hear a bill topped by Bob Dylan.

earlier you got to the hall, the nearer you got to the front. By the early evening of the day of the concert, there were already some 8,000 fans waiting for admission. The show was scheduled to start at 8pm, but at seven o'clock the doors were still closed. Possibly because someone heard the band doing a sound check inside and thought the show had started, possibly also because of the size and impatience of the previously good-humoured crowd, a glass door was smashed and the fans swept into the hall. Before the show had even started, there were eleven people dead and eight injured.

Blame has since been directed at festival seating (which increases the gate while decreasing the need for ticket staff), and the lack of sufficient guards or police with large enough powers, at the tardiness of the hall or the band, and even at the fans themselves described as 'animals' by one editor. In an echo of every official criticism of rock'n'roll since the fifties, New York's deputy police chief, Gerald Kevins, accused the Who – along with Kiss, Led Zeppelin and Earth, Wind and Fire – of 'whipping the kids into a frenzy'.

Whatever the precise cause of the tragedy, it is only surprising that a similar tragedy had not happened before Cincinnati. Indeed, the Riverfront Coliseum itself had been the scene of two earlier 'serious crowd incidents', as *Time* magazine wrote, at a 1976 Elton

John concert and a 1977 Led Zeppelin concert. Pete Townshend thought the problem was the wrong sort of control. 'People in large numbers *need* controlling,' he admitted. 'They're like cattle.' But the question remains, as Townshend himself noted, whether fans are willing to be controlled.

Back in the sixties, the sense of the rock community on the West Coast was a powerful myth. But on the other hand, the history of Haight-Ashbury has already had to be rewritten to counterbalance the summer of love with an influx of weekend hippies, hard drugs and bad vibes. Things were never as rosy as they seemed, love was never as universal as it was imagined to be. The famous Woodstock Festival in August 1969, when half a million fans gathered in a field in upstate New York was rather less of a celebration of love and peace than most people assumed at the time and, like Monterey, rather more like a sordid story of rip-offs, near-disasters, mismanagement and bad acid. But, deluded or not, people spoke of 'Woodstock Nation' with conviction – they wanted to believe in the ability of people to organize their own lives, in the community of rock, in the shared commitment of performers and fans. Even the established press, amazed at the generally peaceful demeanour of 500,000 fans, could credit that this might just be, as Grace Slick had said on stage, 'a new dawn'.

The rude awakening came with Altamont, the free festival at a California speedway track, held on 6th December 1969, and organized by the Grateful Dead and the Rolling Stones as a sort of West Coast Woodstock. The promoter of the Stones' 1969 nationwide tour of America, John Ellsworth Jaymes, said: 'It's a Christmas and Hanukkah gift from the Stones and other groups to American youth.' In view of later events, Mr Jaymes was being a trifle starry-eyed. Early reports from Altamont were equally starry-eyed. 'The scene was very peaceful,' said the San Francisco *Examiner and Chronicle* as the event was just ending. 'The youthful auditors sat on the soil, smoked pot or drank wine, talked or slept – and listened.' 'We should be together,' trumpeted the headline, adding, 'and boy, were they together.' But the newspapers had not heard the news.

From the start, things went wrong. The show, originally scheduled to be held in the Golden Gate Park, had to be switched to the Altamont venue at the last minute, because of a disagreement about film rights. As a result, tens of thousands of fans got lost and the roads were blocked for miles around. As the music started (the first set was from Santana) things began to look bad among the 300,000 strong crowd.

- Hell's Angels battled with fans who tried to mount the stage. The Angels had been hired to keep the peace and they were paid with a few hundred dollars' worth of beer. As a result, they grew increasingly violent – perhaps in response to an increasingly worked-up audience. They knocked Jefferson Airplane's singer Marty Balin unconscious during a performance, but when the band stopped playing, tension in the crowd

142

Ants are better organized. An aerial view of the Altamont festival, 6th December, 1969, where the festival scene found some perspective.

grew worse and another Angel threatened to beat up Paul Kantner. Four of the 'peace-keeping force' beat up a drunk who had kicked one of their precious choppers; some others decided to punish a grossly fat young man who had removed all his clothes – offended by the sight, the Angels clubbed him to the ground. Things got so bad that the Grateful Dead decided not to play, but the Stones reckoned that they would cause even more trouble if they pulled out at this stage.

Jagger was brought face-to-face with the simmering violence as soon as he stepped from the Stones' helicopter. A young man leapt out of the crowd and hit him in the face. 'I hate you!' he was screaming; 'I'm gonna kill you!' Once on stage, Jagger went into his diabolic routine, prancing around for *Jumping Jack Flash* and *Sympathy For The Devil*. Meanwhile the Angels saw a young black called Meredith Hunter pull a gun and aim it at the stage (or so they testified at a

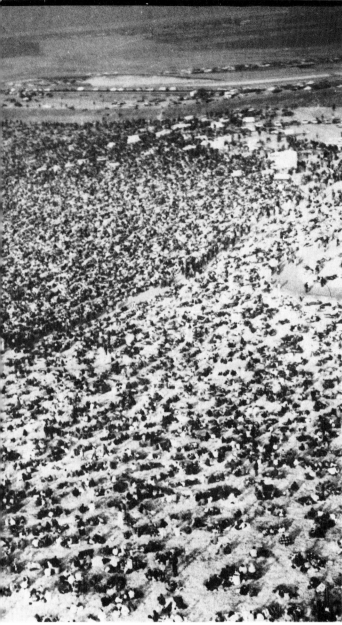

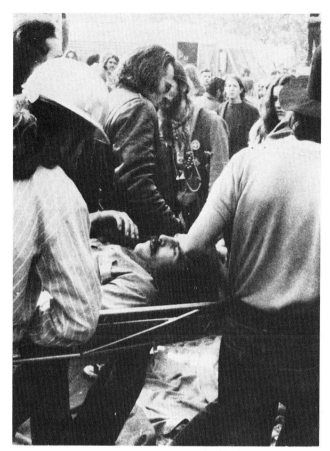

A Christmas and Hanukkah present from the Rolling Stones, the Altamont festival in December 1969 brought the Love Generation to a halt. With four deaths, three births and countless other trip-outs, ODs and injuries, first-aid teams ran out of essential medication.

subsequent trial). They clubbed him with pool cues, beat him with fists and chains and stabbed him five times in the back and once under his ear so that he bled to death. Hunter's gun was never found, but a court agreed it was 'justifiable homicide'. Justifiable or not, nobody seemed able or willing to stop the madness that seemed to take over Altamont.

Robert Santelli, in a book about rock festivals, points out that at Woodstock, for all its faults, the stage became a channel for messages, warnings, information and reassurance. At Altamont it was merely a stage. The Stones, scared to keep playing, at first appealed to the crowd. When that had no effect, they became even more scared to stop, playing for their lives as the rock 'community' shattered all around them. They were stars, the fans were fans – and that was that.

Within two days, the press had changed its tune about Altamont. Most of the fans there had already changed theirs. The *San Francisco Chronicle* headlined a front page piece, 'The Black Aftermath of Altamont'. While three babies were born during the event, three

other people besides Hunter died, and there was a host of serious injuries. Two people died when a car ploughed into their campfire at around midnight on the night after the concert, and another man was killed when he slid into the California Aqueduct Canal while on an acid trip. A man and a woman were hospitalized with severe head and internal injuries. Four medical teams at the site reported treating numerous people for overdoses and bad trips – an emergency supply of sedatives had to be flown in when the medical teams ran out. 'A sea of empty wine bottles and other refuse covered the speedway area...' said the *Chronicle*. 'Officers said several hundred cars were left at the scene, apparently broken down, out of gas or lost by their owners in the mass exodus ...' It would take a week to clean up the remains of this particular present for Christmas and Hanukkah.

As for the Hell's Angels security guards, Melvin Belli, the lawyer retained to represent the Stones said, 'They might have been a little too enthusiastic.' 'If Jesus had been there,' said Jagger, 'he would have been crucified.' Keith Richard commented lamely that 'lots of people were tired and a few tempers were frayed'. The Angels themselves defended their behaviour, saying that they had been hired to 'keep people off the stage'. 'I'm no peace-creep in any sense of the world,' said Sonny Barger, president of the

143

Oakland Chapter of the Angels, who provided the guards. 'If a man don't want to be my friend, I'm going to hurt him and he's going to hurt me.'

The violence and deaths at Altamont have made that festival part of the 'rock'n'roll frame of reference', while Cincinnati, though more recent, is all but forgotten. The reason of course is that no-one was surprised by Cincinnati – shocked, certainly, but not surprised. The deaths of those eleven unfortunate fans failed to impinge on the rock culture because, during the seventies, violence, whether pre-meditated or accidental, had become commonplace. Ten years earlier the deaths at Altamont were unexpected, brutal and not all accidental, producing both a collective revulsion and an endorsement of gratuitous violence that was to reverberate throughout rock for a decade.

The sense of failure that overtook rock in the wake of Altamont especially affected the fans. The age of the lookalike flowered. At one time vast numbers of fans may have styled themselves on Elvis or the Beatles, Bob Dylan or Janis Joplin. They did not consider themselves lookalikes because the look was often more or less universal and unstructured. But care, attention and money were necessary to look like the glitter and glam stars of the early seventies. Among Marc Bolan's, David Bowie's and Bryan Ferry's fans, there were coteries who assiduously cultivated the clothes, make-up, hairstyles and mannerisms of their idols. The look had become the key to the whole style, and rock gigs often became arenas in which fans could achieve a sort of stardom themselves as simulacra of the unreachable hero.

In time, the process became institutionalized. Clubs held Bowie nights when fans tried their hardest to look like the man. BBC TV publicized a Deborah Harry lookalike contest (won by a receptionist from Newcastle-upon-Tyne); Alice Cooper even organized his own Alice lookalike competition (won by a Vietnam veteran on day release from a mental hospital).

Lookalikes even took to the professional or semi-professional stage. Today, there are dozens of Elvis impersonators – some who merely dress up like Elvis (including a Dr Reco H. Shane who, despite rhinestones and jet-black pudding basin hair, looks and sounds exactly like the Beverly Hills dentist that he is), some who look like Elvis (Malcolm Halsall from Scunthorpe, for example, who performs professionally under the name Rupert), some who change their names to Elvis, some who have plastic surgery to make themselves look like Elvis (professional impersonator Dennis Wise says he underwent surgery for over a year because 'I wanted to do something for Elvis').

There has been at least one Jimi Hendrix impersonator (an old friend of his named Randy Hansen), and there have been several Mick Jagger impersonators (including, though he might not admit it, Bob Geldof). In the late seventies, a group of five necrophiliac performers billing themselves as 'Rock'n'Roll Heaven', underwent plastic surgery to make themselves look like Janis Joplin, Jim Morrison, Jim Croce and one male and one female Elvis. What is remarkable about all these people is not the lengths to which they have gone to impersonate dead (or living) stars, but the fact that audiences are often willing to recognize them as acceptable substitutes.

While some fans try and bridge the gap by physically copying their heroes, the increasing inability of rock stars and their fans to achieve a genuine intimacy has also led to violence by fans against performers who distance themselves on stage. In Germany, fans have learnt to throw cans at groups who displeased them. Toledo, Ohio, is known as the firework capital of rock'n'roll since fireworks are popular missiles at rock concerts in that city. In 1976, flying cans and bottles injured more than 50 people at an open-air Queen concert in London. The year before, a fan threw ketchup onto Elvin Bishop's jeans while he was performing in Florida and then broke a roadie's hand with his buckled belt. Lou Reed has been threatened with a knife on stage and in 1979, Cheap Trick's road manager, Kirk Dyer, was cut in the chest, ribs, arm and thigh when he tried to stop a knife-wielding fan from storming the stage at a Texas gig. In the same year, an Australian fan decided to pick a fight with Jerry Lee Lewis on stage. The two men fell against a monitor and Lewis broke several ribs, forcing him to cancel the rest of his tour. In one truly bizarre incident, the American group Wild Cherry were threatened with physical assault as they arrived for a performance. The threat was not, as one might imagine, intended to dissuade the group from playing but to *encourage* them. At the end of their set some of the group and their entourage were attacked anyway.

British punk groups (and some Americans), partly inspired by an antagonism towards the accepted ideas of stardom, cultivated violent abuse as a mode of performance. But punk was a style of dress and attitude almost before it was a type of rock'n'roll music, and more than most other styles, its fans were responsible for its existence in the first place.

It was composed of disparate strands. Out-of-work East End kids with no focus for their discontent, who only found that authority and other people's wealth were oppressive; art college students with a heady disregard for convention and a need for a style of their own; fans whose dreams of a passionate democracy of music had been trampled on by the lumbering mammoth of mid-seventies rock; experimentalists, anarchists and the ill-fitting rebels of a society in mid-collapse; kids who were having no fun, and found that even their anger had no outlet. 'Bored, denied, used, cheated, manipulated, ignored – this is what happens to the youth, the future of Britain,' wrote one London punk in one of the scores of fanzines that sprang up as

145

Rock'n'roll heaven: five singers who were surgically altered to resemble dead stars, 1978. Standing from the left are Elvis Presley (Erin Rhyne) and Elvis Presley (Jesse Bolt). Sitting from the left are Janis Joplin (Mona Caywood Moore), Jim Croce (Marc Hane Brouck) and Jim Morrison (Duke O'Conell).

Spot the difference. Deborah Harry 'lookalikes' pose during a competition run by a British magazine in October 1979. The judges agreed that Ruth Merritt, aged eighteen (top row, second right), was a ringer for Debbie.

an integral part of the punk scene. 'I'm seventeen-years-old and haven't got one qualification at all,' said another, proud to possess 'the most important asset ... common sense.' 'In July 1976 I was knocking around with a few Bowie/Roxy freaks,' said a third. 'They were going to see Slaughter and the Dogs ... also on the bill were the Buzzcocks and the Sex Pistols. It was exciting, raw, funny. I knew straight away it was for me. It was the first time I'd really got into anything.' The punks talked of energy, spontaneity, a life without rules, a life with 'nobody to answer to, nobody to satisfy, nobody to call "sir",' as Danny Baker, co-founder of *Sniffin' Glue*, the best-known of all punk fanzines, put it. Somebody split a T-shirt and held the rent together with a safety-pin – a fashion was born. Somebody liked a certain band and had access to a photocopier – a magazine was born. It was that simple.

Picking up on the New York scene, some people adopted music which had for a long time been called 'punk' because it manifested the same youthful disregard for convention, skill and morality suggested by the word's earlier meaning – the young, homosexual companion of a male tramp. The fetishistic clothing of the increasingly evident sexual fringe was taken up because it, too, pointed to experimentation, youthful sexual licence and a desire to shock.

It all gelled around the music: anger, frustration, rebellion, experimentation and delight focused on the sound and sight of groups of often incompetent musi-

Remember me this way. The 1980 Sid Vicious Memorial Demonstration on the first anniversary of his death. Stars get the fans they deserve – or is it the other way round?

cians playing as if their lives depended on it, but not really caring. It didn't matter what the music was like – because it was the music that had created, in Johnny Rotten's words, 'the entire superband system' and which, accordingly, stood in the way of rock'n'roll touching its audiences. If you were a punk fan, you felt you could become a punk musician.

Spitting (or gobbing), hurling insults and sharp objects, or merely sneering and snarling were as important a part of late seventies' punk performances as playing. As if to demonstrate their contempt for stardom, groups like the Sex Pistols or the Damned turned abuse and violence on their audiences, and the punk fans, who understood what was going on, retaliated by fighting, clawing each other or throwing cans and bottles.

Too often, however, punk groups found themselves gobbing against the wind. In becoming stars, (albeit small-scale ones), they would often have to face audiences who came specially to witness the spectacle of violence. Critic Richard Cromelin of the *Los Angeles Times* panned the Damned on the 1977 tour of the US for not being 'as rude and obnoxious as advertised'. The day after the Cromelin review appeared, the Damned took the stage at an LA club under a hail of ice cubes, bottles and coins. Drummer Rat Scabies threw his drumsticks at the audience, challenging them to a fight. Bassist Captain Sensible took off all his clothes (a nurse's dress and tights) and paraded round the stage. The band's manager joined them on stage to shout 'I'm

fucking sick of you fucking Californians driving your fucking Cadillacs! You're so fucking bored, you don't know what to fucking do!' Instead of simply negating stardom, the band had become anti-stars, with a massive anti-following of anti-fans. They were out of context, and their punk violence was a sham.

One way of avoiding the problems of confronting fans on stage is of course not to appear on stage at all. That was the solution the Beatles hit upon when, by 1966, they began to see their performances as meaningless and potentially dangerous ritual appearances. They retreated into the studio, never to perform live again. Since then, many star rock groups have spent extended periods avoiding live performance. But at the time the Beatles retired, the step was sufficiently risky to convince many people that it meant the end of the group's career. At around the same time, Bob Dylan took an enforced eighteen month break from performing and recording, following his near-fatal motor cycle crash. Most people assumed that nobody could ever come back after eighteen months out of the public eye. The effect of these retreats was, however, quite the reverse of most predictions. Both Dylan and the Beatles continued to be even more successful recording artists.

When Dylan returned to live performance in the seventies, he seemed to have acquired an extraordinary popularity. His first 'come-back' tour, eight years after the crash, attracted six million ticket applications from American fans alone – ten applications for every seat available. Similarly, Bruce Springsteen's 1981 European tour was a complete sell-out, after a five year gap and a disastrous tour in 1975 preceded by a risible media hype. But then Springsteen is one of the few present-day superstars who does seem to comprehend the importance of the star-fan relationship.

But his attitude was all but submerged from 1966, until the punks insisted on bringing it back ten years later. In the intervening decade, confronted by the barrier of the stars' physical absence and by the mysterious depths of songs no longer designed for live performance, fans frequently adopted a sort of code-breaking mentality. To learn the secret language of Bob Dylan and the Beatles would somehow compensate for not being able to see them perform. One would at least be hearing their *authentic* voices. Superstars like the Beatles and Dylan, no doubt fuelled by artistic pretensions and large amounts of halluginogenic drugs, were only too happy to oblige.

Secret messages – hidden in stereo tracking or run-off tracks or disguised in cover artwork – were all the vogue for a while. By late 1969, it was even possible for an elaborate hoax about secret messages to gain credence across the world. An American student publication, *Rat Magazine*, printed an alarming and arcane article in its issue of 29th October, 'proving' that Paul McCartney had died and the fact had been covered up. 'Knowing that perhaps the ruse couldn't last, the Beatles have hinted at the truth in every successive album,' the article said. 'On the *Sgt. Pepper*

Diabolical wizard, proto-punk or plain murderous con? Charles Manson believed the Beatles were sending him messages in songs. His lawyers tried to call John Lennon as a defence witness for his trial on murder charges (23rd April, 1971).

album centrefold (*sic.* – it's actually on the cover), only Paul faces away from the camera . . . On the *Magical Mystery Tour* insert, only Paul wears a black rose . . . *Revolution No. 9* on the double album contains the phrase "I buried Paul" when played backwards . . . *Abbey Road* shows the Beatles walking in single file. The first two, John and Ringo, wear mourning clothes, "Paul" is barefoot and dressed for burial, George follows in the work clothes of an English grave-digger.'

In no time at all, the clues mounted: the juxtaposition of the two final tracks on *Revolver*, *Got To Get You Into My Life* and *Tomorrow Never Knows*, clearly pointed to McCartney's death in a car crash (*Tomorrow* was loosely based on Tim Leary's interpretation of *The Tibetan Book of the Dead*). *Sgt. Pepper* contained a picture of a fat man waving (an Eastern death symbol, said the secret agents), a four-stringed guitar (clearly an electric bass) outlined in flowers and Paul with his back turned. On *Sgt. Pepper* Paul is shown wearing an arm-band with the initials O.P.D. – said to be London police terminology meaning 'officially pronounced dead', in fact standing for nothing more sinister than Ontario Police Department. *Magical Mystery Tour*'s walrus was supposed to be a Viking death symbol. One photograph of McCartney in the 'M.M.T.' booklet shows him seated above a sign that says 'I Was'. The

White Album was littered with secret messages hidden in the tracks – things like 'Miss him, miss him' and 'Turn me on dead, man'. Then, of course, there was the Volkswagen pictured on the cover of *Abbey Road*. Its number plate read, in part, 281F, or, the afficionados pronounced, he'd be *28 if* he was still alive.

Even a sound analyst from the University of Miami got into the act by announcing that scientific evidence proved that Paul's voice had changed more than it was humanly possible since the first Beatles' records. Others discovered a more direct route to the 'truth'. Gazing long enough at the cover of *Magical Mystery Tour* a sufficiently stoned fan might detect a seven figure telephone number picked out in the stars that made the 'Beatles' (I came up with 832–7135). Most of those who undertook this exercise, (and many did, ringing up to try and contact the ghost of Paul McCartney), found themselves connected to the hapless industrial editor of a national British newspaper, but the 'Paul is dead' story itself took a long time to die. McCartney's only comment was to say that he hadn't heard of his own death, but then he was 'always the last person to know of anything in the Beatles'.

The success of this hoax demonstrated just how loony fans can be. But there have been worse examples. Most tragically was the case of the Tate-LaBianca killings in 1969, when the psychotic petty criminal and failed song-writer Charles Manson deluded himself and his Californian followers into believing that the Beatles' White Album contained confirmation of his lunatic neo-Nazi theories. Having predicted a bloody race war from which he and his followers ('the Family') would emerge as survivors and leaders, Manson interpreted several songs on the White Album, (*Blackbird*, *Piggies*, *Revolution 1*, *Revolution 9* and, most notoriously, *Helter Skelter*), as support for his fantastic visions. 'The Beatles are telling it like it is' he used to say to the Family. 'Helter Skelter' became Manson's name for the race war. Convinced that the conflict needed a little encouragement (and, presumably, imagining that he had the tacit backing of the Beatles), he ordered Family members to commit a series of brutal murders (including that of movie actress Sharon Tate and her house party). To help throw blame onto black militants, Manson instructed his assassins to daub slogans like 'Death to pigs', 'Pig' and 'Helter Skelter' around the murder sites in the victims' blood.

For the Beatles themselves, even this particularly gruesome association was no more than an embarrassment. Despite a much-publicized but somewhat half-hearted attempt to call John Lennon as a witness for the defence at Manson's trial, it barely impinged on their lives.

Even when fans actually pursue stars after-hours, the result is usually little more than a mild irritation. They hang around the stars' houses, or outside recording studios, hotels and stage doors, but usually they will settle for a glimpse or an autograph. For some stars, even such relatively harmless displays of interest and affection are more than they would wish to handle. 'Imagine sitting in a house like this, nice as it

House-husband to be: on 15th September, 1975, two months before the birth of their son, Sean, John and Yoko go out to eat. Despite temporary retirement, Lennon couldn't help being a public phenomenon, a target for intrusive journalists, photographers – and fans.

Daily Mail

MONDAY, DECEMBER 15, 1980

12p

Archbishop prays as millions join last, silent tribute to John Lennon

THE FINAL FAREWELL

THE Sun

Thursday, December 11, 1980   12p

TODAY'S TV: PAGES 14 and 15

STARTS TODAY

A super Sun exclusive on superstar Lennon

THE WILD WAYS OF JOKER JOHN

TODAY'S FASCINATING EPISODE—CENTRE PAGES

Newsweek

THE INTERNATIONAL NEWSMAGAZINE   December 22, 1980

John Lennon°
1940–1980

Number 51

WHY DID HE MURDER MY DADDY?

From COL ALLEN in New York

HEARTBROKEN Yoko Ono told last night how she explained John Lennon's death to their five-year-old son, Sean.

The bewildered little boy had asked her: Why was my daddy killed?

She spoke out only minutes before the former Beatle was secretly cremated.

Lennon was gunned down by 25-year-old Mark Chapman in New York on Tuesday.

Yoko's sad talk

PRESS 12   2345 HRS   12-8-80   20 PCT
1 W.72 ST., REPORT OF A MAN SHOT.
VICTIM REMOVED TO ROOSEVELT HOSP.
NOTHING FURTHER AT THIS TIME.
OPER UNIT- PO VAN ARSDALE

Left: The first police teletype report of a shooting on New York's West 72nd Street. The victim turned out to be John Lennon.
Below: Bagged for the last time. John and Yoko had appeared publicly in bags during their 'political' period in the early seventies. In a final irony, John Lennon's body was removed for cremation in a bag, 10th December, 1980.

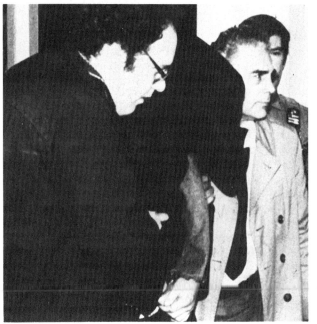

is,' said Barry Gibb of the Bee Gees during the height of their popularity, 'and not being able to go outside because of all those people going past.' 'It's like living in a goldfish bowl,' he said, echoing the star's eternal lament.

Once the illusions have been put on the market, it is no easy matter to withdraw them from sale. For star and fan alike, these illusions are often their most precious possessions – the means of achievement and success for one, the dream of achievement and success for the other. When Mark Chapman killed John Lennon, Lennon had just re-emerged from five years' retirement. He had tried to be an ordinary resident of New York City, made a point of being part of the street scene, chatting to people openly, even autographing an album, a few days before he died, for the man who would shoot him. He may have got away with the pose of Ordinary Joe under other circumstances, but not with a new album in the charts. That made him a star again and reminded the public that he had once been a

Left: Mark Chapman, handcuffed and hidden by a blanket, is led away to face charges for the murder of John Lennon.

Beatle. To try and be an ordinary, home-loving, bread-baking husband and father *and* an ex-Beatle was a supreme exercise in cake-eating and having. To do that in public through the medium of press and broadcast interviews, releasing records celebrating his ordinariness and his successful passage through the dark night of Beatleness, was an affront to a fan like Chapman who virtually worshipped Lennon.

The consensus among many commentators on the circumstances of the Lennon shooting was that Chapman thought he was destroying a symbol, not killing a human being. This is a comforting thought, perhaps, but entirely wrong. Chapman knew he was killing a man – the man that he was not. But he was also murdering himself, or at least that part of himself that had made the journey with Lennon from stardom towards an attempted ordinariness. 'I don't believe in God . . . I don't believe in Beatles,' Lennon had sung. In the ten years that followed, Lennon's rough edges were planed down and he re-emerged, with Yoko, on the *Double Fantasy* album as a complacent homebody, but still a star. If he had kept his passion or lost his popularity, things might have been different. As it was, the 1980 version of John Lennon measured for Mark Chapman his own failure. Lennon was privileged enough to *want* to be ordinary. Chapman could never accept such an ambition for his idol, any more than he could come to terms with his own in-

ability to be extraordinary.

After the shooting, the BBC interviewed some people on the streets of Liverpool. One of them said that Lennon should never have left his home town. It had been a kind of betrayal, and his death a kind of punishment. When the Beatles moved to London in the sixties, their local fans in the north west held a demonstration against them. London meant stardom, meant separation, and the local kids who had breathed life into the Mersey scene knew that it was they who would be left behind. One of the group's earliest fans recalled to Liverpudlian writer Mike Evans how they felt the night Bob Wooler, the Cavern's DJ, announced that *Please, Please Me* had reached Number One. 'It was awful, because the reaction was the opposite to what they expected. Everyone was stunned. That was the end of it as far as we were concerned.'

There is an ironic postscript to the Chapman story. The killer's autographed copy of *Double Fantasy* was left outside the Dakota building after Lennon had been shot. It was propped against the wall at the spot where Chapman had been standing, reading *Catcher In The Rye*, while he waited for John and Yoko to come home on the night of 8th December, 1980. A fan picked it up and handed it in to the police. They returned it to the finder, who at once became the possessor of one of rock's most treasured relics. From the jail cell where he is now serving twenty years, Chapman announced his intention to sue for the album's recovery. His aim, said his lawyer, was to auction the album and give the proceeds to the American hand-gun control lobby.

I know what it's like to be dead. Fans mourn John Lennon outside the Dakota Building in New York, where he lived and was shot by one of their number.

BLINDED BY THE LIGHT

In 1956, an American Pentecostalist minister named Albert Carter condemned rock'n'roll as irreligious. 'The effect of rock and roll on young people,' said the minister, 'is to turn them into devil worshippers; to stimulate self-expression through sex; to provoke lawlessness; impair nervous stability and destroy the sanctity of marriage. It is an evil influence on the youth of our country.' While most teenagers might have answered, 'Right on!', the first flush of rock'n'roll resulted in moral panic – an outburst of fervent condemnation which ran from Reverend Carter's diatribe through the censorship of songs and performers to the elevation of an American payola investigation in 1959 to the status of national crisis.

The rockers themselves were deeply affected by all this. Many of them came from religious backgrounds from among the black or poor white communities; Elvis, for instance, never cast off the yoke of belief that supports Southern fundamentalist Christianity. He acknowledged his debt to God as a matter of course; it was more significant by its casual acceptance than any debt he might have thought he owed to human beings, his fans or the democratic system. Under attack for his lewd performances, Elvis would appear in public as a humble, god-fearing boy. He survived the moral outrage of the time because he thought he could challenge God on His own ground. Others, however, were less certain of their righteousness.

Confused by the significance of what he was doing and condemned for marrying his thirteen-year-old cousin, Jerry Lee Lewis was forced into temporary retirement. Rock'n'roll, he has always said, will send him to hell. 'I *know* the right way,' he said. 'I was raised a good Christian. But I couldn't make it.' Despite his conviction that Jesus Christ is not inclined to do 'a whole lotta shakin'', Jerry himself (like Elvis, a member of the evangelical Assembly of God), is unable to break himself of the habit. Riding the conflict has required a vast consumption of booze ('I used to have to drink a fifth of tequila to sober up and do my shows,' he once said), and a variety of drugs. As a result, Lewis's career has been marked by violent swings of mood and catastrophic incident. In 1979, 'strung out on pills . . . like a wild Comanche', he was pulled off stage at Baton Rouge by his cousin, TV and radio evangelist, the Rev. Jimmy Swaggart. Jimmy took him home, poured all his whisky and pills away and looked after him for a week. 'I guess it saved my

life,' said the old reprobate – a reformed character, at least until the next time.

Little Richard Penniman became a gospel student following that 'vision' on an aeroplane over Australia in 1958. ('It was at the time they sent the satellite up,' he said, 'and I was on tour with Eddie Cochran, Gene Vincent, and it was a fantastic, monstrous tour.' They couldn't, as the song goes, get much higher.) Perhaps becoming a preacher was just like joining another branch of show business, but the lure of rock'n'roll for this most flamboyant of the early black rockers was too great. He found the perfect excuse – rock'n'roll was to be the way he could 'teach love, because music is the universal language'. The Reverend Carter can't have approved, but Little Richard was not the only rocker to try and square the circle.

British rock'n'rollers were also prone to the call of God in those early days, though generally in a more quiescent manner. Brian Locking, who had backed Terry Dene before replacing Jet Harris in the Shadows, became a Jehovah's Witness, like Dene, in 1963. Hank Marvin, also from the Shadows, waited until 1973 before joining the same sect. Marvin, a father of six, seems to have been something of an exception – a successful performer who came to religion out of a positive sense of wonderment. 'I'd started to question the amazing things in nature that couldn't happen by chance,' he explained. 'I felt there really must be a creator and decided to get involved.'

The best-known convert of all in early British rock'n'roll remains Cliff Richard, who became a committed Baptist in the early sixties. Ironically, in Cliff's second film – *Expresso Bongo* (1959) – he played an innocent pop star whose manager devised the crafty strategy of having him present himself as a god-fearing, mom-loving boy in order to make the transition from teen-rave to star performer. The strategy, of course, had already been demonstrated in real life by Elvis Presley. Cliff, however, discovered a well-spring of sincerity which has enabled him to be actively involved in the evangelical movement, while periodically reviving his reputation as a raunchy rocker. When questioned as to how he can sing rock'n'roll and still support moralistic and ultra-conservative organizations like the Festival of Light (anti-abortion, anti-indecency, pro-hanging and so on), Cliff resorts to a philosophy of pop values, innocent love and good, clean fun. Claiming to have remained celibate since 1965, Cliff is the perfect example of a performer who has reconciled one of rock'n'roll's central conflicts by learning how to be in two minds at once.

Christ you know it ain't easy. Johnny Rotten crucified for the Easter issue of Melody Maker, 1st April, 1977. The picture was suppressed.

153

Ham with cheese. Cliff Richard, God's other son, accepts a gift of dairy produce from Miss Teenage State of Victoria, 19th July, 1960, on behalf of charity.

The conflict, of course, is between rock'n'roll's spirit-elevating impact and its crudely physical form and sexual symbolism. Rock'n'roll does not make you fuck, but it might make you want to fuck, or even feel like you already have. Repressive religious morality cannot tolerate anything that suggests that spiritual pleasure can be the result of physical stimulation.

The attacks on rock's irreligiosity and alleged immorality have continued through the years. In 1966, John Lennon told journalist Maureen Cleave of the London *Evening Standard* that 'Christianity will go. It will vanish and shrink. I needn't argue about that. I'm right and I will be proved right. We're more popular than Jesus now. Jesus was all right but his disciples were thick and ordinary.' This display of bravado was probably occasioned by no more than Lennon's increasing antagonism to the Beatles' 'mop top' image. As later commentators have pointed out, it was, in part, an accurate assessment – in the popularity stakes Jesus at that time was probably fourth or fifth behind Karl Marx, Mao Tse Tung and the Beatles (maybe Mohammed or Buddha or Elvis could also have given Him a run for His money). But Lennon was speaking in a Christian country and did his case no good by an ignorant comment about Christ's disciples. Inevitably a fuss ensued. It was worst in America where the extreme right of politics had already discovered the Beatles had to be communist atheists. It was only too easy for many people to believe that Lennon had advocated Beatlism as a state religion or that he had

154

claimed that Ringo Starr was the son of God.

It all added fuel to the fire of such men as the Rev. David Noebel from Billy Hargis's Christian Crusade. 'In the excitatory state that the Beatles place these youngsters into,' the Rev. David somewhat inelegantly pronounced, 'these young people will do anything they are told to do . . . One day, when the revolution is ripe, the Communists could put the Beatles on TV and could mass hypnotize American youth. This scares the wits out of me.' To the followers of David Noebel and his ilk, the day of ripeness seemed to be drawing nearer. Radio stations across the Southern states organized 'Beatles bonfires' to burn the group's records and ephemera. At first Brian Epstein and then Lennon himself were obliged to make some sort of apology. The fuss died down, but the group's image never quite recovered its middle American appeal.

Anti-rock sentiment has never disappeared among some evangelical Christians. At the end of the seventies, two 'born again' Minneapolis brothers, Steve and Jim Peters, began a career for themselves in this area. As ordained ministers, the brothers (in their mid-twenties when their crusade began), took as their text the warning that 'listening to rock music will be harmful to your spiritual, emotional and mental health'. In a little over a year, the brothers reckoned to have burnt and otherwise destroyed more than half a million dollars' worth of records, tapes and memorabilia associated with performers as diverse as Led Zeppelin and John Denver, Kiss and Linda Ronstadt (not forget-

Which one's Cliff? Evangelist Billy Graham recruits Cliff Richard (right) to the cause, at Graham's London rally, 16th June, 1966.

ting the dear old Beatles). The brothers' act featured a lecture, cunningly entitled 'What the Devil's Wrong with Rock Music?', in which they make some farcical claims, including that Mick Jagger is a 'proud and practising' homosexual, Barry Manilow is evil, Janis Joplin would have died of venereal disease if the drugs hadn't got her first, an album by the Alan Parsons Project features on its cover the veiled faces of girls with syphilitic sores, John Denver intends to become God, Kiss is an acronym for 'Kids In the Service of Satan', and the Eagles' *Hotel California* is about Satanism. Most of this is on the same level as earlier claims of extreme rightists about the Beatles. ('Norwegian wood is British teenagers' slang for marijuana' said the John Birch Society's rock spokesman, Gary Allen, about one song title; *Strawberry Fields*, he said, referred to the practice of planting marijuana in strawberry fields

because, according to Allen, the plants looked alike.)

Predictably, the Peters' paranoid version of rock'n'roll is replete with secret messages. The boys' mother, Josephine, first discovered such messages in a Beach Boys album brought home by a third brother. 'I sensed it wasn't Christian,' she said, and went on to describe how the family got rid of such Satanic instruments as the television set. 'The life-styles, lyrics, intentions and album covers of many of the rock stars,' said Steve Peters before each burning, 'are perverse, immoral, profane and unscriptural.'

It's fair to say that rock'n'roll has always stepped outside the boundaries of the established Christian churches. It is, after all, a music that espouses rebellion and eschews the order so necessary to official religion. But it has the energy, faith and abandon of less orthodox religious experiences. Theologically inclined propagandists who detect the dangers of mass hys-

Happiness is a hot disc. After Lennon remarked that the Beatles were 'more popular than Jesus', during summer 1967 Beatle burnings – like this one organized by station WAYX in Georgia – were repeated across America.

MAHARISHI'S FLYING CIRCUS

teria in rock performances are only observing a genuine emotional power from an external point of view. Rock'n'roll, at its best, has always been a spiritual music with roots in devotional forms (black gospel music, for example), as well as music celebrating secular ecstasy.

Two important things happened to rock in the sixties to transform the music's spiritual nature. The first was the tremendous success of large numbers of musicians who found that their power on stage was not, after all, matched by the ability to survive off it. The second was the education of a generation into a philosophy of 'love', inspired at first by the western world's infatuation with permissiveness and liberalism and fuelled by the apparently mystical revelations of LSD.

By 1967, the Beatles had stopped touring, there was growing and destructive over-indulgence among the members, Brian Epstein was being increasingly suicidal (he made his first, unsuccessful attempt in September 1966), in fact the group seemed on the verge of complete collapse. George Harrison reacted particularly strongly to the group's personal failure. Late in 1966, George and his wife Patti went to India, for George to study the sitar with one of its leading exponents, Indian musician Ravi Shankar. George's musical ambitions had already led him to experiment with the sitar in 1965. The ostensibly pastoral and mystic orient exercised a strong pull on many young westerners in the sixties, and for George Harrison, swamped in the mire of the Beatles' confusions, the sitar was more than just a novel instrument with an unusual sound – it was a repository of faith, spiritual awareness and beauty. It pointed to a way out. Ravi Shankar introduced Patti and George to his guru, Tat Baba, and the couple – who had already flirted with acid-inspired mysticism – became more and more attracted to the oriental view of life.

Back in England, word reached Patti about the Maharishi Mahesh Yogi, an Indian guru with a marketable line in meditation – a mantra-based technique backed up by some simplified and easily assimilable Hindu philosophy. The Maharishi's system was known as Transcendental Meditation (TM). The guru himself giggled a lot, clutched flowers and claimed to be bringing the West some profound and spiritual message that its materialistic, militaristic culture had ignored. (TM turned out to be so deeply spiritual and pacifistic that it was subsequently adopted by the US Navy as part of basic training, while the Maharishi eventually formed an investment organisation called The Age of Enlightenment Company.)

Patti Harrison joined the Maharishi's Spiritual Regeneration Movement in 1967, while the Beatles themselves were too busy with *Sgt. Pepper* for much meditation. The seed was sown, however, and when news broke that the Maharishi would be visiting

Britain in the summer, all four mop-tops decided to give him a try. The Beatles met the yogi in August, 1967, at a lecture in the London Hilton Hotel and agreed to accompany him to a weekend retreat in Bangor, North Wales, for a further dose of spiritual castor oil. Accompanied by wives, girlfriends, Mick Jagger and Marianne Faithfull, the Fab Four journeyed by special train from London to Bangor. The press and fans were out in full strength. The stars were sent off with screams and popping flashbulbs, the whole scene seemed awash with flowers. Jagger sneered that it was all 'more like a circus than the beginning of a religious event', and Cynthia Lennon got left behind on the platform.

While they were still in Bangor with the Maharishi's 300 other students, the press reporters brought the Beatles the news of Brian Epstein's death. It was, without doubt, a shock. Whether it had been accident, suicide or murder, it could not, however, have been a surprise. Under the circumstances, the Maharishi's advice to 'be happy' (spoken, no doubt, with a giggle) was probably as much as they could have expected from anyone, but his presence did act as a buffer. Media coverage soon guaranteed the Maharishi a solid reputation as someone who mattered to the Beatles, and the group members sang his praises and lauded meditation to the skies.

Beach Boy Dennis Wilson was the next big-name rock star to discover the Maharishi, who was, by later 1967, touring the world with his somewhat banal message. 'I shook his hand, and all of a sudden I felt this weirdness, this presence, this guy had,' said Dennis, who would later say much the same thing about Charles Manson, before the latter was revealed to be a psychopathic killer. (Dennis knew Manson as 'the Wizard' and put him and the Family up in his house for a period, during which, according to an acquaintance, the Family ran up – and Dennis paid – the biggest gonorrhoea bill in history.) Nevertheless, the Beach Boys (Mike Love in particular) were sufficiently taken with the Maharishi to become involved in TM. Can they really have been attracted by the appalling predictability which he displayed the first time he spoke to Dennis Wilson? '"Live your life to the fullest,"' remembered Dennis, 'was the first thing he ever said to me.'

The Beach Boys, like the Beatles, were in something of a mess. In 1964, their leading light, Brian Wilson, had had a nervous breakdown and had collapsed on a plane. 'I was run down mentally and emotionally because I was running around, jumping on jets from one city to another on one-night stands,' said Brian. He was also producing, writing, arranging, singing, planning and teaching, in a punishing schedule that allowed no time for relaxation. On the occasion of his crack-up he had only been in the air five minutes when he told Al Jardine he was no longer able to cope. 'I started crying,' Wilson recalled. 'I put a pillow over my face and began screaming and yelling, and I started telling people I wasn't getting off the plane . . . The rubber band had stretched as far as it would go.'

Brian Wilson retired to his home where he continued to compose and produce, becoming increasingly eccentric over the next couple of years. He installed a sand-box in his dining room containing eight tons of sand so he could bury his feet in it while playing the piano. He experimented with LSD and other drugs and sought to investigate 'the mind-expanding possibilities of music and the mind-expanding possibilities of drugs'. He picked up on astrology and health-foods (even opening a shop called 'The Radiant Radish'); he picked up on numerology and the *I Ching*. He radically revised his sex life ('refrains from coming' was how his wife described it). He also managed (he has since said) to destroy the tapes of an entire Beach Boys album, to have been called *Smile*, because it 'was destroying me . . . it just wasn't my kind of music'. Rumour had it that he had actually burnt the tapes, as a result of an apparent delusion that some tracks on the theme of fire had caused some buildings in Los Angeles to burn down. It may be, of course, that the appearance of *Sgt. Pepper* in 1967 was the real reason why Brian shelved *Smile*. The Beatles' album certainly ruined his self-confidence and, although many tracks from *Smile* were eventually revamped, appearing on a variety of records, Brian never again displayed the sure touch of his early career.

The rest of the group moved further adrift from their main creative talent. They refused to put their name to his songs. Brian himself has said that his drug consumption in the mid-sixties was phenomenal. 'I'd bought a lot of hashish,' he recalled on one occasion. 'It was really a large purchase, perhaps $2,000 worth . . . and the music was getting so influenced by it . . . I mean, we had to lie on the floor with the microphone next to our mouths to do the vocals.' By 1967, the group were having immense business and legal problems with their record label, Capitol, as well as bitter internecine disputes. These generally revolved round the creative hub of Brian Wilson and concerned how close each of the others felt to him; brothers Dennis and Carl Wilson tended to line up against Brian's cousin, Mike Love and his old school friend, Al Jardine.

In 1967, TM seemed to be the glue that could prevent the imminent disintegration of the group. They embraced it wholeheartedly, at least for a time, following Dennis Wilson's conversion. Mike Love and Al Jardine became teachers of TM (Love remained closely involved), and even Carl Wilson endorsed the Maharishi's system. 'I meditate regularly,' he said. 'Bad things, or rather difficult things, affect me less. I find that it relaxes me very deeply and gives me energy. I recommend it highly.' If TM seemed like some new superdrug – tranquillizing, stimulating, non-addictive, cheap and safe – that was perfectly acceptable to rock stars who were, whether they knew it or not, still looking for the perfect high.

When assorted stars followed the Maharishi to his Indian hideaway at Rishikesh in early 1968, the guru

fad really began. Of course, not everyone wanted a guru. Mick Jagger had already condemned the Maharishi as a fraud during his stay at Bangor. Life in the Meditation Training Centre was not to everyone's taste, although it did allow them to escape the prying eyes of the press. The trainee meditators, including the Beatles, Mike Love, Donovan and Mia Farrow, had been booked in for three months: but Ringo and Maureen left after ten days, complaining that the Centre was rather like a holiday camp with too many flies, too much heat and too many spices in the food. Paul McCartney and Jane Asher found the whole episode tedious – although it gave McCartney time to write several songs. When they left Rishikesh, Paul told the press that while the Maharishi was 'a nice fellow', neither he nor Jane were 'going out with him any more'.

John and George held on until, as John later said, 'There was a big hullaballoo about his trying to get off with Mia Farrow and a few other women.' Even George felt uneasy and Lennon himself wrote *Sexy Sadie* (in which Sadie, who 'made a fool of everyone', was meant to be the Maharishi) for inclusion in the White Album. The yogi's technique, said Lennon, was just 'coloured water'. And yet religion and the yogi's style of leadership grew in popularity. 'Pop is the perfect religious vehicle,' said Donovan at the time, in a flower-power echo of Little Richard's earlier pronouncement. 'It's as if God had come down to earth and seen all the ugliness that was being created and chosen pop to be the great force for love and beauty.'

One could hardly miss the message of love, but the appeal of gurus and mystical faith generally for rock stars seems to have had far more precise foundations. They promised some sort of order and therefore some sort of control in the chaotic and unbalanced world of rock'n'roll, and they offered inspiration, energy, and not least, a justification for doing what some rock stars were increasingly doing mechanically, lackadaisically and without conviction. Even the doubting Lennon eventually found a guru of his own in Dr Arthur Janov, a psychiatrist who had developed primal therapy, a form of treatment which required its patients to scream their way through repressed experiences. Brian Wilson also settled for psychiatry in the seventies when he put himself temporarily in the hands of one Dr Eugene Landis, after flirting with several other faiths, including the guru cult of Subud, which he heard about from the Byrds' Jim McGuinn. This cult was founded by the Indonesian mystic Pak Subuh and promotes the concept of a universal church. (It also demanded of McGuinn that he change his name to Roger – Subuh's name had been changed on the advice of a passing beggar while he was still a child and the change apparently effected a miraculous improvement in the infant guru's health.)

The Who's Pete Townshend discovered the Persian Sufi mystic, Meher Baba, during the group's US tour in 1967, when he met some of the guru's followers in California. He spent a great deal of energy devising new rock strategies to define himself as a spiritual seeker, and was joined in this exercise by former member of the Faces, Ronnie Lane. As with most gurus, Meher Baba – whose motto was 'Don't worry, be happy' – seems to have been content to let his message work at a very subtle level. (He died in 1969, after a self-imposed silence of over 40 years.)

Townshend doesn't proselytize, despite creating works like *Tommy* and *The Seeker* which revolve round his appreciation of Baba's philosophy. In fact his attitude to Baba is distinctly pragmatic. At the beginning of 1972, he made the trek to India where he stayed with Baba's family and disciples, visiting Baba's tomb and kissing the holy ground. 'I felt like a speck of dust,' he said. 'It was fantastic.' Baba's followers stood round the tomb singing the guru's favourite song, *Begin The Beguine* and Pete Townshend felt deeply moved. It was not, he said, 'a flirtation with the Maharishi thing', but neither has it solved the manifest problems of being a rock star. It has given him some equanimity, however. 'Jaded and worldly' as he confesses to be, Townshend said in 1981 that 'this is where Baba wants me to be. The rock business is a lousy world but I've got to work through it.' Any excuse, as they say.

Sufi mystic, Meher Baba, averts eyes from his disciple, Pete Townshend. Baba's motto was 'Don't worry, be happy.' Townshend doesn't seem so sure.

Guitarists John McLaughlin and Carlos Santana found a spiritual mentor in the seventies in their own Hindu guru, Sri Chinmoy. McLaughlin (who was known as Mahavishnu) has since rejected Chinmoy but used to say that 'my music is an offering to the Supreme Being . . . God is the Supreme Musician, the soul of music and the spirit of music. I'm trying to reach him by allowing myself to become his instrument.' Devadip (Santana's spiritual title) told *Rolling Stone* in 1980 that his conversion followed directly on his rapid rise to stardom. 'I got slapped by reality,' he explained. 'Platinum albums in my house, drugs, food, flesh and all those kind of things, but I felt such an emptiness . . . I was not taking my time to acknowledge my inner body.' Nowadays, his inner body tells him that 'perfect perfection . . . is the goal. Being at absolute oneness with the creator.'

Former Spooky Tooth vocalist, keyboard player and songwriter, Gary Wright, was introduced to the teachings of his guru, Paramahansa Yogananda, by George Harrison. The result was, according to Wright, 'the complete re-channelling of my energies'. A best-selling album, *The Dream Weaver*, followed in the mid-seventies. During the recording, said Wright, 'for the first time I took real control,' which is an understandable ambition for someone who emerged from a band as inconsistent and badly organized as Spooky Tooth. After his conversion, Wright expressed the view that 'groups are psychologically obsolete . . . Ideally,' he said, 'if you're in a band it should be, "Well, fellows, let's function as a company. We're in here to make money." But it never happens, so someone's got to take charge.' No doubt, it has made his manager's job easier to have been told by Gary, 'Dee, you may be my business manager, but Paramahansa Yogananda is my spiritual manager.' Manager Dee Anthony was blunter but nearer the point when he said, 'I told him, "Don't spiritualize yourself out of the business." If hymns were hits I'd be managing Moses – right?'

In a relentless pursuit for spiritual well-being which had already taken him up a hill in Cornwall for several days and nights and over to the mountain retreat at Rishikesh, George Harrison himself moved on to His Divine Grace, Guru A. C. Bhaktivedanta Swami, founder of the International Society for Krishna Consciousness. George had become infatuated with Hinduism – giving up meat, drugs, drink and (almost) cigarettes. He meditated for hours on end and recorded devotional ditties like *My Sweet Lord* (which sold a million) and albums with weighty philosophical titles like *All Things Must Pass* and *Living In The Material World*. The former Beatle seemed to find a certain peace of mind in Krishna Consciousness; when he wasn't turning hymns into hits he performed hits as though they were hymns.

In 1969, the Swami was seen leaving London Airport in a Rolls Royce lent by John Lennon. By 1973, he was able to afford to buy a fleet of his own. George Harrison, meanwhile, produced records by the Swami's followers – a group of saffron-robed, shaven-headed monks of both sexes who habitually danced up and down major thoroughfares of big cities wherever their temples were situated, jingling bells and chanting 'Hare Krishna, Hare Krishna.' (Hence George's irreverent nickname – Harry Georgeson.) In 1971, this chant, produced on record by George and released over the name 'Hare Krishna Temple', became a top ten hit.

The next year, George bought an Elizabethan manor house and seventeen acres of ground just outside London as a religious headquarters for the sect. The 55-room mansion houses 63 sect members and cost £250,000. George also helped to buy a building for their London temple. By 1973, it was revealed in the press that the Hare Krishna organization in England was making £400,000 from the sale of incense. Their merchandizing company was known as the Spiritual Sky Scented Products Company.

George's religious fervour was soured by his split with Patti, and by a plagiarism suit which accused him of stealing the melody of *My Sweet Lord* from the old Chiffons' hit, *He's So Fine*. He was eventually found to be guilty of 'partly unconscious plagiarism' and had to pay damages of around £250,000. By the mid-seventies, the man who had once described himself as 'just the servant of the servant of the servant of the servant of Krishna' was finding it hard to cope with the realization that while his life might have belonged to 'the Lord Krishna', the Lord Krishna steadfastly refused to live it for him.

Keeping his options open, Carlos Santana lights a candle to his guru, Sri Chinmoy, while Jesus looks benevolently on.

I wanna hold your hands. George Harrison poses with Shiva in 1971.

The guru followers have rendered unto Caesar that which is Caesar's and unto their Lords . . . a prayer of thanks, perhaps, that they need no longer question what they are. The poor old superstars can feel so burdened by their position out front that they need a god or a guru to put themselves back in perspective. Sometimes, the burden may seem intolerable – or so dangerously attractive, that substantial compensation is needed to ease the 'sacrifice'. Repressive faiths may be the solution.

Cat Stevens, after toying with Buddhism for a while, converted to Islam, assumed the name of 'Yusuf Islam' and has now retired from the mainstream music business. Leading English folk-rockers, Richard and Linda Thompson, also converted to Islam, but continued to perform. Mike Heron (formerly with the Incredible String Band), disappeared into Scientology. Michael Schenker of UFO joined the Christian sect, the Children of God, as did Fleetwood Mac's Jeremy Spencer, who was last seen selling tracts on a street corner in London's West End, and confessing to his former sins as a godless rock star.

Some performers are drawn the other way. Led Zeppelin's Jimmy Page discovered Aleister Crowley,

Cat among the Muslims. Yusuf Islam – formerly Cat Stevens – marries a Turkish woman named Fawzia in a London Mosque, 7th September, 1979.

Led Zeppelin as a group have had a peculiarly tragic record of untimely death and severe accident associated with themselves and their entourage.

In 1976, Zep associate Keith Harwood died in mysterious circumstances; Keith Relf, formerly of the Yardbirds, which formed the nucleus of Zep, committed suicide; and the wife of Zep's road manager, Richard Cole, also died. In 1977, Robert Plant's five-year-old son Karac died of a virus infection while the group was touring America. The next year was relatively disaster free but in 1979, Philip Hale, a photographer friend of Jimmy Page's, died at one of Page's homes after ingesting too much morphine, cocaine and alcohol and, in 1980 – at another of Page's houses – John Bonham met his untimely end.

Graham Bond, one of Britain's finest R&B organists, was also fascinated by Aleister Crowley. (At one time he fronted a band called Magick.) In the seventies, lack of recognition seemed to compound an unfounded and paranoid belief that he was Crowley's bastard son. In 1974, the delusion got the better of him and he killed himself by throwing himself under a train 'while the balance of his mind was disturbed'. It took the police two days to identify the body.

For the most part, however, black magic, satanism and the occult are merely fertile sources of shock imagery for bands devoid of any superior resources with which to get themselves noticed. Like the similar crop of late-seventies groups employing the symbols and styles of Nazism, their goal is outrage for its own sake. It is an indication of how bankrupt much of rock'n'roll has become that it should so readily accept diabolical imagery as an acceptable, not to say familiar, part of 'entertainment'.

Another aspect of this creative bankruptcy has been the recent spread of 'Born Again' Christianity among the rock community. Bob Dylan was rock's most notable convert – along with many of the performers on his mid-seventies' 'Rolling Thunder' American tour. Born-Again Christians – now something like a startling 40 per cent of all Americans – include Roger McGuinn (in yet another conversion), Donna Summer, members of the group Kansas and many others. As a religious movement, born again Christianity is a hodge-podge of differing ideals and philosophies, encompassing views from the centre to the extreme right of the moral and social spectrum. What unites it is the sense of reaction, a feeling of having gone too far or far enough on the wrong road, a desire to turn back and try another route.

Bob Dylan is hardly a conservative in the traditional mould, however, nor was his conversion a sudden acquisition of spirituality. On the contrary, Dylan has always been one of rock's most spiritual and most challenging performers. But now he has channelled his spirituality into a safe bywater. The poetry and intensity of Dylan's work in the early sixties may have been secular and political in a fairly narrow way, but it was always infused with a humanism that was more than merely mechanistic. After his motor-cycle crash, he began to trace his cultural heritage which eventually led him to flirt with

the leading Satanist of his day, who claimed to practise 'magick'. Page was involved in an occult bookshop in London and even bought Crowley's old mansion, Boleskin House near Loch Ness, where, he says, strange things have been known to happen. Jimmy Page is loath to talk about his beliefs or 'involvement in magick' in any detail, merely hinting darkly at mysteries experienced and as yet unexperienced. He claims, too, not to be interested in making 'converts' to Crowley, whose ideas are attractive to him because, he says, they are aspects of 'the unknown'. Among those also associated with Crowley have been experimental film-maker Kenneth Anger (for whom Jimmy Page once wrote some soundtrack music) and Robert Beausoleil, one of the Manson gang, currently doing time for torturing and murdering musician Gary Hinman.

Despite the fact that Page is careful to say he 'takes precautions' with his 'magick', it was rumoured at the time of Led Zeppelin's retirement that one reason for their split was an uneasy feeling that Page's activities might have had something to do with John Bonham's death. This is patently absurd – Bonzo's death was the result of years of over-indulgence of one sort or another. On the other hand, Page's mysterious association with 'magick' is bound to lead to that kind of superstitious sensationalism. It is certainly true that

The Born-Again Christian nearly saved . . . Bob Dylan still on the edge of sanctity, during his 1978 world tour.

Judaism (the religion of his parents). Some critics have detected in his work an obsession with the Tarot, and, some time in the seventies, Dylan employed a 'psychic guide' to assist his passage.

Unlike John Lennon, whose evident spirituality was far more diffusely expressed, Dylan seems to have remained untouched by either left-wing politics or feminism in the seventies. Certainly, the break-up of his marriage and the ensuing messy battle for custody of the five children revealed Dylan as something of an old-style patriarch. In this light, Dylan's conversion makes a good deal of sense – especially when, in 1979, a friend of his revealed that 'he hasn't given up Judaism, he just discovered Jesus.' Indeed, while fans barracked him as he returned to the stage with a 'gospel' show, an organization called 'Jews for Jesus' gave him their blessing and Pat Boone – one of the first of the Christian pop singers – 'lent his support to the Dylan crusade', as a newspaper put it at the time.

If Dylan's Christianity means anything, it is that all the conflicts and struggles that emerged in the sixties and were embodied in rock'n'roll have not been resolved. There is, of course, no reason why they should have been after only a few short years, but Dylan and his Christian cohorts feel the need for such a resolution and, in being 'born again', they have rendered the life of the spirit itself quite unthreatening to themselves. They have wiped away the sense of risk that gives true rock'n'roll its edge.

Once upon a time, Dylan believed in rock'n'roll and it caused a furore – but in a 1977 interview with Jonathan Cott he said, 'There's no more rock'n'roll, it's an imitation, we can forget about that; rock'n'roll has turned itself inside out – I never did do rock'n'roll.' Once he believed in the here-and-now. Not any more: 'I believe in life, but not this life.' Once he believed in the power of feelings to move and in the power of music to make feelings happen. But now he 'doesn't believe in emotion'. 'The highest purpose of art is to inspire,' Dylan said before his Christianity was fully formed. But afterwards, he produced art which was so much a caricature of inspiration – patriarchal, sloganizing or sentimental drivel, for the most part – that even (or perhaps especially), life-long fans booed him at performances which occupied the cosy niche of Lord-praising. One thing of course remains. 'I have to play in front of people just to keep going,' he says.

The banality of most rock conversions is, without doubt, their single outstanding feature. For the most part, a reassuring smile or being taught a breathing exercise are enough finally to destroy the last vestiges of rationality clinging to the wasted skulls of rock stars. If you lead a life of such ineffable confusion as is generated by mass adulation, large-scale drug abuse and late nights, it is probably only to be expected that nothing but the simplest of things will hold any mystery.

Eric Clapton's conversion was effected backstage during the Blind Faith tour of the US in 1969. 'Two guys came to my dressing room,' he later told Steve

162

Turner (himself a Christian). 'They were Christians and they said "Can we pray with you?" I mean, what do you do?' Clapton got on his knees and prayed. The experience evidently made him 'feel much better' – something like 'the blinding light', he said. For some unexplained reason, he wanted to show the two men a poster of Jimi Hendrix but, when he unrolled it, there was a picture of Christ inside it which, he said, 'I had never seen in my life before.' The possibility that someone might have put it there without his knowledge doesn't seem to have occurred to him. At once, he became a devout Christian.

That this trite experience effected a conversion suggests that the need for faith was already there, waiting for a trigger. Whatever else religion was for Eric Clapton, it was clearly something bigger than him, something that could control events as he had discovered himself unable to do. But Clapton discovered that if faith can move mountains, it often fails with considerably smaller things, like people. One of them was himself – for whom love and heroin were destined to become far stronger influences on his life than faith. The others were George and Patti Harrison. When Clapton learned their relationship was breaking up, his faith was shaken. 'The fact that George had been into TM for so long yet couldn't keep his wife . . . I mean, his wife just didn't want to know,' said Clapton. 'All she wanted was for him to say "I love you" and all he was doing was meditating . . . It caused him to treat her bad. Although it wasn't Christianity, I can

see Christianity in the same situation doing the same thing.' Once Clapton's heroin addiction was defeated and his career on the up, he and Patti finally got together. An embittered George now had *his* faith shaken, but Eric's found its pragmatic level. 'I still pray,' he told Turner, 'and I still see God in other people more than I see him in the sky or anything like that.'

Clapton did at least write and record one superb religious song – *Presence Of The Lord*. Perhaps for some, conversion is a sign of complacency and advancing age, rather than a symptom of continued struggle. Like most of the musics from which it has borrowed, rock has never accepted the 'civilized' distinction between spirituality and physicality. As such it cannot be acceptable to the puritan (of whatever denomination) but it can be, in the widest sense of the word, a religious music. It is only when it stops working that the need is felt to inject faith from the outside.

Perhaps the last word should come from the Reverend Joel Agnew, black-satin clad and dog-collared pastor of the First Church of Rock'n'Roll, based in Niles, California. His leather-jacketed and denim-clad congregation pay $2 each a time to worship and they number in the hundreds. The church plans to start its own record label, Behemoth. 'For thousands of years the devil has been getting the credit for Saturday night,' said Agnew in 1980. 'Rock'n'roll has always been a religion – an alternative to the bullshit.' While Bob Dylan's badly-received Christian album, *Saved*, lay about in unsold piles in the shops, the Rev. Agnew announced that *his* church's aim was 'to work towards the more perfect party'.

In the presence of the Lady. Having lost Christianity Eric Clapton found Patti Boyd Harrison, seen here at the premiere of Tommy, *1975. They were married in 1979.*

FAKING CARE
OF BUSINESS

The rock'n'roll business is probably no more corrupt than any other business, but it is extremely sensitive to allegations of malpractice. Its operations are entirely based on the idea that it is selling talent and popularity, which is why allegations of record hyping have always been greeted by dismay, denials or excuses. 'Sure, there was hype,' said the then president of Capitol Records, Voyle Gilmour, commenting on the breaking of the Beatles in America. 'But all the hype in the world isn't going to sell a bad product.'

Hyping can take many forms, but its ultimate aim is always to create exaggerated reputations for records and acts through expensive, elaborate advertising and promotional campaigns. In the late sixties, subtlety came to be all important; record companies supported magazines like *Rolling Stone* even though they sometimes criticized the industry, because such magazines had the necessary 'counter-cultural credibility'. In the same way, the industry brought in so-called 'company freaks' like Danny Fields at Elektra or Billy James at Columbia, whose very belief in the acts they hyped charmed away all suspicion of corruption. The record industry put on a counter-cultural face and annual sales went through the billion-dollar barrier. The companies held parties at which journalists, disc-jockeys and TV producers could mingle with the rock elite; the straight-laced accountants and cynical businessmen who ran the industry stayed at home; at Christmas time, they gave away tasteful little *objets d'art* instead of envelopes containing bank-notes. This sort of hype was so much more effective once rock had become established as the dominant area of the music market, stressing the values of artistry, integrity and youth identity rather than the more traditional values of earlier kinds of mass appeal music. In the fifties, things had been a little different. The major form of hype took an altogether less subtle form. Its name was payola.

Payola is a particular kind of corruption involving the payment by direct or devious means of disc jockeys and broadcasters for playing specific records. Not only is it intended as a form of promotion, generating extra record sales, but it also makes money directly in the form of royalty payments. Payola had been an established part of the music business, since the late nineteenth century when composers, publishers and song-pluggers would pay performers to feature their

songs, employ them as 'consultants' or give them spurious song-writing or arranging credits. But in 1959, the music business was changing beyond all recognition. In that and the following year, Congress investigated the fixing of popular quiz shows on American television. Not only were the contests often fixed, but several music publishers were also kicking-back a percentage of their song royalties to quiz-show producers who had featured the publishers' songs on their programmes. There had already been murmurings from another Congressional committee about gangsters fixing juke-box plays, and from the Federal Communications Commission (FCC) and the music business trade papers about payola itself.

Most of the publishers concerned in the quiz show scandal were members of the American Society of Composers, Authors and Publishers (ASCAP), a licensing and royalty collecting agency that represented the old tin-pan-alley establishment of Hollywood and Broadway. But since 1940, ASCAP had been in deep rivalry with a new organization, Broadcast Music Incorporated (BMI), which represented much of the new rock'n'roll business and was specifically geared to dealing with the burgeoning community of radio DJs. So, as an issue of the trade paper *Variety* noted at the time, 'ASCAP songsmiths . . . take the credit for switching the spotlight from TV quiz rigging to disc jockey payola'.

The major record companies and radio networks came out of it relatively unscathed. The investigations had done them a service by focusing on rock'n'roll – a monopoly-breaking music that had been nurtured by independent record companies, was heard mainly on independent radio stations and was published by independent publishers. The payola scandal stifled the entrepreneurial spirit that had pushed Elvis Presley, Chuck Berry and Buddy Holly to the fore. Rock'n'roll became a dirty word among broadcasters. Radio playlists came under increased scrutiny and tighter control so that anything risqué, raucous or merely innovative would almost certainly be thrown out along with the records that might once have clearly been hyped. Of course, by 1959 many of the innovative companies were themselves turning to a safer, cleaner sort of teenage music than rock'n'roll had been in 1955 and 1956, but the payola investigations set a sort of legislative seal on the process: this was 1960, election year, and right-of-centre America was asserting itself once more.

Payola, of course, wasn't an invention of ASCAP, major companies or government agencies. The boss of one small record label admitted to paying out $2,000

Who's kidding? Elvis tries a novel method of slimming Colonel Parker's share. The bogus Colonel Tom set the tone for rock'n'roll personal management when he took Presley over in the mid-fifties.

165

Alan Freed had been promoting mixed rock'n'roll package tours like this one from the early fifties – and ensuing riots brought him to the notice of the courts twice before the Payola scandal broke in 1959.

each month in payola and most of the DJs who lost their jobs confessed to accepting excessive amounts of cash or expensive gifts to play records. But for a small company, without the resources of the majors, payola was often the only way to get a disc-play and, in any case, the investigative dice were loaded.

A number of the FCC commissioners were themselves receiving bribes from major broadcasting companies – a fact which threw a new light on their threats to revoke the licences of over 5,000 smaller radio and TV companies under investigation. A counsel for the Congressional Committee investigating payola expressed views which were distinctly anti-rock. 'Suppose John Smith owns a record company,' he said, 'and then buys a broadcast station. Suppose he dumps its personnel and its good music format to push his own label, generally only rock'n'roll . . . Now, that's not in the public interest.'

The most tragic victim of the investigations was DJ Alan Freed, the man who claimed to have coined the expression 'rock and roll' back in 1952. Freed always promoted an 'authentic' version of rock'n'roll. He was not well liked by the powers that were, and over-enthusiastic response of fans at his concert promotions twice led to his arrest. Although a popular and successful figure, he always remained on the fringe of the entertainment industry. He certainly took payola in spite of earning a substantial salary and receiving money for public and film appearances and from concerts he promoted. He was given spurious writer's credits on several hits and he confessed to taking gifts 'if I've helped somebody . . .'. 'But,' he said, 'I

166

wouldn't take a dime to plug a record. I'd be a fool to; I'd be giving up control of my programme.' This by now familiar argument didn't stop him losing his job on a New York radio station – he sobbed as he announced his resignation over the air – nor did it prevent him being sacked from the *Big Beat* TV show. He was arrested for receiving $30,650 from six record companies, eventually receiving a six month suspended sentence and a $300 fine on a partial guilty plea. In 1964, he was indicted for evading the tax on this payola income and the next year he died drunk, broke and all but forgotten in a Florida hospital, aged 42.

Dick Clark, *American Bandstand's* clean-cut 'emcee', had no such problems. Clark owned or part-owned six music publishing companies, three record labels, one pressing plant, one record distributor and one management company. He owned sixteen songs as a publisher, most of which were 'free gifts'. Clark's network TV show was, of course, immensely influential in popularizing clean-cut Italianate pop idols. The show was aimed at a family audience and was specifically designed to launder rock'n'roll of its rebellious, arrogant, black and sexy image. It also brought in between $10–12 million a year in advertising revenue. When Clark was due to appear before the payola investigations, ABC told him that he would have to give up either *American Bandstand* or all of his other interests which conflicted with it. He chose to stay with the show, and at the hearing where he was star witness, the committee chairman told him, 'You're not the inventor of the system or even its architect. You're a product of it.' The chairman, who had himself been obliged to give up a 25 per cent share in a TV station,

Above: Payola roll blues. DJ Alan Freed arrives with his wife Inga at the New York District Attorney's office, 30th November, 1959. Implicated in the Payola scandal, Freed refused to testify before a Grand Jury. It marked the end of his career.

Rock jocks busted shock – Alan Freed (second right), programme director Mel Leeds (third right) and DJ Peter Tripp (fourth right) arrested in New York after being accused of commercial bribery by the Grand Jury investigating Payola, 10th May, 1960.

Below: Good guys wear white. 'American Bandstand's' Dick Clark shows his ring of confidence as he testifies that he never took Payola before the House Legislative Oversight Sub-Committee, 29th April, 1960. Clark gave up all his other interests rather than lose his position as host of 'American Bandstand'.

had a final testimonial to make. Clark, he said, was 'a fine young man'. When Alan Freed made his last, tearful, appearance on his (non-network) TV show, a young girl was heard to sob the teenagers' testimonial: 'They've taken away our father.'

If the 1959 payola scandal achieved anything of moment, it was to make sure that the next phase of musical innovation came from outside America and that many American musicians of originality with any sort of commitment to a genuine popular music were turned off rock'n'roll until 1964. The one thing it didn't do was put a stop to payola. Gifts and free records may have replaced direct cash payment, but in one area at least the gift-giving seems to have reached dramatic levels. They even labelled it 'drugola'. Certainly, in the mid-seventies, record company offices and studios were often the most reliable places to find an itinerant drug dealer if one was needed, and drug use is almost universal in rock today. One notorious recording studio was well-known in the seventies for debiting drug purchases to the accounts under the guise of 'gardening expenses'. 'In the advertising world, it's martini,' said one record producer in 1973, 'in the music world, it's cocaine.'

The record industry in Britain has long been less susceptible to classic payola than in the USA – largely because airplay is governed by the charts and these are compiled exclusively, if unreliably, from record sales. The energy of the British record business is thus centred on chart hyping. One easy and relatively undetectable way to guarantee airplay is to buy a record a chart position. With a few hundred pounds and a list of the 450 shops that now make sales returns to the market research organization which compiles the BBC charts, it is a matter of little more than legwork to push a record into say, the bottom of the Top 40 or to nudge it from second place to number one. The effect is of course even better than with advertisements because once in the charts a single will sell on almost guaranteed airplay.

In fact 'shopping' (which is how the practice of buying records into the charts is known) is often considered too inefficient and obvious for successful chart hyping. Since a 1978 press investigation in the London *Sun* and *Daily Mirror*, which dealt with a number of well-known artists on the A&M label, it has become clear that one of the most popular techniques is now to offer 'favours' (free records) to dealers in return for entry in the sale diary which is used to compile the charts. This is particularly useful for hyping albums which might otherwise prove too expensive to buy into the charts. In return for recording a non-existent sale, the record dealer gets a free record of a different title. These come under the category of promotional albums for the record company, so there are no royalties to pay and the whole deal is very cheap to operate. There need be no secret shopping trips, no special agents and no disguising of intent – the ordinary record company reps. give 'favours' as a routine aspect of their work. In addition, it means that whatever

happens, more of the company's product gets around – so everybody, except for the deluded public and the performers and writers concerned, is happy.

Ironically, the most notorious British payola scandal to date focused on precisely the kind of music – traditional sentimental ballads – that hardly ever makes the pop charts but which can earn an awful lot in royalties from continued record play on light music programmes. The details were first revealed in 1971 by the *News of the World*.

The newspaper reported how orgies had been organized for BBC producers and disc-jockeys at a flat in Mayfair; how former singer Janie Jones had procured girls and arranged yet more orgies for radio figures; how a young female record plugger offered herself as an inducement along with free copies of the record she was handling and sealed envelopes containing used banknotes. All stirring stuff, despite the fact that nobody had ever heard of most of the people involved. Fifteen arrests were made but most were cleared of all charges. A loudly-trumpeted Scotland Yard investigation into chart-rigging followed on the newspaper exposé but without result. Accusations against singer Dorothy Squires were dismissed when she was shown to be entirely innocent of any involvement in the scandal. One freelance TV producer (who had already made a clean sweep of it before the exposé was published) was fined £100 for accepting £25 from one of Jones' associates to feature a group called Demon Fuzz (of all things) on his BBC show. Janie Jones herself was jailed for a few years for doing something immoral, which was an affront considering that all the men who were only too eager for her to do it got off scot free. And that was the end of that.

DJ Peter Myers, questioned at the time of the American scandal in 1959, commented that what was wrong with payola was 'the siphoning off of money in front of the artist's anticipated royalties'. Indeed, in all this wheeling and dealing, it's sometimes easy to forget that it is the performers and the public who prop up the whole edifice. The public at least has the illusion that it is getting what it wants, but performers often get precious little of anything. The standard argument is that without the industry pushing from behind, the artists would have no hope at all. 'Godammit,' says the archetypal music biz fat-cat, 'they ought to be proud that I think they're worthy hyping.' For many, proud is all they'll ever be.

In both the UK and the US, ripping off performers is virtually a music business institution. The musicians concerned too often accept it as just one more way in which they 'pay their dues'. In America particularly, black musicians have always been the most frequent victims of contractual rip-offs. The small record labels in the fifties – like Atlantic and Chess – were able to attract black artists because majors were often dilatory in paying royalties or giving composer credits.

If they don't actually falsify returns, or refuse to pay royalties, record companies (large and small, alike) often charge a contracted artist for studio time, hotel expenses, the cost of hiring instruments or vans – almost anything they can get away with. Under the terms of some contracts, the profits made by one record could be appropriated to pay for the next or any subsequent follow-up. Since much more care is invariably taken over follow-ups and since successful acts are supposed to make albums as soon as possible after hit singles, the resulting expenditure sometimes leads performers into a sort of debt-bondage.

In the fifties, Leonard Chess of the Chicago-based Chess Records (where Chuck Berry, Muddy Waters and numerous other R&B performers recorded), gained a reputation as a particularly exploitative record company boss. Chess – a Polish immigrant who started out running a number of downtown dives with his brother Phil – had an undeniable talent for money-making. His musical ear was more debatable. 'He knew nothing about it,' said Etta James, who went to Chess in 1960. If Chess was an astute businessman, it was an astuteness largely informed by venality. That he discovered many important performers and nurtured others cannot be doubted, but he never let musical sentiment interfere with his money-making drive.

Many companies in the fifties felt that the gift of a Cadillac or a new wardrobe of smart suits was enough to discharge their responsibilities to their artists. Atlantic Records' Jerry Wexler once defended such an attitude by saying of Leonard Chess's relationship with his artists, 'He recorded them – that's what's important.' Important it was and important it remains, but it didn't pay the bills.

In the early days, rock'n'roll performers were the 'white niggers' of the music business. The managers looked upon them as short-term talent and short-term investments. A typical rock'n'roll operation was run during the late fifties and early sixties by Irving Micahnik and Harry Balk in Detroit. These two managed Del Shannon and Johnny and the Hurricanes, among other less successful acts. They took 20 per cent of their artists' earnings and signed them to their own record label, Twirl, at the ludicrous royalty of $1\frac{1}{2}$ per cent, which was low even by the standards of the day. (Atlantic paid between three and five per cent.) Out of this royalty, artists often had to pay their own recording costs. Meanwhile, Twirl would lease its recordings to other companies at a rate of 8 per cent – giving Micahnik and Balk $6\frac{1}{2}$ per cent of every record sold to the public.

Businessmen could make a small fortune if one record hit, but there was no incentive to nurture a performer's career. Performers with hit records, meanwhile, could all too easily find themselves in debt as recording costs mounted for follow-ups and as they spent money on hotel accommodation, new equipment and all the accessories of stardom. Such performers might make money on live appearances (at least, until the concert circuit also became subject to grossly exploitative business operations), but it was rarely enough to cover the costs of the recordings and promotions that were considered necessary by the business as a whole to sustain a career.

Even performers who were regarded as long-term prospects, could become suspicious of the way their affairs were being handled. A well-known example is Norman Petty's dealings with Buddy Holly and the Crickets. Holly himself broke with manager-producer Petty in 1958, partly because he wanted to handle his own affairs and direct his own career and partly, so it seems, because of the arrangements Petty had imposed for the disposal of Holly and the Crickets' income. Petty seems to have had absolute control over almost all the money that Holly and the Crickets made. As a result, suspicion grew that he was withholding money that was not legitimately his. After splitting with Petty, Holly actually took legal action to try and recover money from his former manager – and in the end it was lack of cash that forced him to undertake his last fatal tour.

This case is complicated by the split between Holly and the Crickets and by Holly's death – more so by the way that all parties concerned seemed to rely on verbal agreements. Petty denies all accusations of malpractice and the surviving Crickets express few recriminations, noting Petty's crucial role in the development of their careers. But, after speaking with everybody involved (except, of course, Holly himself), Holly's biographer, John Goldrosen concludes: 'It is my own judgement that Holly and the Crickets probably never saw much of what was rightfully due to them. Though they may well have been paid all that was *legally* due them, in the entertainment business more than in any other industries [sic], what is fair and what is legal is [sic] often worlds apart.'

The music business changed quite dramatically in the wake of the Beatles. For one thing, many of the managers and new industry figures who emerged were little more than amateurs. Their motives for entering the world of rock'n'roll were often complicated by personal attachments to the performers with whom they dealt, or by private ambitions which went beyond the simple goal of money-making.

Brian Epstein, a masochistic homosexual, was sexually attracted to the Beatles (Lennon in particular). His liking for 'rough trade' was damaging in more than one sense. After his death, dark rumours circulated about the exact cause, which, it is said, had more to do with rubber masks and suffocation than overdose or suicide. At times during his life, he would disappear for days, eventually turning up bruised and blackened by one of his anonymous acquaintances. At other times, he would phase himself out of the daily struggle between his respectable middle-class background and his turbulent, guilt-ridden sexuality with the help of large quantities of sleeping pills. His was, inevitably, a desperation suffered in silence and remorse and he would go to almost any lengths to live out his fantasies and then to live them down. Spurned by Eric Burdon, with whom he had quite hopelessly fallen in love, he took LSD to 'get closer to Eric's mentality'. At home he would dress up in drag and sing songs – Lionel Bart accompanying him on the piano. In 1966, he was rushed to hospital suffering from an overdose and a

The Brian Epstein stable – from the left, four Beatles, Gerry and three Pacemakers, Brian Epstein, and two Dakotas on each side of Billy J. Kramer. Where are they now?

year later he died as the result of another.

No doubt, Epstein's sexual proclivities extended to a fondness for the paraphernalia of the torture chamber so beloved of masochists, and there is perhaps somebody who can say for certain how Epstein spent his lonely last weekend, but they're not telling. The chances are that another decline into the sado-masochistic twilight was followed by familiar dreadful recriminations, only this time – with the Beatles drifting from him, weekending in Bangor with a new, if short-lived, father-figure in the Maharishi Mahesh Yogi – on August 27th, 1967, he took one or two pills too many and escaped forever.

Perhaps it is no more than the traditional showbiz link with homosexuality, but a substantial number of rock's successful managers (especially those with British operations) are gay – a situation that seems to have been current since the first days of British rock'n'roll. No doubt, the sexual ambivalence of the male rock star's image – much remarked on since Elvis – has encouraged this trend. The managerial role itself combines power and benevolent paternalism in a way that echoes a distinctly male notion of sexuality.

Like Epstein, the Who's co-manager, Kit Lambert, was homosexual. Like Epstein, too, the very success of his wards seemed to leave him in an emotional vacuum, increasingly filled by drugs and casual sexual encounters.

Lambert began his career in film-making. He planned to make a film of a pop group with a fellow assistant director, Chris Stamp (brother of actor Terence). While casting round for a suitable subject, they came across the Who playing a gig at the Railway Hotel in the London suburb of Harrow, and took over their management.

170

Brian Epstein, clutching a Queen, arrives at a press conference, 5th August, 1966, to apologize for John Lennon's 'blasphemy' about the Beatles and Jesus. Within just over a year Epstein would be dead.

Lambert was soon indulging a taste for drugs which eventually began to take over his life. In Los Angeles, he was introduced to cocaine and a variety of other more-or-less exotic drugs and, while continuing to work with the Who, he rapidly became preoccupied with drug-taking. He evidently harboured an ambition to die young (his father, composer Constant

Daily Mirror

•NO WONDER
THE MIRROR
OUT-SELLS
THE FIELD..'

EPSTEIN
(The Beatle-Making) Prince of Pop
DIES AT 32

BBC 'News-Stand' pays a remarkable
tribute to the favourite daily
newspaper of 15,786,000 readers

Bottles
taken
from
his flat

Broadcaster
Connell

ELECTIONS

Unknown

**THE QUIET MAN FROM LIVERPOOL
WHO RAN A 'STABLE' OF STARS**

Lambert, had died of alcoholism at the age of 40). By the time the Who had actually achieved a level of success which guaranteed their independence and continued profitability, Lambert – whose inherited wealth, efforts and inspiration had been crucial to the band's survival – had effectively dropped out of the managerial picture. In 1972, he bought himself a small, decrepit palace in Venice. When not buying drugs, he spent much of his money on rebuilding the foundations of this property. He called himself Baron Lambert and, living in one room, he entertained himself by taking heroin and indulging in a succession of good-looking Italian boys. By 1976, his friends and family had made him a ward of court and he was persuaded to return from Italy to live at his mother's house in London, where they could keep an eye on him.

On 5th March, 1981, he returned home at 2.30 in the morning from an evening spent at a regular night-club haunt. The owner said he had been only a little drunk when he left, but added that Lambert was an habitual drug user who craved company and frequently lied to gain sympathy. 'I would describe him as paranoid,' said this man.

He arrived home penniless, claiming to his mother that he had been mugged and had had his wallet and keys stolen. However despite blackened eyes, the inquest found no sign of injuries beyond those 'consistent with the manner of his death'. At home he had fallen off a chair, dropped a cup of coffee and fallen over on his way to the bathroom. On leaving the bathroom, he had fallen downstairs and fractured his skull. He died in hospital three days later when his family agreed to switch off his life support machine. He was 45 years old. His blood, tested in hospital, had

The world's press waits for news outside Brian Epstein's house on 27th August, 1967. Epstein had been found dead in bed that morning but no details were released until later in the day. He had apparently overdosed on pills but a question mark still hangs over the precise cause of his death.

171

Finders and minders of the Who in the sixties. Chris Stamp (left) was the son of an East End tugboatman (and brother of actor Terence Stamp), while Kit Lambert (right) was the son of composer Constant Lambert, a product of public school and Oxford. No class distinction here.

contained significant levels of alcohol, heroin or morphine, and tuinal.

Whatever the private motives of men like Epstein and Lambert, the illusion they fostered about their professional relationships with their acts was one of mutual support. The model, of course, was Presley's manager, the self-styled 'Colonel' Tom Parker – a former carnival hustler and erstwhile manager of country singer Eddy Arnold.

Parker single-mindedly devoted his entrepreneurial efforts to Presley – or rather, to the Presley empire. The kindest argument is that such a relationship between performer and manager comes about because certain managers realize that only by nurturing a talent can it be brought to full flower – the implications being that such managers care for their performers, that the performers respect and trust their managers and that money only enters the relationship as the due reward for unique artistry. In fact, self-interest is more likely to be the true foundation of such management practice.

Much of the mystery about Elvis clears once you consider his relationship with Col. Parker. The measure of this relationship can be gained from the fact that, while Parker took 25 per cent of Elvis's earnings as a performer according to the terms of their first contract, by 1963, the two had signed a merchandizing deal in which Parker received 50 per cent of net earnings from the vast range of Presley souvenirs and memorabilia which still flood the market. Since his first studio sessions in 1954, Presley has sold around 300 million records and generated an estimated $5 billion worth of business, by far the greatest portion of

which derived from merchandizing, the apparently interminable series of lamentable Hollywood movies he made in the sixties and his later appearances in Las Vegas cabaret. All of these aspects of Presley's career reveal the hand of Col. Parker – ever concerned with where the most money could be made with the least fuss and bother. Parker's personal financial requirements became particularly extravagant during the seventies, when approaching his own seventies, he was doubtless concerned to get the most out of his remaining years. Parker's particular vice was gambling. 'Colonel Parker is the best customer you ever had at this hotel,' the general manager of Hilton Hotels Las Vegas International told the owners in 1972. 'He's good for at least one million dollars a year.' (Indeed, in 1973 Parker sold the complete Elvis catalogue to RCA for $5.4 million and a guarantee of $500,000 a year against royalties for seven years, just to raise some cash.) Before Hilton took over the hotel, Parker had signed Elvis to a five year exclusive deal at the International which paid a bare quarter of the going rate for an entertainer of Presley's stature. While Presley's earnings were severely limited by this deal, the hotel found itself in the remarkable position (for a Las Vegas establishment) of making vast profits from its live entertainment. In return, the Colonel was treated royally, given unlimited credit on the gambling tables and, on top of his cut of Presley's earnings, eventually received a $50,000 annual fee from Hilton Hotels for 'promotional services'.

Elvis Presley was not a clever man, and his extravagance was notorious. In spite of much outraged surprise at the diminished size of the Presley estate at the hands of Colonel Tom (which is the subject of a long-running legal wrangle, as yet unresolved), at least Parker had tried to guide Elvis from the start, even if it was sometimes into arenas unworthy of the King's talent.

Brian Epstein also thought that he had nothing but his clients' best interests at heart. But unlike Col. Tom, Epstein had four wilful and determined clients able to act with the assurance of their own collective strength. They grew away from Epstein and the evidence suggests that, in doing so, they found themselves ill-equipped to run their own affairs – ultimately almost breaking themselves in pursuit of the utopian fantasies epitomized by Apple, where money was lost hand-over-fist through mismanagement, idealism and plain stupidity.

Well-intentioned or not, Epstein actually left much to be desired as a businessman (possibly because *no-one* had had any experience of running this sort of business before). Like Colonel Parker, he became heavily involved in merchandizing and increasingly distant from any notion of his clients' developing talent. Parker, Epstein and their like were managers who saw their clients as long-term investments. Instead of taking a quick profit on a high turnover of short-lived acts, these managers stayed with their acts and 'nurtured' them. They may have been less than competent businessmen, but they knew (or rapidly became aware) that if successful rock performers could be an almost inexhaustible well of money, they could also dry up artistically in the process. In an attempt to

reconcile art and commerce, a new kind of manager was born.

'People see now that they can become millionaires by doing it right,' said Elliot Roberts who, through an interconnecting network of friendships, came to manage Crosby, Stills, Nash and Young, Joni Mitchell, Jackson Browne and the Eagles in the sixties, eventually founding Asylum Records with a young booking agent named David Geffen. Roberts' hip management style – 'doing the right thing by the artist' – is different from the approach of a Colonel Tom Parker because his idea of 'the right thing by the artist' is different. But in terms of artistry, independence or taste, the manager's prime concern remains the making of money – even if no longer just for himself. If that goal demands the contentment of performers, then contentment is what's offered – it may be a little harder to arrange than a Cadillac or a regular supply of heroin, but then it may actually keep the performer making records and concert appearances for a lot longer.

The long-term contracts which became standard industry practice in the sixties by no means satisfied all performers – even when they offered apparent security. The Beach Boys, for example, used to call Capitol Records – to whom they were signed – 'Captive Records' and tried to set up their own label, Brother Records. Other performers have found that low royalty rates – which might have seemed suitable for a new career being financed by a risk-taking man-

---

A picture speaks a thousand words: Colonel Parker, saving breath.

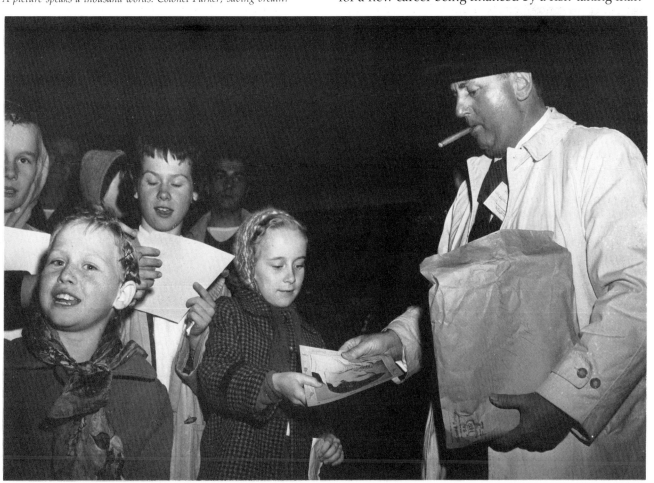

ager or record label – have allowed the business people to enrich themselves disproportionately after success has been achieved.

Some managers have gained reputations for intemperance, understandable in anyone involved in such a competitive arena as rock. In New Zealand, John Reid, the fiery Glaswegian who manages Elton John, once flattened two local journalists who had spoken disparagingly of Elton's sexual preferences. He spent three weeks in jail. On another occasion, he hit a San Francisco hotel doorman over the head with a cane. 'I've given him more than a black eye,' Reid said about Elton, displaying a certain fecklessness even in anger. Always prepared to lay blame wherever convenient, Reid fired two of his executives after Elton's record, *Ego*, failed to make the charts. Reid's 'workaholism' and his apparent lack of sentimental attachment ('I have Elton, family, friends, work,' he says, 'I can't give to a woman as well'), may well explain his temper.

Peter Grant, Led Zeppelin's manager, is a veritable whale of a man who worked as a wrestler for some time just to make money, and harboured an ambition to become an actor, even doubling for Robert Morley in films. In the fifties, he collected tickets at the 2 I's coffee bar in Soho and subsequently became a tour manager for Gene Vincent, Little Richard and Jerry Lee Lewis. Later he managed the New Vaudeville Band. The band were thrown out of Italy in 1967 after a row about fees – one member, Mick Wilsher, and their road manager, Richard Cole (a long-term associate of Grant's) were arrested. Grant threatened to sue, but the band were later accused by the Italian authorities of 'fraudulent insolvency' and 'unlawful appropriation'. Peter Grant became manager of Terry Reid and Jeff Beck in 1968, and then masterminded Led Zeppelin's meteoric rise through 1969 and 1970.

In 1973, following the unsolved theft of more than $200,000 in cash from a safe at the New York hotel where Zeppelin were staying, Grant pleaded guilty to a charge of harassment, resulting from an incident in which he seized a roll of film from a press photographer at the scene of the crime. In early 1978, Grant, Richard Cole, Led Zep's drummer John Bonham and one of their 'minders' (John Bindon) were found guilty of battering security guards during a backstage altercation at a Led Zep concert in Oakland, California. The four were sentenced to probation in their absence. 'I won't stand for people taking advantage of the group,' Grant used to say about Led Zeppelin – and, no doubt, he meant it.

Don Arden was a singer who worked as a compere on early rock'n'roll package shows in Britain. After compereing one of Gene Vincent's early tours, Arden decided to manage him. By the seventies, he was overseeing the career of one of the world's top-selling groups, the Electric Light Orchestra. His image is of an uncompromising businessman, but it is, he insists, *only* an image. 'That's the biggest joke of all,' says Arden, 'and everyone has fallen for it . . . In this business you've got to be tough and that kind of image

174

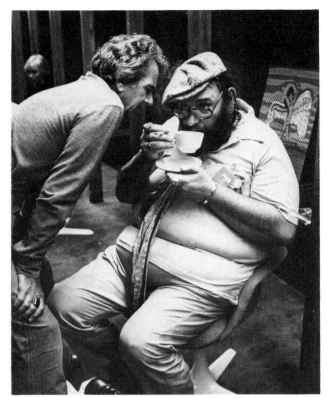

Peter Grant, the man behind Led Zeppelin, takes coffee (1977).

does come in useful.'

Indeed, Arden once prided himself on being one of the few real men left in an industry riddled with 'drug addicts, homosexuals and hangers on'. These days he describes himself as a 'pussycat', a man whose motto may well be his own comment that 'you don't succeed by being a softy'.

Sensational gossip is notoriously rife in the rock world, full of preposterous stories about people who send wheelchair catalogues to their enemies or who threaten to nail recalcitrant promoters' feet to the floor. Periodic rumours that certain rock'n'roll deaths have been the work of contract killers are backed up with little or no evidence. Yet death threats *are* made – and not always by warped fans. Elton John received several as a prelude to his retirement in 1976. He came close to leaving the business altogether at that time as a result, although he was also tired of the blind adulation of the public ('I could have read out the cricket scores,' he says, 'and still got a full house').

The fact is that rock stars are likely to suffer as much from legitimate business practice as they are from clearly criminal operations. Even the Beatles in their heyday discovered that it was easy to lose money in the labyrinthine complexities of the rock world. 'We didn't have anything in the bank really,' said John Lennon of the period after Brian Epstein's death. 'None of us did . . . When Klein heard me say that he came over right away. Now I've got lots more money than I ever had before. Allen got me more real money in the bank than I've ever had in the whole period.'

'One of the few real men left' in the music business, Don Arden, buried in flesh during his early days as a singer.

Allen Klein was one of the rock performer's attempts at a solution to the problem of being ripped off. He was a sharp New York accountant who made and saved the Beatles' millions in the two years during which he handled their affairs. His specialities were negotiating better deals with record companies and unearthing money they owed their performers through a studious investigation of company books. In 1965, he won $1.25 million in advance payments for the Rolling Stones. He became their manager for a time. Klcin, who in his time has handled the affairs of Sam Cooke, Bobby Vinton, the Dave Clark Five and Jeff Beck, as well as the Beatles and the Stones, attempted an early coup when he bought a controlling interest in the Cameo-Parkway label and announced ambitious expansion plans which resulted in nothing except a reverse take-over of his own management company and a tenfold rise in the value of Cameo-Parkway shares until the American stock exchange suspended trading in them. In 1971, Klein was the focus of attention in Paul McCartney's suit to dissolve the Beatles' partnership. The judge pointed out that Klein's company, ABKCO, 'made grossly excessive claims for commission and ... received commission grossly in excess of that specified in the appointment' (the specified figure was 20 per cent of all the Beatles' income generated under Klein's management). A New York court found him guilty of failing to make and file tax returns relating to employees' taxes at around the same time and, in 1979, he was found guilty of filing a false tax return for 1970, relating to the sale of $170,000 worth of promotional albums on the Apple label. He was fined $5,000 and served two months of a two-year suspended sentence. Clearly, Klein was not the shining knight he had once seemed.

When George Harrison was sued for plagiarism following the success of his song, *My Sweet Lord*, Allen Klein, who had lost control of the Beatles six years previously, bought the rights to *He's So Fine* (the song which Harrison had allegedly plagiarized), as soon as they became available. Three years later, the expected judgement was made that Harrison had indeed plagiarized the earlier song, albeit unconsciously. Noting Klein's ownership of the rights to *He's So Fine*, the judge declared damages against George of a little over half-a-million dollars – exactly the same amount, in fact, that Klein paid for the rights in the first place.

The vitriolic disputes between Lennon and McCartney which marked the last days of the Beatles as the group's assets were sold off and individual Beatles hurled abuse and law-suits at each other, were also marked by a choice of champions. John, Ringo and George plumped for a money man – the ubiquitous Klein. McCartney, however, chose Lee Eastman, Linda McCartney's father, and a respected New York lawyer. The lawyer and the accountant, together or apart, now stand as symbols of rock'n'roll.

Survival and success have become key words in rock'n'roll – and, although nobody can doubt the wisdom of performers wishing to control their own des-

tinies, the end result often seems like a caricature of what rock'n'roll once hoped to be. Today's successful bands are probably more in control of their professional lives than ever before. But because success is measured in millions, they sometimes seem as soulless as any corporation turning a comparable profit. At the peak of their popularity, Kiss were grossing $130 million a year. The lion's share came from merchandizing Kiss comics, T-shirts, badges etc, all sporting the notorious SS slash symbol. Lead singer Gene Simmons (real name Klein but no relation) said proudly, 'Sure, we have regular meetings on merchandizing. I'm a good Jewish boy from Brooklyn and all four of us are members of the board. I don't have any respect for bands who get ripped off. Christianity and Disney have got nothing on us when it comes to merchandizing.'

Other sources of income include major investments. Abba (second biggest money-spinning industry in Sweden) got into the oil business when in 1977 they negotiated a barter deal with Rumania, exchanging records for part-payment in millions of dollars' worth of crude. In 1981 Paul McCartney and Yoko Ono got together behind closed doors to offer £25 million to

Allen Klein in 1966. Klein had a genius for getting unpaid royalties out of record companies for grateful rock star clients, including the Rolling Stones and Jeff Beck.

The world watched us the Beatles disintegrated all over the papers in 1970. Paul McCartney relied on a lawyer (his father-in-law Lee Eastman); the others on a moneyman (and in came Allen Klein).

Sign here and baby, you're a rich man. Allen Klein was brought in by John Lennon to help sort out the break-up of the Beatles. John and Yoko continued their association into the late seventies.

buy back the rights to all the early Beatles' songs sold in 1969 to Lord Grade's ATV company.

'It's like a job,' said Freddie Mercury of his life fronting Queen. Queen was a planned operation from the start, because, said Freddie, they were never prepared to be 'out-of-work musicians'. Listening to him talking about Queen's 1980 tour of South America, one could easily imagine one was listening to a chairman's statement at a shareholders' meeting, full of references to 'new territory being opened up' and markets being conquered.

Freddie Mercury sees bands these days being geared to survive in the business: 'It's a growth process. I can't analyse every band, but take the Police – they're more geared up than we were ten years ago to taking this business, step by step, and finding a way through it.' The Police present the perfect image of the modern rock group, from the tips of their dyed beach-boy blond hair to the toe-tapping rhythms bought but not paid for from fashionable reggae music. Somewhat too old to be punks and definitely too experienced to be fools, they have incorporated only the largely uncontroversial aspects of the punk image into an entertainment form. 'Musically, the band is evolving at its own rate, and we're in control of that,' said Sting (real name Gordon Sumner), the band's bassist, vocalist and chief appointed spokesman, pointing out at the time (1980) they were 'generating large amounts of money' and hence found themselves at the mercy of image-builders who, he said, were 'trying to soften the group to make it acceptable to even more people'. It was, perhaps, a trifle disingenuous, considering the values that the band readily admit to. Drummer Stewart Copeland argued against punk's 'politically oriented' music saying that 'I don't feel responsible for the ills of the world, and the only thing I'll go into battle for is my music.'

The result is a band run on the lines of a business venture. 'We're ambitious,' Sting said during a 1980 tour which set out to 'break new territory' in Mexico, Egypt, India, Thailand and Greece. 'We want power and I think occasionally you have to compromise yourself. The opportunities presented themselves and we took 'em. There's a very clear, very simple *gestalt* to the Police. There are three blond heads and that's it. That sells.'

One result of this heightened awareness of rock as commerce has been a number of dinosaurian battles between performers on the one hand and 'the business' on the other. The most notable of these to date was the case between Robert Stigwood and the Bee Gees. In 1980, the Bee Gees filed the largest lawsuit in showbiz history against their manager and the head of their record label, Robert Stigwood. They accused him of fraud, conflict of interest and unfair enrichment at their expense. The suit, for $125 million from Stigwood and his companies and $75 million from Polygram (the multinational conglomerate which owns Stigwood's label, RSO), cited 'grossly inadequate' contracts that Stigwood had made, apparently featuring royalty rates significantly below the industry norm, alleged that he registered their song copyrights in his name and pocketed money that was rightfully theirs. The Bee Gees, lest it be forgotten, had the biggest selling album of all time in *Saturday Night Fever*. Stigwood, on the other hand, has been no stranger to disaster in his chosen business.

Stigwood started in the entertainment business in Britain in 1961 managing actor-turned-singer, John Leyton, and singer-turned-film director, Mike Sarne, among others. Soon he was heavily involved in concert promotion. In 1965, the 29-year-old Australian put his company into liquidation having lost £15,000 on a cancelled Chuck Berry tour and £10,000 on a cancelled P. J. Proby tour. Proby was sacked because, according to Stigwood, he insisted on using his personal compere, Kim Fowley, who had still not received a work permit a week before the tour began. The promoter replaced Proby with Chuck Berry, only to find that 'contractual obligations' kept Berry from performing. At the liquidation, Robert Stigwood Associates owed a total of £39,000.

Stigwood worked for Brian Epstein for some time before moving into business on his own account with the Robert Stigwood Organization (RSO) and his own record label, Reaction. The deal he made with major acts like Cream and the Bee Gees reinforced his reputation as a cautious businessman. His public response to the Bee Gees' suit was to call it a 'cheap stunt'. But within weeks of this comment the group and their manager had achieved a reconciliation apparently as sweet as the split had been bitter.

If the enormous success achieved by rock'n'roll worldwide has to be celebrated for anything, it should be for providing us with the sweet irony of law's majesty and accountancy's order becoming entangled in a music that was described, barely twenty-five years ago, as lawless, anarchic and immoral. 'Money doesn't talk,' as Bob Dylan once sang, 'it swears.'

HEADLINE VIEWS

The rock'n'roll business is all about selling mass illusions – and for that you need the mass media. Consequently, the most effective hypes in rock have been those that turned rock'n'roll into news, not merely an entertainment for a specific audience, but a part of the general public consciousness. In some cases, incidents have been manufactured and the truth coloured by invention. This is not to say that every time rock'n'roll hits the headlines the event has been staged, or that the stories are themselves lies. Hype can just as easily be based on truth, because it is essentially a process of image building. Whatever materials come to hand are grist to its mill. The right image and the right approach are the keys to media interest. But, once aroused, the beast is often dangerously insatiable. If you give the non-rock press riots and rebelliousness, they crave more. The Rolling Stones found interest could soon turn to hostility.

The Stones were among the first rock groups to be deliberately hassled by the press – although they tended not to turn up drunk or drugged for interviews, and, for the most part, managed to keep a sensible division between their riotous public life and their quieter (but at times much seamier) private lives. That is until Brian Jones revealed his drug habits to two people he had met at a night-club. Ever eager for scandalous stories with which to assail its prurient readership, the *News of the World* ran the story of the conversation in the second part of their special series, 'Pop Stars and Drugs', in February 1967 and gained a libel suit from Mick Jagger for their pains.

At the Redlands trial in 1967, Jagger claimed that the paper had intentionally set out to discredit him in order to kill off his libel action. The paper admitted only that it had informed the police on the night of the Redlands' raid that drugs *might* be found at the house. That in itself was enough to inspire vociferous criticism – not least by the British 'quality' press. It was a matter of journalistic ethics – a newspaper should not act as a police informant, especially having failed to check its sources and with no intention of running a story on the matter. The ethics of newspaper coverage of rock'n'roll in general were never actually questioned and the traditional attitudes survive today as strong as ever: alternately celebrating the innocent joyousness of teenage music and condemning (usually with gleeful relish) the 'dangers' and 'immorality' of rock'n'roll.

The non-rock media can be extremely fickle – one moment courting you, the next condemning you, and after that ignoring you, exactly as they see the wishes of their readers, listeners and viewers. The Beatles first made the national press in the *Daily Mirror*, with a story of how John Lennon hit Bob Wooler at McCartney's twenty-first birthday party on 20th June, 1963. Wooler was a DJ at the Cavern club, and, like most other Merseyside music personalities, attended the party at Dinas Lane, Huyton, in Liverpool. As usual, Lennon – who later and rather disingenuously described Wooler as 'my best friend' – was drunk as a skunk. When Wooler insinuated that John and Brian Epstein were having an affair (common local gossip at the time), Lennon's macho working class upbringing took over.

'I was so high, I didn't realize what I was doing,' Lennon told the papers afterwards, adding that 'Bob is the last person in the world I would want to have a fight with.' In the end, Epstein intervened, driving the DJ to hospital and offering money and an apology on John's behalf – both of which were accepted. The press story treated the incident as the exceptional act of a drunken man, completely ignoring both Lennon's habitual drug-taking and drinking *and* the comments that caused the fracas. Even so, John Lennon's violence was scandal enough to arouse the interest of the press.

Soon, however, scandal gave way to praise: ballet critic Richard Buckle called the Beatles 'the best song-writers since Schubert', while music critic Tony Palmer went one better and called them the greatest composers 'since Beethoven'. As Lennon himself pointed out, there was, by that time, too much in the way of goodies and good times for anyone to risk the Beatles' wrath by raking up the muck. Swinging London had become the gravy train.

In time the swinging had to stop and the Beatles, increasingly tarnished with drugs, politics, religious heterodoxy and sex, became a freak show. The legal battles between McCartney and Lennon were gloated over; John and Yoko's 'political' activities – 'bed-ins', acorn-planting ceremonies, the 'War Is Over' campaign – were watched by the media with the wry amusement one affords a naughty child who has found a worthwhile, if naively pursued, hobby. When John and Yoko split up in 1974 and he ran off to Los Angeles with his Chinese secretary May Pang, the newspapers, once again, were interested only in his indiscretions. Visiting the Troubadour Club one night with Harry Nilsson, he became objectionably drunk,

179

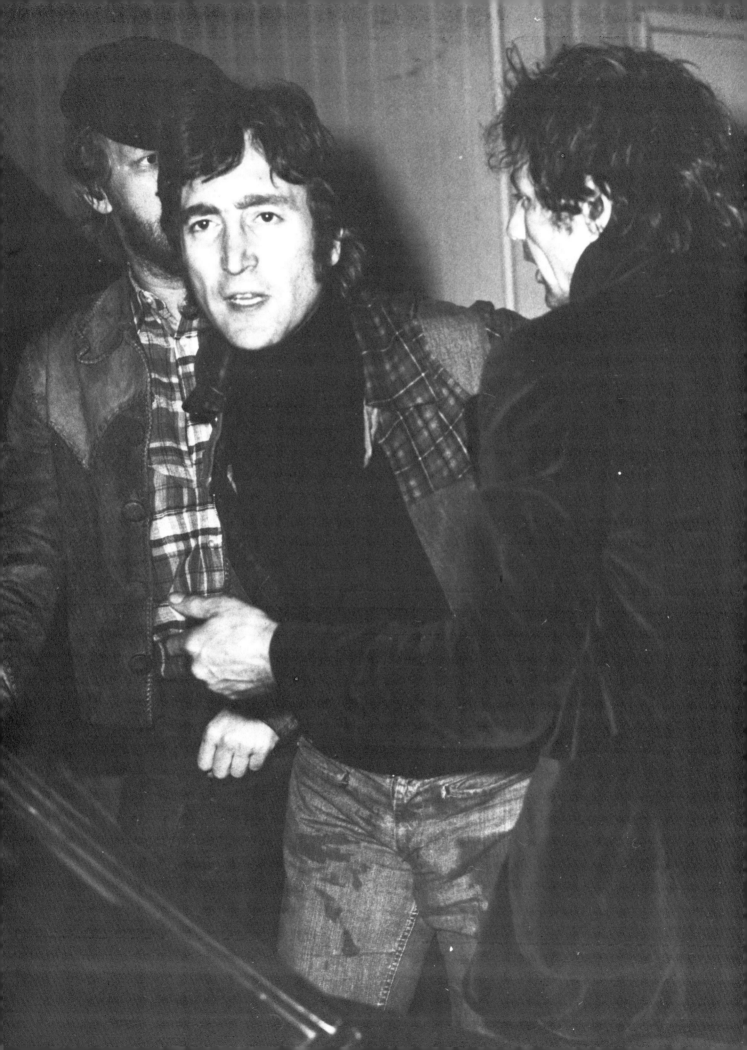

heckled the Smothers Brothers who were trying to perform and paraded in the club with a sanitary towel fixed to his head. Lennon and Nilsson finally succeeded in getting themselves ejected and Lennon tried to attack a woman photographer recording the scene. The press lapped it up – perhaps out of their contempt for their earlier sycophancy during the Beatlemania period, the newspapers revelled in the vision of shoeless idols displaying their feet of clay. The nutty, noisy, happy, handsome, unbelievably brilliant, incredibly attractive, wonderful, wonderful Beatles were dead, said the supercilious media men and women; long live the next big thing.

The Boomtown Rats' Bob Geldof, often considered to be one of the most articulate new wave rock stars, was once the next big thing himself. Finding himself on the sharp end of media attention, this former journalist began to object vociferously to the wrong kind of attention. In particular, he found the way the rock press treated his realtionship with Paula Yates upsetting. 'They were really nasty about Paula,' he said. 'They'd say, "Geldof made an appearance with that ugly cow he calls his girlfriend" . . . or, "They're so boring, who do they think they are? The Rod and Britt of the new wave?" Jesus. You go somewhere with your girlfriend, and that's what happens.'

This outburst, made to the *Melody Maker*, seemed like a case of protesting too much, since neither Paula nor her swain were ever particularly shy of joint or individual publicity. Throughout most of 1978, the British press was lightly bombarded with stories of the Geldof–Yates affair. In April 1978, Bob was making news with earnest declarations that, while living with Paula 'very happily', he had no inclination towards marriage. Geldof, it was widely reported, claimed that his three ambitions were 'to get rich, to get famous and to get laid'. By June, Paula was telling the *Daily Mail* that her eight-month relationship with Bob was 'a mad passionate affair'. 'I shall go mad before the end of the year if he doesn't marry me,' she announced breathlessly. Less than two weeks later, Bob and Paula announced their intention to get married – and so on. If that's not asking for it, I don't know what is.

In the end, Geldof claimed his self-confidence was shattered by all this coverage. He found he could not handle bad reviews and they were becoming more frequent. The Rats were associated with the general punk negative attitude to stardom, probably wrongly, but Geldof had put himself forward as a sort of spokesman for the new mood in rock while remaining unaware of the incompatibility of that mood and his role. Not surprisingly, members of the press wanted to deflate what was (even by his own admission) his overbearing ego. Geldof himself has learnt (so he says) to keep a lower profile. 'No more riding around in limos,' he said in 1980. 'I won't do any more interviews unless I've actually got something to say.'

Geldof at least had some control over his own movements and his own orientation. He was well aware of the power of image but understood how destructive it can be. This is more than can be said of the Sex Pistols when they allowed Malcolm McLaren to take them over. McLaren's choice of Johnny Rotten to front the Sex Pistols and of Sid Vicious to replace Glen Matlock were entirely based on looks and attitude; musical ability did not even enter the picture. The Stones, the Beatles, Bob Geldof, even Bill Haley, had some musical substance behind the froth of media interest: the Pistols only had the froth.

Like the Stones, the Pistols soon learnt that the press expected them to be monstrous, and the group lived up to expectations. Every carelessly-worded complaint or angry response was turned in the press into a 'flood of four-letter words' or an act of 'vandalism'. To the traditionally intemperate popular newspapers, the Pistols were 'wreckers', 'hooligans' and 'degenerates'. A slight fracas at Heathrow Airport in which one of the group may or may not have been sick, became 'an uproar' in the London *Evening News*. 'They shocked and revolted passengers and airline staff as they vomited and spat their way to an Amsterdam flight,' said the paper. A similar vomiting incident at the London offices of A&M records (the Pistols' second label) was totally fabricated, according to the executive who signed the group to the label and then dismissed them a week later.

If the Pistols' manager, Malcolm McLaren, had decided that his group needed to break new boundaries of outrageousness, he failed to realize that the media like outrageousness to be contained and controllable: just an image, in fact. If Rotten spat and snarled on stage, threw chairs at amplifiers or – as he did on one occasion – ended a show by stripping punk fan Jordan, they were all outrages safely restricted to the stage itself. In October 1976, EMI – one of the giants of the record industry – had no compunction about signing the group to a two-year contract for an advance of £40,000. (In fact, they beat their competition by drawing up the fastest contract in their history – it only took one day.) 'For me the Sex Pistols are a backlash against the "nice little band" syndrome,' said EMI's A&R man, Nick Mobbs, 'and the general stagnation of the music industry.' But the backlash could not be contained. The public fuss over the Pistols' first release, *Anarchy In The UK*, took off uncontrollably in the wake of the group's notorious appearance on Thames Television's 'Today' programme in December.

The Sex Pistols' interview took a course that was no doubt unplanned. The Pistols, who appeared as a last-minute replacement for another group who dropped out of the peak-hour, family news and chat show, were displaying their usual crass public face, and Bill Grundy, the presenter, was doing his best to show them at their worst. During the exchange, Grundy made an aside to some punk girls in the audience. 'I've always wanted to meet you,' simpered one of them, to which Bill Grundy replied, 'We'll meet afterwards, shall we?' One of the group remarked that

Harry Nilsson (left) and John Lennon being ejected from the Troubadour in Los Angeles, March 1974. 'Do you know who I am?' said Lennon to a waitress while he was wearing a Kotex on his head. 'Yeh,' she said, 'you're an asshole wearing a Kotex on your head.'

The real stars of the Sex Pistols' scenario. Malcolm McLaren impersonates Winston Churchill while Vivienne Westwood hangs onto a dream, 20th December, 1977.

make a statement in an attempt to defuse angry criticism from shareholders. By the beginning of January 1977, the group had been dropped by EMI – after receiving a total of £50,000 from the company.

Despite headlines detailing the Pistols' less savoury personal habits, *Anarchy In The UK* continued to sell (55,000 copies after only five radio plays). In March, A&M stepped in to sign the group in a staged ceremony outside the gates of Buckingham Palace (it was the year of the Queen's Silver Jubilee). A&M dropped the group within a week of handing over £75,000 in advance payments and having pressed but never released the group's second single, *God Save The Queen*. The Sex Pistols were rapidly becoming seen as a contagious disease. In April, the group played their first live concert since the 'Today' fiasco, before an invited audience at a cinema in Islington, London. 'The first number is dedicated to Bill Grundy and the Queen,' said Rotten, opening the Pistols' set. 'It goes, "Fuck You!"' Once more, the press were outraged.

Effectively unable to perform or get their records released as a result, the Pistols might then have fallen apart, had not Virgin Records stepped in, figuring, no doubt, to revitalize their ageing hippy image. *God Save The Queen* was released at the end of May 1977 and climbed to the top of the charts – despite the fact that the BBC refused to mention its name, let alone play it. The fuss continued – the Pistols were reduced to performing under assumed names to avoid bans. Johnny Rotten – the victim of physical and verbal assaults –

he considered Grundy 'a dirty old man'. Grundy, mindful of his live audience and with one eye on the studio clock, pushed them to their limit. 'You've got another five seconds,' he taunted. 'Say something outrageous.' To which one of the group replied in kind: 'You dirty fucker. What a fuckin' rotter.'

Of course there was an explosion of disgust in banner headlines. Grundy found himself suspended for two weeks and removed from the show to safer pastures elsewhere in the network for his part in the fiasco; but his career survived. Nevertheless, it was embarrassing to all concerned and potentially, if not actually, damaging to some people's careers. It certainly led to the cancellation of a number of Pistols' gigs and the eventual severing of the band's association with EMI (albeit for a very substantial 'golden handshake'). The facts that Malcolm McLaren had carefully cultivated the Pistols' outrageousness, Grundy goaded them on and encouraged their hostility and EMI had suggested that the programme feature the Pistols in the first place, all indicate that the interview was intended to work as hype, sealing their image as the latest and greatest 'group you love to hate'. But the media were beginning to discover that the Pistols did not respect anybody else's ground rules. Their response was to build the group into even bigger monsters than they intended to be. A planned tour was cancelled and the EMI packers refused to handle copies of the Pistols' single, *Anarchy In The UK*. At EMI's general meeting a few weeks later, the company chairman, John Read, felt constrained to

Melody Maker

MARCH 26, 1977 15p weekly USA 75 cents

ROTTEN: •**They've given us up through fear and business pressure. They've kicked us in the teeth. W mean what we say. A recor company is there to market records —not dictate terms** •

FIRING OF PISTOLS —TURN TO PAGE 3

182

hired a bodyguard. Sid Vicious, who had joined in February 1977, became increasingly dependent on heroin. The band failed to write any new material and became tied up in McLaren's grandiose ideas for a feature film, originally to be entitled *Who Killed Bambi?* and to be directed by cult 'sexploitation' director, Russ Meyer. Internal disputes and bad press ensured that the film's backers would pull out – which of course they did in November 1977. Arguments amongst the group members and between Johnny Rotten and McLaren continued unabated. The American tour early in 1978 was greeted with bad reviews, audience hostility and a menacing atmosphere of simmering violence. After a gig in San Francisco, Rotten walked out; he confessed in New York that he had 'hated it in the Sex Pistols' all along. McLaren and the other three continued gamely but, by 1978, even the press had become bored with their increasingly futile antics. Gradually the whole Pistols operation ground to a halt, probably because, as Oscar Wilde once wrote, 'There is only one thing worse than being talked about, and that is not being talked about.'

The media, of course, like to control everything. If they must be part of the hype, they want it to be on their own terms. Their periodic investigations into corruption sometimes seem less courageous investigation than sour grapes. But it takes a very clever hustler – or a great deal of expense in bribes – to ensure that they

Whose round is it, anyway? Johnny Rotten (left) and Sid Vicious, accompanied by the habitual photographer, giving their drinks' order to a 'bluebottle', in Kensington, London, October 1977. The Pistols attracted attention wherever they went.

toe the line. In fact, most groups these days tend to restrict their contact with reporters to communications issued from behind those brick walls known as publicists, press agents or public relations officers.

At the simplest level, publicists are the source of the basic information that daily floods into the offices of newspapers, magazines, radio and TV stations. They supply photographs and sometimes autograph them in the star's name, and they act as 'gatekeepers', arranging interviews and promotional events and selecting which journalists will be allowed access to which stars.

Publicists create and sustain images, so they tend to have a strange grasp of truth and reality. Creating an image is a sort of Frankenstein process in which a performer can all too easily become a monster inhabiting a misty no-man's-land somewhere between truth and fiction. Elton John's bisexuality (although widely discussed by industry and media people), remained a furtively-whispered rumour, until, that is, Elton himself spoke of it in 1976 at the time of his first retirement from live performance. 'I would have said something all along if someone had asked me,' he told an interviewer who had actually had the temerity to broach the subject. This just confirms the idea that the public relations image was independent of the person whom

Melody Maker

of the gloriously raucous, ted melee of British rge the mus generation crucial or pl

PUNK ROCK ROTTEN RAZORED

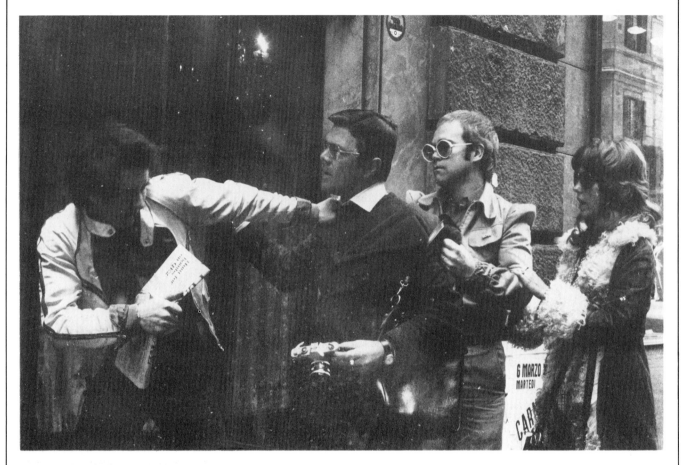

it was intended to represent.

There are a number of different approaches to image-building, any and all of which are at the disposal of the publicist. The simplest is the straightforward lie, in which performer, publicist or both offer the media unvarnished falsehoods. 'Kit Lambert used to brief us before we went into interviews about what to say,' Pete Townshend recalled, 'sometimes to be as objectionable, arrogant and nasty to reporters as possible. And oh, those outrageous lies we told: I remember telling Jonathan Aitken, "I have got four cars, a Lincoln Continental, a Jag XK150, a Cortina and a London taxi", and all I had was an old banger.' According to their early hype, the Who were 'a band with built-in hate', they were 'a new form of crime'. 'We didn't want any boy-next-door image,' said the group's co-manager, Chris Stamp.

In rock, it seems, there is sometimes such a thing as bad publicity. MGM's efforts in late 1967 to hype several groups from Boston as successors to the Liverpool and San Francisco groups, went strangely awry. Within a matter of weeks of MGM arriving in Boston with contracts in one hand and press releases in the other, *Newsweek* ran a lengthy piece on 'the Bosstown Sound'. An alleged quote from one local fan set the tone of the hype: 'They're Thomas Wolfe in sound,' she supposedly said of one group, 'with words that make you gloomy but always gladder.'

But by the middle of 1968, articles in *Vogue*, *The*

When in Rome ... Tempers flare as Elton John (second right) and an associate tangle with an unwelcome Italian photographer, 13th April, 1973.

Village Voice, *Time*, *Jazz and Pop*, *Rolling Stone* and *The Wall Street Journal* (this last accurately titled 'Selling a New Sound'), were noticeably critical. Jon Landau asked in *Rolling Stone* whether 'there is anything lying beneath the hype' and answered himself in the negative. *The Wall Street Journal* seemed content to let the hype speak for itself. Quoting the then head of MGM Records, Mort Nasatir, it reported on the most heavily backed of the Boston groups, Ultimate Spinach (yes!). 'Some of this music is so intellectual,' said Nasatir, 'that it is a little like the poet T. S. Eliot with his seven layers of ambiguity in each line'.

No group could live up to this sort of hype, and Ultimate Spinach were no exception to the rule. Despite the fact that the record trade papers continued to hype the success of the Boston sound, it was born a very lame duck. The groups were just not good enough, they were signed up too early in their careers and they never built up the kind of local fan following that could sustain them. All this was important at a time when live performance, musicianship, skilful lyric writing and the appearance of seriousness were at a premium in the kind of market into which MGM and their fellow labels were attempting to plug. You could fake a group like the Monkees, as Don Kirshner did with the Archies – a group of cartoon characters – but not the Grateful Dead.

Jon Landau, whose position as reviews editor of

184

Rolling Stone was influential enough to inspire his description as 'dean of rock critics', was himself indirectly responsible for another and similar classic hype. Having seen Bruce Springsteen in 1974, he wrote a piece about the performer for the Boston *Real Paper* in which he made the exaggerated and tendentious claim, 'I saw rock'n'roll future and its name is Bruce Springsteen.' Columbia Records (Springsteen's label) picked up on this outrageous but timely comment. Until Landau's review, CBS had been thinking about dropping Springsteen – despite critical acclaim, his first two albums had not sold well enough to recoup their huge initial investment. They decided to continue backing their performer. Landau was brought in to rescue Springsteen's new album from a mire of production difficulties and a campaign was planned. It opened with a number of full-page magazine ads quoting Landau's review prominently and at length. 'The future of rock'n'roll' became the best-known misquoted phrase in rock music.

In what is effectively an official biography of Bruce Springsteen, Dave Marsh argued that the subsequent build-up was not so much hype as 'auto-hype' – self-generated publicity triggered by fans in prominent positions on leading journals. This suggestion seems remarkably naive, even if one accepts that critical admiration for Springsteen grew rapidly by word-of-mouth. The co-ordination of the release of *Born To Run* in 1975 with the appearance of major features on the performer in the *New York Times* and in *Time* and *Newsweek* cannot be explained away by such simple-minded reliance on critical approbation.

In fact, interest in Springsteen seems to have followed on from interest in Columbia's promotional effort itself. The company spent an estimated $250,000 on pushing *Born To Run*. Without the already expressed approval of Landau and his fellow rock journalists, Columbia would doubtless have felt the expenditure unjustified. It was not the critics' approval that made Springsteen newsworthy, but the financial backing he was being given. *Newsweek* was particularly impressed and decided to carry a feature on 'the making of a rock star'. Springsteen's manager, Mike Appel, was meanwhile refusing all magazine interviews except those tied to cover features. *Time* was trying not to be caught out by *Newsweek.* And so an actual hype was born.

In Britain, the hype became almost feverish. Springsteen's first-ever performance there (in 1975) was heralded by the appearance of starkly dramatic black and white posters over London shouting out that 'At last London is ready for Bruce Springsteen'. Anybody who was anybody was invited to the show, and many accepted. After all, the future of rock'n'roll wasn't just going to breeze into town, play three chords and leave. The hype generated enormous expectations which were bound to be disappointed – even by a rock'n'roller as outstanding as Springsteen. Springsteen and his band were particularly affected by the excessiveness of the hype in Britain and the mini tour passed in an atmosphere of some gloom. Bruce was unhappy at having to perform the impossible task of living up to an impossible reputation (he even took to tearing Springsteen posters off walls in London).

Despite all this, the hype seemed to work. Bruce Springsteen was rapidly becoming, in theory at least, a very wealthy man. Unfortunately, his deal with Appel became increasingly a subject of conflict (Springsteen confessed to not having read his contracts with sufficient care). In July 1976, the writs started flying and for almost a year Bruce was effectively banned from recording (although he continued to play live). However his career hardly suffered and the break with Appel finally cemented Springsteen's business relationship with the man who had started it all – Jon Landau.

Another classic hype was perpetrated in Britain. This one was a disastrous failure. Brinsley Schwarz was a band formed in 1970 from the remains of Kippington Lodge, a BBC radio house band. They signed a management contract with a company called Famepushers whose intention was to launch them with a record released through Liberty/UA, a concert at the Fillmore East and a film of that concert. The idea was that each enterprise would both help pay for and promote the others. It was a complicated financial manoeuvre which absolutely depended on getting the right publicity.

Famepushers chartered a plane to carry rock and

Kissing Cousins. Pete Townshend gets close to Binkie Baker, husband of rock journalist and media personality, Anne Nightingale, at a promotional party for Ian Hunter.

non-rock reporters from Britain to the New York gig. But things went terribly astray. The three British members of the band (Brinsley Schwarz, Nick Lowe and Bob Andrews) had difficulty in getting visas into America, and eventually arrived tired, hassled and well below form. Meanwhile, the press plane flew in ten hours late after a delay at London and an enforced stopover at Shannon. The journalists arrived hotfoot and drunk at the Fillmore to find a nearly full house and no seats booked for them. The few that got in missed most of Brinsley Schwarz's woefully inadequate set. Reporters from the national press discovered a couple of celebrities in the crowd who were of more interest to them than some unknown rock group. And, to cap it all, the Famepushers' film crew were refused admission to the concert hall.

When it was all over, it had cost Famepushers more than £20,000 plus room service – the drinks bill for one hotel room alone came to £300. Those journalists who did not totally ignore the event wrote scathing reviews of the hype or dismissive reviews of the band. Despite the fact that the album heralded by the hype was the band's best-ever seller, the Brinsleys retired for some months to reconsider their position, eventually re-emerging as kings of the pub-rock circuit. It wasn't until six years later that the group's split-up freed Nick Lowe to become a successful new wave producer and solo performer and Brinsley Schwarz and Bob Andrews to win recognition as members of Graham Parker's backing band, the Rumour. At least two of the people associated with Famepushers went on to greater things, however – Dai Davies as a publicist, agent and the original manager of the Stranglers, and Dave Robinson as one of the founders of Stiff Records.

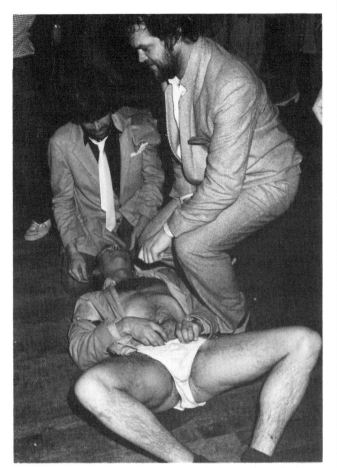

The fourth estate – down but not out. Smiling all the while, two of Rod Stewart's associates debag journalist Simon Kinnersley at a party for Rod, London, 1980.

Governments tend to be very sensitive about the control of broadcasting. For example, in the sixties, the British government outlawed the offshore 'pirate' radio stations that sprang up just outside Britain's coastal waters, despite the fact that most of these displayed a non-controversiality guaranteed by their dependence on payola and record company advertising. A more subtle process overtook America's 'alternative' FM stations in the seventies.

With an eye to both their advertisers and their FCC licences, FM stations were all too eager to discipline or sack any DJs who displayed too radical or too controversial an approach to broadcasting. In particular, the FCC pressured FM stations on the question of drug lyrics or allegedly obscene song references. This was part of a Nixonian tendency which embraced vice-president Spiro Agnew, the then chairman of the FCC; the head of MGM records at the time, Mike Curb, who, in 1970, announced very publicly that his label had terminated the contracts of 'eighteen groups . . . that are associated with hard drugs'; and a variety of unsavoury right-wing groups, including the John Birch Society and the Ku Klux Klan (who, in 1970, bombed a community radio station in Houston).

In Britain, the BBC claims never to actually *ban* records, merely to refuse to play them. The distinction

is too fine to be visible. The BBC (and the commercial broadcasting authority, the IBA) have 'refused to play' a long list of songs in which references to drugs, sex or distasteful politics have been noted. These include the Beatles' *Sgt Pepper* track, *A Day In The Life*, X-Ray Spex's *O Bondage, Up Yours!* and Paul McCartney's *Give Ireland Back To The Irish*. Despite revelling in the most lurid sexist imagery, some record companies have been quick to clamp down on 'unsavoury' sleeves too. One Beatles compilation album cover design depicted the boys as blood-stained butchers. It was banned. The Rolling Stones' original cover for *Beggars Banquet* showed a picture of a graffiti-laden urinal wall. It was banned. EMI refused to distribute John and Yoko's *Two Virgins* which depicted the couple naked on the front. Other albums featuring a little too much of the naked body (Hendrix's *Electric Ladyland*, for example, and an album by a group named Boxer called *Below The Belt*) have been withdrawn from display or 'censored' by prudish shops. Virgin Records was taken to court in December 1977 over the Sex Pistols' album *Never Mind The Bollocks . . . Here's The Sex Pistols* on the grounds of indecent display, following a complaint about a poster advertising the album in a Nottingham shop window. The case was dismissed but many records shops took to concealing the album all the same.

The most famous cases of broadcast bans involve Elvis, the Stones (again) and the Doors on the Ed Sullivan TV show. Elvis, of course, was filmed only from the waist up. The Stones were required to alter the words of *Let's Spend The Night Together* to 'let's spend some time together' – and acceded. Jim Morrison, asked to sing an alternative line to 'Baby, we can't get much higher' in the song *Light My Fire*, caused much consternation when he actually sang the original during the show after agreeing to censor himself at a rehearsal.

The rock press might seem to be a better place to seek rock's radical vision but in truth it's no less reliable than radio or TV on the patronage of record companies and concert promoters – patronage that takes the form of advertising, the supply of records and concert tickets and the provision of information and access to performers. It also takes the less direct form of subsidy to journalists through the supply of promotional records. Most of the time this subtle patronage encourages self-censorship by the rock press. Not wishing to offend the industry, criticisms are toned down and touchy subjects are often ignored completely. But threats to withdraw support and the actual withdrawal of support are by no means unknown, while patronage is often made explicit to the point of bribery. A magazine may be offered an exclusive interview in return for a favourable review, or ads may be placed on condition that they are backed by editorial. Many rock journalists are also part-time DJs, record company publicists or A&R people. The forms of bribery are many – job opportunities, exclusive stories, freebies – and even include offers of cash payments. 'I maintained my illusions about the value-free purity of rock,' critic Richard Goldstein wrote in *New York* magazine, 'until the day in 1969 when my agent informed me that a large music publisher would pay me $25,000 for three presentations on the state of popular music. It was understood that I would favour this company's artists in my reviews.'

But beyond this formal sort of bribery there is a more insidious informal process helping to diffuse criticism in which rock journalists are seduced by the glamour of their vocation. Promotional parties are where most of the stardust rubs off. Usually they are relatively routine occasions, at which the assembled hacks, publicists and general parasitic riff-raff get routinely drunk. At one end-of-tour party thrown by Rod Stewart at London's Embassy Club in December 1980, the unfortunate rock music critic of the *Daily Mail* was debagged by two of Stewart's henchmen. Journalist Simon Kinnersley, also involved in the *Sounds* libel suit, found himself set upon as if in jest, and unceremoniously divested of his trousers. It appeared that the writer had been less than flattering in his review of Stewart's gigs – so Rod's over-zealous associates turfed the unfortunate ex-public school journalist out into the street in his underpants. It may not sound too glamorous – but it *was* in Mayfair.

At the vertiginous, self-congratulatory heights of superstardom, glamour is often synonymous with excess. The end of Wings' 1976 tour of America was celebrated by a party on the estate of the silent comedy star Harold Lloyd. The pool was drained to provide a disco floor. There was entertainment from a chamber orchestra playing Beatles' songs, the cast of the Broadway musical *The Wiz*, the Los Angeles Ballet and comedian John Belushi (the high point of whose act was an insulting impersonation of Joe Cocker). An estimated 400 guests – including Bob Dylan, Elton John, Cher and Natalie Cole – cavorted into the night at a cost to the Wings tour budget of some $200 per person.

In 1981, Deborah Harry's record company arranged a party to celebrate the release of her solo album, *Koo Koo*, at the ultra-exclusive women's health club in London, the Sanctuary. The 400 guests desported themselves amidst the jungle foliage eating their way through mountains of seafood and drinking themselves silly. By the end of the evening there was so much food left that the guests (many of whom could afford to buy their own fishmongers) were wrapping up crabs, lobsters and prawns and taking them home. At an earlier seafood do for Harry's group, Blondie, the guests of honour arrived in a specially hired US Army tank!

The single most important aspect of these events is, of course, their prestige value. In some cases, record companies will arrange a plush event for a performer whose prestige value is more important than his or her popularity might suggest. Most performers are greatly impressed by a company's willingness to spend money on them. Hype they may be, but they certainly work towards general goodwill, improved artist relations and a good image for the industry. And, of course, a good time is usually had by all – so that the hype itself is clouded in the mists of mellow booziness and made to seem of little significance.

The surprising thing is that occasionally (very occasionally, it's true) rock journalists balk at the whole process. They are not, it then seems, fawning sycophants but merely people with a blind eye to turn on the machinations of the record industry. Sometimes the layer of comfortable privilege that isolates them from the world outside of recording studios, concert-halls and plush hotels is pierced, and they rally (or think they are rallying) to the defence of rock'n'roll.

For all its faults, the punk movement did pierce a few layers of privilege and open a few blind eyes. The rock press as a whole was made aware of what can only be called the glaring inhumanity of the industry's star system – a system which had reached Hollywood Golden Age proportions and was being more or less uncritically supported by the vast body of rock journalists occupied in their own versions of being 'on the make'. Suddenly, negativity was all the rage. New writers (and some old ones in disguise) emerged calling themselves 'Savage' and 'Suck' and so on. Sudden conversions to the dole queue ethos became all the rage. For a time, rock journalism acquired a social conscience. Political issues were vigorously discussed and even the record industry came in for some overdue criticism. For example, the British division of RCA

Records flew 200 assorted rock biz persons and journalists to Amsterdam for two days in September 1980, so that they could (at an estimated cost of £50,000) spend some time in a luxury hotel and between breakfast, lunch, dinner and drinks, visit a gig by RCA band Sad Cafe and the unveiling of Sad Cafe's new album. On that occasion, the British rock press wasn't slow to point out that not only had Sad Cafe previously sued RCA for allegedly failing to support them adequately, but that the company was, at the time of the trip, a week away from sacking 21 employees in a recession-inspired cut-back designed to save money. But such radical posturing could hardly survive, let alone flourish, given the cosy relationship between the rock press and the record industry. History could have shown the punk-era journalists how expert the record industry is at undermining the independence of writers.

In May 1973, 140 rock journalists gathered in Memphis for the 'First Annual National Association of Rock Writers' Convention'. Most came from America, two or three from Britain. They were there, it may be assumed, to assay the common problems of the rock writer. Among the questions discussed were the low rates of pay, the rock writer's lack of negotiating strength, and the difficulties of dealing with conservative publishers and a fickle record industry. In four days, the writers held a number of sessions at which the arguments ranged far and wide. Richard Meltzer suggested, not entirely in jest, that record companies should pay for reviews. Greg Shaw of *Phonograph*

Beggars can be choosers. To mark the release of their album, Beggars Banquet, *the Rolling Stones threw a launch party (complete with boar's head) and several 'custard' pies, 6th December, 1968. Aristocratic guest, Lord Harlech – former escort of Jackie Kennedy – wiped foam from his face and beamed: 'An absolutely topping party.' Presumably, dream topping.*

Record Magazine, which was funded by United Artists, argued that there were too many complaints about writing fees. 'I'm a fan,' he pronounced with disarming candour, 'not a writer.'

The discussions went on through the convention. Meanwhile the assembled rock journalists took notes on pads provided by MCA Records, their evenings were spent popping in and out of hospitality rooms run by MCA, Blue Thumb, London, Stax and Polydor, or maybe they were out to dinner with executives from CBS, Mercury, A&M or Motown, who were all present. Perhaps they just reflected on the fact that the whole event had been sponsored by Stax Records and organized by Stax's publicist who, not entirely coincidentally, was trying to break the British band, Skin Alley, into the States. The cost of the convention was estimated by one writer at $40,000 – a figure confirmed by one of the others present, who commented that it was quite reasonable compared to a recent one-night promotional event for Jefferson Airplane's RCA-sponsored Grunt label, which had cost $100,000. The writers made no decision of any significance except to call themselves by the grandiloquent title, 'Rock Writers of the World'. They never met as an organization again, Skin Alley never took off in the States, but the partying continues.

ACKNOWLEDGEMENTS

There are many thanks to be made, not least to the numerous writers and critics whose books, articles and interviews have provided me with invaluable insights and source-material. It is a measure of my indebtedness that I must forbear to mention each and every name and that I may omit one or two of the more general or less significant books or publications that I consulted while preparing this book. Space is just too limited to allow a comprehensive listing.

Among the periodicals I found most useful, I should like particularly to acknowledge *Rolling Stone*, the *New Musical Express*, *Melody Maker*, *Sounds*, *Crawdaddy*, *Creem* and *Circus* – these have been a fund of useful interviews and thought-provoking comment. It is appropriate that I should express my immense gratitude to the staff of the British Newspaper Library at Colindale and the *Daily Express* cuttings library in Fleet Street. Particularly helpful newspapers have been the London *Sunday Times*, the London *Observer*, the *Daily Mail*, the *News of the World*, the *Los Angeles Times*, the *New York Times* and the *San Francisco Chronicle*. Specifically, I would also like to thank the following newspapers for their permission to reproduce cuttings from past issues: *The Sun*, the *Daily Mail*, the *Evening News*, the *Daily Mirror*, the London *Times*, the *Evening Standard*, the *New York Times*, the *New York Daily News*, the *Sunday People*, *Newsweek* and *Melody Maker*.

Writing this book would have been considerably harder without the previously published work of the following authors and editors: Robert Santelli (Aquarius Rising); Steve Chapple and Rebee Garofalo (Rock'n'Roll is Here To Pay); Jerry Hopkins (The Rock Story, Elvis and Elvis: The Final Years); Jim Miller (ed. The Rolling Stone Illustrated History of Rock'n'Roll); Ellen Sanders (Trips); Tom Wolfe (The Electric Kool-Aid Acid Test); Michael Lydon (Rock Folk and Boogie Lightning); Jonathan Eisen (ed. The Age of Rock I and II and Twenty-Minute Fandangos and Forever Changes); Albert Goldman (Elvis); Simon Frith (The Sociology of Rock); David Dalton (Janis and The Rolling Stones – The First Twenty Years); Tony Sanchez (Up and Down With The Rolling Stones); Dave Marsh (Born To Run); Phil Hardy and Dave Laing (eds. The Encyclopaedia of Rock); Steve Turner (Conversations With Eric Clapton); Hunter Davies (The Beatles); Philip Norman (Shout); Geoffrey Stokes (The Beatles); John Blake (All You Needed was Love); Fred and Judy Vermorel (The Sex Pistols); R. Serge Denisoff (The Sounds of Social Change); Bev Bevan (The Electric Light Orchestra); John Goldrosen (Buddy Holly); Ian Hoare (ed. The Soul Book); John Pidgeon (Rod Stewart and the Faces); Curtis Knight (Jimi Hendrix); Jenny Fabian and Johnny Byrne (Groupie); David Leaf (The Beach Boys and the Californian Myth); Michael Cable (The Pop Industry Inside Out); Greil Marcus (Mystery Train); Virginia Boston (Shockwave) and Tony Palmer (Born Under a Bad Sign).

It should go without saying that any mistakes, misconceptions and misjudgements included in this book are entirely my own responsibility – however, I should like to thank John Pidgeon, John Tobler, Phil Hardy, Dave Laing, Penny Valentine, Frances Kennett and Richard Barber, all of whom in various ways helped with the original research of this book. I would also like to thank Lisa Hardy, Sue Holland, Debbie Geller, Fran Pelzman, Thaddeus O'Sullivan, Bob Ughetti and Jonathan Read for their help in researching visual material. Thanks are also due to Barry Plummer, Terry Norman of London Express Features, John Halsall at LFI, Steven James of Flicks, Joe Canale at Wide World, Colin Crawford of Syndication International, Simon Crocker at the Kobal Collection, Tony Gale of Pictorial Press and Lynn Facey at *Record Mirror* for assistance with photographs. Special thanks are due to Jim Marshall for his co-operation in supplying his copyright photographs featured on pages 4, 36, 38 and 121, and to all the following who have supplied photographs elsewhere in the book: Associated Press, John Beecher, Camera Press, Chet Flippo, Bob Gruen, Dan Hardy, Keystone Press Agency, Laurie Lewis, MPL Communications, Denis O'Regan, Popperfoto, Neal Preston, Chuck Pulin, Rex Features, Shep Sherbell, Joseph Sia, Carter Smith, *Sounds*, Syndication International, Allen Tannenbaum, Virginia Turbett, UPI, Burk Uzzle, Virgin Records, WEA, Michael Weinstein, Valerie Wilmer and Michael Zagaris. It has not been possible in all cases to trace the copyright sources, and my publishers would be glad to hear from any such unacknowledged copyright holders.

I would also like to express my gratitude to Harvey Weinig, Alice Morey and Sue Cochrane for specialist assistance; to John Parker for support; to Robin Allen for his design; to Sandra Wake and Terry Porter at Plexus; and, especially, to my editor Nicky Hayden, without whom . . .

Index of names